BRITISH LIGHT MUSIC

A personal gallery of 20th-century composers
Philip L. Scowcroft
with a Foreword by Ernest Tomlinson MBE

DANCE BOOKS

The author and publishers would like to thank Hilary Ashton of the Light Music Society (see p. 178) for her help in providing the cover illustrations for this book, and Nick Barnard of the Tin Pan Alley Orchestra (see p. 179) for generously donating a copy of the original edition of this book.

First published in 1997
This edition published in 2013 by Dance Books Ltd.,
Southwold House, Isington Road, Binsted, Hampshire GU34 4PH

ISBN: 978-1-85273-163-2

© 2013 Philip Scowcroft

Printed and bound in Great Britain by Lightning Source UK Ltd.

CONTENTS

Preface	1
Foreword (Ernest Tomlinson)	4
Richard Stewart Addinsell	17
Charles Ancliffe and Sydney Baynes	19
Kenneth J. Alford	21
John Ansell	23
Hubert Bath	25
Ronald Binge	28
G.H. Clutsam	30
Eric Coates	33
Samuel Coleridge-Taylor	36
Frederic Curzon	39
Robert Docker	41
Percy Fletcher	43
Harold Fraser-Simson	46
Henry Geehl	48
Edward German	50
Archibald Joyce	56
Albert Ketèlbey	59
Reginald A. King	63
Leighton Lucas	65
Billy Mayerl	67
Frederick Norton	72
Walton O'Donnell	74
Montague Phillips	77
Roger Quilter	85
Alfred Reynolds	88
Frederick Rosse	93
Wilfrid Sanderson	94
W.H. Squire	100
Arthur Wood	102
Haydn Wood	104
The Best of the Rest	108
Select Discography	171
Select Bibliography	177
Light Music Societies	178
Illustrations	81-84

PREFACE

What is 'light' music? Opinions may differ on its precise definition; but in general it occupies the middle ground between 'classical' music – symphonies, concertos, grand opera, oratorio, etc – on the one hand and 'pop' (or in earlier days 'folk') and indeed jazz on the other, while inevitably taking something from all its neighbours. While being easier to assimilate than most classical music, it should have an artistic, as well as an entertainment element about it, with due regard for attractive orchestration and craftsmanlike construction. It should be listened to, if not necessarily with the same concentration as a symphony or a sonata but certainly not as background music. I found, as a teenager in the late 1940s, that listening to light music led to the appreciation of something more serious; yet I have not grown out of the former. It can include – and this is a personal view – music for orchestras, of the type common earlier this century in theatre or cinema pits, in hotels and restaurants, in seaside (and some inland) resorts and from 1922 on the BBC – suites, sometimes derived from theatre music, and individual genre pieces; it can include the counterpart of that music, written for piano solo or small instrumental groupings, often, though not always, for performance in drawing-rooms; it can include the lighter end of the song repertoire, familiarly called 'ballads', again often performed in a domestic ambience, but also as interludes in orchestral concerts, as happened at resorts or, at one period of their history, in the Henry Wood Promenade Concerts; it can include a substantial part of the repertoire of brass and military bands; it can include film music; it can even include so called 'mood music', though this is often just a background; and it can include operetta and musical comedy.

However one defines light music – and I dare say many, even most, readers will differ from me in detail as to its extent – it seems clear that today it is an endangered species. Few, if any, theatres have resident orchestras, finding taped music a cheaper option. Most of the resort orchestras have disappeared, again largely on account of economic reasons, although a few, like those at Scarborough, Bridlington, Felixstowe and Broadstairs, have remained to enhance the enjoyment of holiday-makers. Bournemouth, the most famous of them all, has become a highly regarded regional symphony orchestra and thus ceased to be a light music institution. Other resorts, among them Worthing and Eastbourne, still have orchestras which give only perhaps five concerts a year instead of several per week, as their predecessor orchestras once did, but perhaps these still derive some inspiration from those predecessors. The BBC, even as late as the 1950s a great focus for, and stimulus of, light music – 'Music While You Work', Light Music Festivals and 'Grand Hotel' among many other programmes – now has relatively little time for it, although a series of Radio 3 talks by Stephen Banfield were welcome. Up and down the country a few light orchestras and smaller ensembles do exist but, excellent though they are, many of them have the look almost of, say, railway or canal preservation societies. Fortunately several record companies (of which Marco Polo must be singled out for special commendation), avid for new repertoire for their CDs, have rediscovered the pleasures of light music and especially British light music, to our delight and, one hopes, their profit.

Light music has a sufficiently long history for us to begin attempting to provide some basic information about its composers, many of whom are conspicuously absent from the main musical dictionaries, although I must except *The New Grove* from such implied criticism. Some writers have covered aspects of the subject (see bibliography), but much remains to be done, and this book, while it is in no sense a last word on the subject, is an attempt to continue this process and perhaps encourage others to delve further into it. The present writer is a musical enthusiast rather than an expert, and is a listener rather than a practising musician: this book is written from those standpoints. There is no attempt to make a lofty historical or musical survey, with appropriate PhD analysis and extensive value-judgements.

The pattern of the book, after the introductory essay (for which I am grateful to Ernest Tomlinson, whom I have long admired as a light music practitioner, whether as conductor or composer), is a series of 30 short essays on selected British light music figures active after 1900. The 30 names (actually 31) are, I stress, a personal selection and do not include anyone still alive, even though there are a number of excellent light music composers, like Robert Farnon and Ernest Tomlinson, of course, who are still active. Such figures and the most memorable of the remaining deceased practitioners (again a personal selection) appear in an Appendix with, of necessity, much shorter entries. In many cases, biographical information has not been easy to come by. If anyone's favourite composer has been missed, I apologise in advance; I suppose there is always scope for a revised edition or a further book on the subject. In particular, one or two eyebrows may rise at the omission of Edward Elgar, despite his output including such masterpieces of light music as *Wand of Youth*, *Chanson de Matin*, *Chanson de Nuit*, *Salut d'Amour*, the *Nursery Suite* and the *Bavarian Dances*; but Elgar is primarily a 'serious' composer and it was felt inappropriate to include him in the 30 'headline' articles, while to relegate our premier composer to an Appendix might be seen as insulting. Much the same considerations have governed the omission of Vaughan Williams, despite *The Wasps*, the *English Folk Song Suite* and *Greensleeves*, Delius despite *La Calinda*, Benjamin Britten, despite *Soirées Musicales*, *Matinées Musicales* and much film music, Gustav Holst, despite his suites for band, and so on. If anyone knows of significant light-music composers I have missed I shall be delighted to hear about them.

A few more acknowledgments of indebtedness are necessary. First to John Bishop of Thames Publishing for the original idea and his subsequent encouragement. Then to the British Music Society and Vintage Light Music Society, in whose Newsletters or Journals some of the material herein originally appeared, albeit in a different form, and especially to Rob Barnett of the former society and Stuart Upton of the latter society for their well-informed support. Then to Malcolm Smith of Boosey & Hawkes for much useful information. Then to Terry Wilkinson, guiding light of the Midland Gershwin Mayerl Society, for comments on a draft of my article on Billy Mayerl. Then to the staff of the Central Library, Doncaster, a paragon among libraries. Finally to my wife for typing the manuscript and for her patience and encouragement throughout.

Philip L. Scowcroft

FOREWORD
Ernest Tomlinson MBE

Light music in all its diversity, from near-symphonic to easy-listening, represents some of the most popular and enduring music there is, as we see by the wealth of repertoire covered in this welcome book. It is nevertheless essential, particularly these days, to affirm that light music – for all the inadequacy of the term – is its own distinctive genre, and that conscious effort is called for to keep it alive and flourishing in the face of the competition from other forms of music, backed up by strong marketing forces.

After all, light music has flourished since music began. The justly famous *Sumer is y cumin in* of c. 1240, the light-hearted balletts and madrigals of the 1500s, were perfect foils to the devotional masses and services of church music; the short minuets and gavottes of the keyboard suites of Bach and Handel, the minuets and scherzos of the symphonies and chamber music from the late 1700s onward, offered welcome contrast and relaxation to the profundity of the movements on each side of them.

Composers themselves, however 'serious' their outlook, have always had room in their inventiveness for lighter pieces: Brahms' Waltzes, Tchaikovsky's ballet music, Dvořák's *Slavonic Dances*, the list is endless. Some composers found their most natural bent in light music of real stature: Sullivan, Delibes, Offenbach, Strauss, Sousa and many more. Alongside music whose joys are revealed by dedicated listening there has always been music designed to entertain, to appeal directly to our sensibilities – which is not to suggest that music that is easy to listen to is in some way of little worth. The beauteous simplicity of a Schubert song can stir the heartstrings just as much as the most deeply-felt statement in a symphony, and the same applies to many a 'light' piece right down to those written in the present day.

By the late 1800s, in an ever-developing musical language, the characteristics that distinguish light music from the 'serious' had become clear. I've always liked the definition given by the late Andrew Gold, who was the head of the BBC's Light Music Unit from 1965 until his untimely death in 1969. 'Light music,' he averred, 'is music where the tune is more important than what you do with it.'

Light music is about melody first and foremost. The elements that identify music conceived symphonically – in its broadest sense, including chamber-music and grand opera – the introductions, bridge passages and development sections which explore different facets of themes fashioned for their suitability for such treatment, concentrating interest over long periods of time, play virtually no part in light music.

In light music tunes follow tunes, each one self-contained and contrasting. Where long movements are called for, such as in a light opera overture, a Slavonic rhapsody, or a longish sequence in ballet or operetta, interest is held by way of regular changes of tempo. The one exception is the Viennese Waltz of the Strauss family, Waldteufel and others, consisting in practice of four or five waltzes in turn, each complete in themselves and containing several contrasting tunes.

What really established light music as a genre on its own was the proliferation of light orchestras in the holiday resorts and spas of Europe from the late 1800s onwards, a Golden Age which lasted until World War II and beyond. Nowhere more so than in Britain, the 19th-century transport revolution meant thousands of workers descending on seaside towns for their annual holidays. The opportunity to hear live orchestras, formed from some of the finest players around – they too enjoyed their summer break – playing beautiful, immediately attractive music were highlights of their holiday treats. The Bournemouth Municipal Orchestra under Dan Godfrey was preeminent, but Eastbourne, Llandudno, Hastings, Scarborough, Whitby, Margate, Blackpool and many other seaside resorts, not to mention the inland spas Buxton and Harrogate, all had thriving orchestras. These were large enough in some cases to provide weekly symphonic concerts too. Elgar and Eric Coates were amongst many composers invited regularly to conduct. The finest soloists of the day were invited to perform under famous conductors, including Malcolm Sargent, Basil Cameron, Granville Bantock and Maurice Miles. To the family audience – children, parents, grandparents too – light music is the one musical attraction to which all can respond without reservation, a fact which still applies today.

Light orchestral concerts are quite distinctive in several ways. Classical music (a term even more inadequate than 'light music'), is performed in the instrumentation chosen by the composer. The light orchestra looks at the whole of music's output and says, if our audiences would enjoy it let's play it, no matter whether it was originally a piano piece, a song, a violin solo, a movement from a symphony or a piece from grand opera. No matter that all the most likely pieces – waltzes, overtures, rhapsodies, ballet-suites or whatever – were scored for orchestras twice the size of even a 'large' light orchestra of, say, 35 players; most light orchestras were considerably smaller, perhaps using only 12 players or fewer. A whole industry was built up by publishers producing the special type of orchestrations required, often in quite new arrangements, with lots of cues and revoicings so that orchestras could give a good account of the music whatever their make-up.

Light music as a genre has no equivalent of chamber music, where trios, quartets, sextets, nonets are playable only by the instruments specified by the composer. Light music had salon orchestras, all, however few their players, doing their utmost to simulate the textures of the complete orchestra, with the ubiquitous piano, plus harmonium or organ, later the piano-accordion, now the synthesizer, covering up for whatever was missing. This is not to suggest that classical chamber music does not continue to produce compositions which could happily be accepted into concerts of light music, as several Radio 3 programmes of the 1970s, 'Light Music Miniatures', showed. But only one combination, the piano trio (violin, cello and piano), is common to both 'light' and 'classical'. From quartet upwards there is no common ethos. In the light combination everyone plays, adapting to that particular instrumentation whatever makes suitable programme-material.

Staple fare for light orchestras, large and small, were marches from the parade ground, waltzes, polkas and mazurkas from the ballroom, and a host of entr'actes, intermezzos, etc. There was an emphasis on descriptive titles, and many novelty pieces, featuring, for example, a xylophone soloist. Light music's counterpart of the long symphonic movement is the *selection*, still immensely popular today, a carefully laid-out parade of tunes from the latest stage musical, memories of the ballet, and tunes or dances from particular countries. There were selections from ballet or grand opera with titles like *Fantasie-Mozaique*.

Orchestras in residence morning, afternoon and evening throughout the spring and summer season, and in inland resorts throughout the winter as well, played to highly appreciative audiences. New music and new kinds of music were constantly welcomed, thus offering the best possible stimulus to the practising composer. It is mainly from this classical era of light music that the galaxy of talent outlined in this book is drawn.

If the concert season offered every encouragement for composers of tuneful music, so did the theatre, not just for its musical comedies and operetta but incidental music for plays. Perhaps the biggest outlet was that forgotten area, music for silent films, in an era which spans nearly 30 years. Before the days of sound-tracks many films had music specially written for them, with live orchestras employed to do the accompanying. But only a few cinemas could support large orchestras. Much more important for the workaday composer and his publisher were the host of little orchestras and ensembles employed in every cinema but the smallest. Music was virtually continuous throughout an evening, with players keeping an eye on the coloured tabs on their sheet music so as to switch deftly from one mood to another according to the demands of the action. Published light orchestral music, classical and modern, was put to effective use. But to cater for the spiralling demand came a new range of publications designed specifically for the cinema: vast catalogues of short pieces with titles like *Broken Hearts*, *Dramatic Agitato*, *Cops Chasing Robbers*, *Scene of Terror*, etc. Light music composers – Percy Fletcher, Montague Ewing, Albert Ketèlbey and Charles Ancliffe, to name but four – contributed steadily to such catalogues and no doubt Eric Coates and Haydn Wood too wrote their light pieces with an eye to their use in the cinema.

The coming of talking pictures from 1929 put an end to that trade, though some cinemas continued to employ orchestras for a year or two longer until the 'mighty Wurlitzer' organ came along. For the composer though there came in the 1920s and 1930s a new means of reaching mass audiences: sound broadcasting and recording, with light orchestras and ensembles playing an essential role from the outset.

The peak of broadcasting's influence on light music came in the immediate post World War II period, reaching a climax during the decade 1950-60. The BBC, still having a monopoly of broadcasting, employed eight full-time light orchestras, each presenting several programmes every week, including the prestigious BBC Concert Orchestra, set up in 1953 to perform light music in the composer's original scoring. Other BBC units made their contribution and there were also many freelance light orchestras broadcasting regularly.

The BBC launched its annual International Festival of Light Music in the 1950s, each festival consisting of five or six weekly concerts on Saturday evenings in June and July at the Royal Festival Hall, London. For nine years under the producer Geoffrey Brand, the Festival was truly international, with guest soloists, conductors, orchestras, choirs, bands and ensembles from round the world performing alongside the resident BBC Concert Orchestra. Beginning with Eric Coates and Haydn Wood, the BBC carried out an enterprising policy of commissioning British composers to write works for these concerts, which were broadcast live to a large European audience. In its everyday output too the BBC, notably from the time of the setting up of its Light Music Department under Frank Wade in 1953, actively promoted the work of living composers.

The range of light music broadcast was very wide – from near-symphonic to more overt 'entertainment' music. There were programmes like 'Saturday Concert Hall' for what was then the Home Service, and

'Friday Night is Music Night' for the Light Programme. Vocal music of all kinds played its part in the BBC's light music output. But most music programmes were purely instrumental, such as the two hours daily until 9am of 'Morning Music'; tuneful, happy music. With so many outlets to cater for, the continuing demand for new music was something composers today can only wonder at, music that won its way into popularity by the traditional values of music, good tunes impeccably shaped and textured.

The older masters of light music, Eric Coates and Haydn Wood, were still around and had their music well represented. But there came along a new style of orchestration, sophisticated yet clear-cut. The George Melachrino Orchestra showed how the string section could move around with the panache of a big band; the distinctive scoring of Robert Farnon and Sidney Torch compositions brought something of the show-band sound into light music.

Whereas the starting point of marketing pre-war was one standard orchestral set, published for sale to the numerous light orchestras of all shapes and sizes and degrees of prowess operating in the 'live' field, which tended to produce a play-for-safety, over-orthodox style of orchestration, composers now wrote first and foremost for broadcasting and recording, with some of the finest players in the world on hand to take any flights of fancy in their stride.

The traditional features of light music remained. If it's good, we play it, no matter what it was originally written for. A successful piece could be rearranged dozens of times for the host of small combinations broadcasting at the time, played too by the numerous fine cinema organists also heard regularly.

The build-up of television began to assume increasing prominence during the 1950s without for a time diminishing the dominance of sound broadcasting. It's important to note that in the early years most television music was not especially commissioned for its plays, serials, newsreels and other features. It was selected by producers from the ever-growing libraries of recordings sponsored by music publishers and designed to cover every kind of situation and mood a programme might need. A new industry blossomed, in which Britain was ahead of the rest of the world, offering almost unlimited possibilities to composers. The range of music was remarkably similar to that produced at the beginning of the century for the silent screen, and still a closed book to the general public and even writers on music. Alongside the vast uses for atmospheric and descriptive pieces of all kinds, the demand for unpretentious tuneful pieces was seemingly endless. A high proportion of the light music classics by Trevor Duncan, Charles Williams, Robert Farnon and many a lesser light, were written initially for mood-music libraries and published for wider dissemination later, particularly those chosen as signature tunes for long-running series.

By 1950, however, the Musicians' Union was questioning the whole principle of recording. Publishers refused to accept the severe restrictions on the use of their recordings demanded by the MU, and its members were forbidden to take on this work. With lucrative overseas markets continuing to beckon, as they still do, publishers simply took their work abroad, where quite different policies rule, and the musicians of Frankfurt, Stuttgart and Munich and other centres benefitted from work lost to British musicians. Understandably, the BBC (as did independent broadcasters later) agreed to severe limitations on the use of publisher recordings, nowadays called Library Music or Production Music. Plum spots on television were unavailable to them, and they found their occasional way into radio programmes only in exceptional circumstances, such as when cricket commentaries were abandoned because of rain, or some friendly producer bent the rules.

Around 1968, clutching at straws almost, Chandos (the aim to become one of the great record companies a distant vision) and one or two other publishers spotted a somewhat obscure market on television, the music broadcast for the benefit of engineers installing new sets around the country when only a trade test picture was being transmitted, at that time including long daylight hours. Quite unforeseen, a listening public for this quality light music gradually built up, at first by the chance switching on whilst waiting for, say, 'Watch with Mother', then by the realisation that here were extended transmissions of tuneful, attractive orchestral music of a kind unavailable on any radio channel. In time this hidden following passed the million mark, and the Performing Right Society recognised the fact by, for the first time, allocating significant royalties to the publishers and composers concerned. A new mini-industry came into being unnoticed outside the profession, with consequences 30 years later which took everyone by surprise.

The 1960s saw the beginnings of a process which over the next 30 years was to see the virtual elimination of outlets for light orchestral and ensemble music as composers had known it from the beginning of the century. Developments both on the 'serious' and 'popular' sides of music led to the increasing disparagement of the whole 'middle' range, which, whether we like it or not – and most of us don't – goes under the term light music.

This was nothing to do with its attractiveness, rather to the dearth of devotees, whether performers or administrators, in influential positions in the arts and broadcasting. At a time when state subsidy for the arts was increasing in real terms each year, the High Art lobby exercised more and more influence. Symphony orchestras increased in size and scope; shorter and lighter items, always an integral part of programmes in the past, and of particular value in guiding new concert-goers to the joys of classical music, came to be considered *infra dig*, and programmes became more and more masterpiece-only orientated. As orchestras on the popular front dried up for lack of resources there was a gradual proliferation of 'chamber orchestras' small and large. Though offering some of the world's greatest music, these inevitably look backwards rather than forwards, since their instrumentation offered no attraction to composers after about 1840, and that of the smaller ones was obsolete by 1780. Imperceptibly, the gap widened between the High Art devotee and the general musical public.

Much more serious for the future of music was the belief by those in influential positions, plus some of the most gifted composers themselves, that 'advancing' music's language, doing something 'new', was all-important. Temporary problems of communication with a reluctant public would be dispelled by time, as, in theory – today's discord is tomorrow's concord – they always had in the past. Thirty years on and it's abundantly clear that this simply has not happened. Unfortunately, to pursue the establishment line on contemporary music meant the denigration, implicitly and explicitly, of new music that stayed faithful to the ageless values of music.

Here we come to the crux of the matter, to be affirmed loudly and clearly, in any definition of light music, namely that it is written in music's single, immutable, universal language.

The discovery of music, music based on the flow of harmony, the tonality of being in a key, music that communicates to all, expressing the whole gamut of emotion with remarkable degree of correlation whatever the age or race, is one of the most wondrous achievements of Western civilisation. From its conception some 1000 years ago and 500 years of gestation, music's power grew, then came of age in what is rightly called the classical era, the late 1700s to, say, 1830. All the essentials of what is still adhered to by composers addressing general rather than specialised audiences was fully revealed by that time for future generations to build on.

Of course there were exciting developments to come to enrich music's language: the increasing sophistication of harmony, and the continuing process of discord being revealed as concord by the understanding of its context. New rhythms, new forms – every aspect of music was to be explored to the limit. The 20th century has seen spectacular advances in music's secondary techniques: developments in instruments and performer virtuosity, and with the coming of electrophonics, virtuosities way beyond the capacity of human dexterity, and sounds unrealisable by acoustic means which reveal the ultimate in sonic expression. All of which have been absorbed into music's vocabulary, usable in varying degrees according to the outlet concerned.

But the true and lasting success of any music, to this day, is dependent on the extent to which the hearer – and every listener is different – can relate it to the basic vocabulary and grammar of music's universal language, established for all time in the classical era. The lesson of all the best-loved music is that breaking new ground is of small import compared with the composer's ability to use music's existing vocabulary and grammar in a distinctive and meaningful way.

The coming of jazz and its commercial developments by way of swing and dance-music brought a new dimension into music, based on a revolutionary approach to rhythm, also bringing into everyday music new facets of melody and the chords and progressions explored earlier by Debussy – for me the greatest innovator of them all. A new freedom from older orthodoxies came with the success from the 1960s of composer-performers not inhibited by conventional training, nor by any need to set things down on paper first, their invention going straight into their vocalising and guitar-based harmonising; the most influential was the team of John Lennon and Paul McCartney. Note though that the most enduring of their songs are impeccably harmonised and shaped according to music's time-honoured principles.

With commercialism first and artistry second, it became increasingly apparent to the practitioners in the pop/rock field that what brought in the crowds and sold recordings quickest made musical values a poor second to the personality of the performers – who needs songwriters anyway – and the choreography and show-biz effects that more and more were needed to sell them. Worst of all for the health of music has been the increasingly drug-like dependency on sheer volume of sound hammered in by head-crunching drumbeats. For all the enterprise of the best of pop/rock and the enormous followings such manifestations command, the only items which graduate to standard repertoire (a smaller and smaller percentage – ask any restaurant pianist) are those which can be accepted into music's universal language.

The most powerful force in shaping the course of contemporary music was and is the BBC, for so long having the monopoly in national radio channels. But the step that was to spell eventual disaster to light music was the advocacy, from around 1969, of generic broadcasting. In place of the traditional concept of broadcasting – presenting balanced programmes, different kinds of music interspersed with news, talks, shows, plays and other features, as in the old Home Service and Light Programmes – the modern idea was of each channel offering a single commodity, allowing listeners to make their own choice as to the kind of programme they wanted at any given time.

Leaving aside the fact that listeners prefer to stay tuned to one channel, with variety the obvious way to hold that allegiance, the concept needed far more channels than were available to the BBC. The BBC settled for a 'pop' channel, Radio 1, a channel (Radio 2) for what one might call 'middle-of- the-road' popular music, and Radio 3 for its 'serious music' output. This left a big void between the two extremes, which it would take at least two channels to fill adequately. Radio 4 was set up as a spoken-word programme, with the barest of gestures towards music now and then. An exception was the popular 'Invitation to Music' programme, which for all its attractions to Radio 4 listeners was eventually axed precisely because, as the BBC informed me, a music programme was not appropriate on that channel. Yet a detailed listener-research project commissioned by the BBC in 1963, and kept secret, showed that it was in this wide 'middle' area of music that most listeners' loyalties lay. Despite that evidence, from then on light music had to be sold either to the High Art policy of Radio 3 or the purportedly with-it popular music of Radio 2.

The surprise was that light music stayed on Radio 3 for so long – eg, in 'Matinées Musicales', whose success with listeners over several years (thanks to producer Alan Owen) – and of the living composers performed – was clearly resented. From 1988, when that programme was dropped, it was made perfectly clear to composers that that kind of music was specifically not wanted.

The Light Programme, recast into Radio 2, went for a big increase in easy-listening 'dance-band beat' music, vocal and non-vocal. Instrumental items were expected to be arrangements of popular songs, leaving genuine light compositions out in the cold. Unless, that is, they were eligible under the other stringent directive, namely to perform only music *already well-known*, thus by definition rejecting any new music by practising composers, unless it had achieved success elsewhere, eg, in films or recording.

Determined advocacy by those producers still rooting for light music, and effective pressure group activity by the Composers' Guild, Songwriters' Guild (now BASCA) and the Light Music Society, persuaded the BBC to modify that rule. New music was welcomed so long as it *sounded* well-known. Hence a new genre of music was spawned, known in the trade as shmusic. It took the genius of Ronnie Binge to produce, for one of these shmusic sessions, a piece which was instantly appealing in its simplicity, yet memorable, achieving great success. The piece: *Sailing By*.

Though the 'swing', big-band area continued to flourish on radio, only a few programmes were left to carry the light music flag – 'Melodies for You', and similar programmes, plus the ever popular 'Friday Night is Music Night'.

We need to qualify this talk about the 'decline' of light music. It is concert music we are talking about, notably that at the forefront of critical and artistic notice, and/or feeding into national broadcasting – orchestral and chamber music.

The attraction of light music has never waned in those areas somewhat removed from big-time notice (because of which they don't *need* a term like light music to identify it) such as educational music, organ music and music for the thousands of concert and church choirs. In this latter field, John Rutter, without the aid of constant plugs on radio, has achieved success in the real sense – demand from performers, acclaim from listeners – in an idiom which would be debunked as 'light' by the establishment in other areas of music, but which speaks with Rutter's individual voice, and can be just as moving as many a more 'serious' offering.

Similar claims can be made for Gordon Langford, Philip Sparke and others in the brass band and wind band fields, which again receive scant attention from the broadcasters and High Art establishment. Here too, though, there are influential forces which follow the establishment line on contemporary music, perhaps jeopardising the support of their potential audiences, not to mention that of the nearests and dearests who help finance the instruments and the outings of the performers concerned.

Music written for the stage and screens has an important part to play in light music overall. The light musical stage in this country suffered a decline after Vivian Ellis produced the last of his major musicals in the mid-1950s, but the enormous popularity of the stage works of Andrew Lloyd Webber and his gifted librettists brought Britain to the forefront of world music theatre, at the same time confirming how music's universal language can continue to speak with an individual voice and offer so much enterprise and variety.

Ballet-music, since the earliest times a fruitful source of quality light music, for a time followed the trend to the more arty and esoteric. But the compositions of Carl Davis and Paul Reade suggest that good tunes and other timeless attributes are making a comeback. Many TV theme-tunes and much music for documentary and feature films fall firmly into the light music category. Performances and recordings of such music are enthusiastically received. The puzzle to many music lovers is why concert music written in similar idioms isn't just as common. The fact is that in this topsy-turvy world of contemporary music it takes more courage for a serious composer to write concert-music he knows the ordinary music-lovers would revel in, than music he knows will turn them away.

Paradoxically, the dearth of light music performances, both within broadcasting and without through the 70s and '80s, is one of the keys to the resurgence of interest since the early '90s. Older listeners after the long famine, welcome with nostalgic pleasure the tunes heard constantly in their youth. But the younger end, performers as well as listeners, are experiencing them for the first time, finding the tuneful, impeccably shaped and orchestrated light music a revelation.

A breakthrough came with the Marco Polo British Light Music series of orchestral CDs. The brainchild of New Zealander Murray Khouri, who as a brilliant clarinettist had played in many light orchestras from 1960 onwards, the first four CDs in the series were issued in 1992. More have followed, each featuring a single composer (apart from one compilation CD). There has been much critical acclaim and a great welcome from the public.

HMV and other record companies recognised the potential gold-mine in old recordings of light music, going back as far as Eric Coates' 78rpm records of the 1930s. Especially revealing were the early post World War II records by Charles Williams, Sidney Torch and others, brilliantly performed by the Queen's Hall Light Orchestra. Other companies, like Hyperion, ASV and Chandos, are now offering new recordings of light orchestral music.

Concurrently, publishers of the library music of the '50s and '60s have given selected items a new lease of life on CD, well promoted all over the world, particularly on TV stations. A most unlikely, almost bizarre, success story came with the issue by Chandos in 1996 of the CD 'Test Card Classics'. Sales soon outstripped anyone's expectations, confirming that the following for quality light orchestral music built up from the late 1960s was still there to be rekindled.

Proof of the void left by the BBC's music output, and indeed that of the numerous commercial radio stations that blossomed, came with the success of Classic FM, launched in 1993, with programmes based on popular classics. Inclusion of much light classical music, including that by present-day composers, and their readiness to give repeat broadcasts of potentially popular items (the opposite to BBC policy other than in 'pop' fields) have contributed to the station's success. There has also been increasing interest in light music by other radio stations round the world.

As far as live performance is concerned, there are many more light orchestras and ensembles, both in the light-classical area and of the Palm

Court type, than are known about, simply because they are localised and there is no broadcasting channel to carry their message. The Royal College of Music's Light Orchestra, established in 1993 by the young conductor and arranger John Wilson, shows how much the youngsters enjoy performing this range of music. The experiences, related to me many times, and experienced myself, of listeners full of enthusiasm, eg, surrounding the orchestra at an exhibition, or sitting and listening to the trio or quartet at a wedding reception or other festive occasion, thoroughly enjoying this 'novel' listening experience. 'Why don't we hear more of this?' is a common remark. Even classical string quartets are finding outlets in light music fields, not least because pianos, indispensable in the light combinations of old, are not around like they used to be.

Popularistic concerts abound these days, and 'serious' orchestras are more ready to present lighter programmes. But there are grave dangers for the health of music. First is the constant emphasis on *only* the well-known, indeed hackneyed, items from the past. Then there is the way new orchestras and ensembles press the nostalgia line, even to the extent of believing performances have to sound corny to be authentic. We need to recognise those conductors and performers who really understand light music and give it the dedication it needs. Dull, unsympathetic performances had much to do with its decline.

Most important of all, there must be readiness on all sides to look out for new music. There are many living composers, young and old, deserving the chance to win their way into repertoire on merit. As I've confirmed countless times, audiences *do* welcome new music and show genuine interest in the progress of the composers concerned, when it's in an idiom they can identify with. The worst legacy of the advance-music's-language brigade is to have nullified that aspect, a fundamental joy of music-making since music began.

Unfortunately there are still those in high places who hate the idea even of light music staying true to the fundamentals that characterises all the great light music of the past. Programming of much music is still in the hands of those whose policies have shown them to be quite incapable of getting on to the same wavelength as the ordinary music-lover. Composers' undoubted achievements in 'advanced' contemporary styles, and their acclaim with the dedicated minorities with whom they genuinely communicate, works against them when seeking empathy with the concert-goer in the street.

On the 'popular' side, too, many younger writers signal their lack of discernment when, attempting everyday music, they show non-knowledge of the fundamentals that make music the immensely satisfying art it is.

All too often banality and mindless repetition rule, plus the evident belief that people can't possibly listen to music or even watch TV unless there's a drum-beat banging away.

Nevertheless, there are many encouraging signs that light music is poised to take its rightful place in the esteem of the listening public. For this to come about the devotees of light music must speak out, put to the establishment, whether it's a national or local arts body, a seaside town looking for special attractions or anyone else concerned in concert promotion, that the music represented here has a vital role to play. There is need for the formation of a National Concert Orchestra, and the need for positive policies to direct interest to new light music. What is needed above all is a national radio channel. The BBC, which has done so much for light music since its inception, should surely take a lead here. For starters the BBC Concert Orchestra should return to its full-time role, displaying the repertoire for which it was created.

Whatever can be said about this country's position through the centuries in music generally – and here we must encompass also Ireland and others who share a common musical heritage, notably Australia and Canada – our standing in all the lighter forms of music from earliest times through to the present has been second to none. Let's keep it that way!

THE 'WARSAW CONCERTO' MAN
Richard Stewart Addinsell 1904-1977

Richard Addinsell, born on 13 January 1904 in London, has a secure place in light music's Hall of Fame on account of having composed the *Warsaw Concerto*: not quite a concerto of course, but a Rachmaninoff-inspired fragment for piano and orchestra – the first of many similar ones for films by a variety of composers and written for the spy film *Dangerous Moonlight*. For this he received the Polish Silver Cross of Merit.

He studied briefly at Hertford College, Oxford, and at the RCM (1925-6) and then, between 1929 and 1932, in Berlin and Vienna. During 1933 he visited the United States, where he composed film music for Hollywood. Back home three years later, he began composing for British films and examples over the next 30 years included: *Fire Over England* (1937), based on A.E.W. Mason's stirring novel of Secret Service in the first Elizabethan age, the music appropriately featuring heroic fanfares and marches; *Goodbye Mr. Chips* (1939), with its stirring 'school song' theme; *Blithe Spirit* (1945), whose haunting Waltz was arranged as a popular concert number; *Gaslight* (1940); *The Prince and the Showgirl* (1957), an incredibly tuneful score; *A Tale of Two Cities* (1958), whose main theme was later adapted for piano and orchestra as a second *Warsaw Concerto* but proved to be much less popular; *Beau Brummell* (1954); *The Waltz of the Toreadors* (1962); *Scrooge* (1951); *Passionate Friends*; *The Amateur Gentleman*, with its 'Invitation Waltz'; *The Roman Spring of Mrs Stone*; *The Big Blockade* (1941); *Out of the Clouds* (1954); *Under Capricorn*; *The Day Will Dawn*, from which the charming *Teatime Music*, for piano and strings, was extracted as a concert piece; *South Riding* (1937); *Love on the Dole*; *Greengage Summer*, one of Addinsell's own favourites; *Tom Brown's Schooldays* (1951); and a variety of wartime documentaries of which we can mention *The Lion Has Wings*, as the march *Cavalry of the Clouds* was extracted therefrom.

For some 20 years from 1942 Addinsell collaborated with Joyce Grenfell, writing the music for her one-woman shows. In fact, generally speaking his music, if not for the cinema, was for radio or theatre. Radio plays and features for which he composed music included *England's Darling* (1953) and *Saviours*, the movements from the latter being entitled Hope of Britain, The Light of Britain, Remember Nelson and The Unknown Soldier. His first work for the theatre appears to have been for the revue *The Charlot Show of 1926* and other revues like *All Clear, Living for Pleasure, The Globe Revue, Tuppence Coloured* (1947) and *Penny Plain* (1951) followed. Music was provided by him for many plays, including Clemence Dane's *Adam's Opera*, produced at the Old Vic in 1928, and *Come of Age* (also 1928) and also for *Moonlight is Silver,* which introduced him to Gertrude Lawrence, *L'Aiglon, Alice in Wonderland* (1930), a staged version of J.B. Priestley's *The Good Companions, Ring Around the Moon*, which included a waltz nearly as haunting as that in *Blithe Spirit, The Light of Heart* and *The Happy Hypocrite*.

'Pure' concert works included the *Festival* for piano and orchestra in beguine rhythm, beloved of the Melachrino Orchestra and admired by Percy Grainger (though even this derived originally from a play), the *Smokey Mountain Concerto*, also for piano and orchestra, written in the US in 1950, *Pantion Waltz*, the pastoral-sounding *The Isle of Apples, Journey to Romance, Tune in G*, a charming piece yet again using the forces of piano and orchestra, the *W.R.N.S. March* and the *March of the United Nations*, written in 1943, while songs like *My Heart's Light as Air, The Spanish Lady, I'm Going to See You Today* and *There's Nothing Now to Tell You* appear to be 'independent' ones. It is interesting for us to hear something of Addinsell's besides the *Warsaw Concerto*. The Marco Polo CD release gives us this chance and also I have heard two pieces not on that disc, namely *Teatime Music*, in a live concert, and the *Blithe Spirit* waltz on radio. Such opportunities give us a wider appreciation of his gift for delicately romantic melody supported by subtle harmony. He composed mainly at the piano, much of his work being orchestrated by Roy Douglas, Leonard Isaacs or Douglas Gamley. Addinsell, a quiet, rather introverted man, retired from composition in 1965 and died in November 1977.

I hope the foregoing has shown that Addinsell was something more than the composer of the *Warsaw Concerto*, deservedly famous though that was; since 1941 it has been recorded more than a hundred times and the sheet music has almost incredibly sold over three million copies. He was particularly associated with writing for films, radio and incidental and other music for the stage – music written for those media is so often ephemeral and quickly forgotten. Fortunately various people, both in Addinsell's day and more recently, recognising that he was one of the most rounded and tuneful of our light-music composers, have rescued his work by making concert arrangements of it and so ensured that it has the power to delight us even when the original film or play is forgotten.

NIGHTS OF DESTINY AND GLADNESS
The waltz composers Charles Ancliffe 1880-1952 and Sydney Baynes 1879-1938

Charles Ancliffe (1880-1952) was a bandmaster's son, so it was natural for him to train at the Royal Military School of Music, Kneller Hall, and to become a bandmaster himself, first of the South Wales Borderers, then of the Scarborough Military Band. His creative output reflects this to a degree, with marches like *Ironsides*, a rousing piece which I have heard in a brass band version, *Castles in Spain* and the popular *The Liberators*, but he is best remembered for his waltzes. *Nights of Gladness*, the most famous of them, gave its name to a BBC programme, for which it was the signature tune (he often conducted for the radio) and there were many other waltzes *like Alpine Echoes, April Clouds, April Buds, Dream Princess, Festive Days, Irish Whispers, Shy Glances, Southern Nights, Temptation, Smiles Then Kisses, Thrills, Hesitation, Twilight Time* and *Unforgotten Hours*.

In addition, he composed dozens of short genre pieces often styled 'intermezzo' or 'entr'acte': *April's Lady, Down in Zanzibar, A Forest Wooing, Burma Maid, Peacock's Parade, Waiting, Moon Man, Little Peter Piper, Canterbury Chimes, Cinderella's Wedding, The Flutter of the Fan, Secrets, Valley of Roses, Penelope's Garden, Jeanette* and *Fragrance*, plus the Two Novelettes, the 'Capricietto Italien' *Mariette-Coquette*, the Latin-American style serenade *El Saludo*, the oriental tone-picture *The Call of the Minaret* (surely Ketèlbey-inspired?) and the 'Dutch Silhouette' *Hans the Stroller*. His attractively and ingeniously titled suites include *Southern Impressions*, from which 'Carnival at Nice' was popular in its day, *Below Bridges* (1939, all London bridges, with the individual titles 'Wapping Old Stairs', 'Stepney Church' and 'Poplar') and *The Purple Vine*, in three movements: 'The Vintagers', 'The Purple Vine' and 'Evening at the Inn'. Ancliffe's songs were very popular in character and had titles like *Ask Daddy* (a little cycle), *Someday in Somebody's Eyes* and *I Cannot Live Without You*.

Like Ancliffe, Sydney Baynes is another who was known primarily for one work, the *Destiny Waltz*, one of many waltzes he wrote which had titles ending in 'y': *Ecstasy, Entreaty, Flattery; Frivolry; Harmony, Loyalty; Modesty; Memory, Mystery, Phantasy; Victory* and *Witchery*. He did of course write other things besides waltzes. Again, like Ancliffe, he worked for the BBC for many years and his march *Off We Go* was the Radio Variety march. Other nonwaltz compositions by him included a *Tarantella*, a *Miniature Ballet Suite*, the overture *Endure to Conquer*, first played at the Armistice Thanksgiving in Westminster Abbey in 1918, the genre pieces *The Spider's Thread* and *Pins and Needles* and another march, *Here Goes!* (Surely it was an error of judgement to have a title so near *Off We Go?*). His songs include several arrangements (by others) of the ever-present *Destiny;* of the rest, *First Love* and *Garden of My Love* were adapted as cornet (or clarinet) solos. He also wrote much for piano solo and some church music.

Baynes was arguably even more valuable, to the BBC and to light music generally, for his arrangements than his compositions. These were countless, including *Fifty Years of Song*, *The Gay Nineties*, *Tipperaryland* and other Irish selections, *Leslie Stuart's Songs*, *Ballad Memories*, *Molloy's Songs*, *Sanderson's Songs* (two selections), *W.H. Squire's Songs*, the dances from Sheridan's 'opera' *The Duenna*, in Alfred Reynolds' adaptation, *Supplication* (a 'sacred' medley) and so on. Baynes' fondness for saxophones emerges in his compositions and arrangements.

Born in 1879, he held the position of organist successively at various London churches, including Highgate Hill Unitarian and St Andrew's, Wells Street; he was then accompanist to singers like Edward Lloyd and Ben Davies. He subsequently conducted, as did so many of our light composers, in several London theatres, including the Theatre Royal, Drury Lane, the Adelphi and the Winter Gardens. He formed and conducted his own ten- piece orchestra between 1928 and 1938, which broadcast and recorded regularly. He died on 3 March 1938 at Willesden.

Various CDs of Archibald Joyce compositions have appeared; surely there is enough material for others devoted to Ancliffe and Baynes?

BRITAIN'S 'MARCH KING'
Kenneth J. Alford 1881-1945

John Philip Sousa is *the* March King, but this country can make a strong reply to him in the persons of James Ord Hume (whom unfortunately we have not space here to deal with in detail) and Kenneth Alford, the former particularly associated with brass banding, the latter with military bands.

Kenneth J. Alford was born Frederick Joseph Ricketts in London on 21 February 1881. Like Hume, he played as a boy in a military band, that of the 2nd Royal Irish Regiment; he served in India with them. His instrument was the cornet but he could also play piano and organ. Between 1904 and 1908 he was a student bandmaster at Kneller Hall, then immediately after that Bandmaster to the 2nd Argyll and Sutherland Highlanders. It was about this time that he began composing under the Alford pseudonym. Using it in a march composition competition at Kneller Hall he came last. Alford's marches *The Voice of the Guns* and *Colonel Bogey* have figured in arrangement in two major films, *Lawrence of Arabia* (with parts for five saxophones, accordion and guitar added) and *Bridge on the River Kwai* respectively. *Colonel Bogey*; at least as popular as any of Sousa's marches, was not quite his first published one – that was either *Holyrood* or *The Vedette* – but when it appeared in 1914 it caught on immediately; its opening two-note motif (B flat/G) is said to derive from an experience on a golf course in Scotland, when an irate golfer whistled those notes at Alford to impress upon him that he was standing on the line of his next shot. *The Great Little Army* was composed for the BEF (the 'Old Contemptibles') of 1914, and other Great War marches were *The Voice of the Guns*, dedicated to the Royal Artillery, *The Vanished Army*, introducing snatches of *Tipperary*; and, foreshadowing his later service as a Royal Marines Director of Music, *On The Quarter-Deck* and *The Middy*. From the 1920s came *The Mad Major* (1921), *Cavalry of the Clouds* (1923), a tribute to the RAF, *The Thin Red Line* (celebrating the 93rd Foot's or Argyll and Sutherland Highlanders' stand at the Battle of Balaklava in the Crimean War and indeed written for the Argylls many years before), *Old Panama*, and, also recalling a visit to New Zealand in 1925, *Dunedin*.

In 1927 he left the Argylls after 20 years and became Director of Music for the Royal Marines at Deal, succeeding Walton O'Donnell (*qv*), moving to the Plymouth Division in 1930. For the Marines he wrote the marches *H.M. Jollies*, which introduces bugle calls from all three RM divisions, *The Standard of St George* and, incorporating a reference to the Marines' quick march *(A Life on the Ocean Wave), By Land and Sea.* By the time the last of these appeared a second world war had begun. Alford, who had retired in 1940, was recalled to his duties as a major at Plymouth almost immediately and served four more years before retiring on account of ill-health in 1944.Two more marches, his last, are tributes to two Allied formations in that war, *The Army of the Nile* (1941) – the unofficial title given to Wavell's troops in Libya in 1940-41 – and *Eagle Squadron* (1942), the RAF unit(s) comprising American volunteer aircrew. Alford died just a week after the end of the war in Europe, at Reigate on 15 May 1945, survived by his wife, whom he married in 1907, three sons and three daughters. He left behind his recordings of many of his own works with the Plymouth Divisional Band, records prized and much sought after today.

His marches were not nearly as numerous as Ord Hume's or Sousa's; in fact we have mentioned almost all of them. But most are still in the repertoire because their range of expression, ingenious counter-melodies and finely judged instrumentation make them second to none. Not that Alford (any more than Hume) confined himself to writing marches. The first non-march composition I know of is *Valse Riviera* (1910), and another waltz, *Thoughts,* was a big hit in 1917. The pastoral fantasia *The Smithy* and the rhapsody *The Hunt* were orchestral pieces catering for the British public's love of rural light music. He produced a considerable number of novelty items for one or two xylophones – *Sparks, The Two Imps, Mac and Mac* and *The Two Dons,* of which the first two at least can still be heard in concert today. *The Smithy* also makes use of xylophones in its score. There were also a number of popular arrangements like *A Musical Switch* (1921) and its sequel, *The Lightning Switch,* both potpourris of favourite tunes, and sundry transcriptions. A march fantasia of 1939, *Colonel Bogey on Parade,* introduced his own best-known march, while his later transcription of two march tunes, *Lilliburlero* and the Royal Marines' Regimental March, *A Life on the Ocean Wave,* enjoyed as much exposure as his own marches; he also produced a suite based on themes from Wagner's *Die Walkure* and literally dozens of other classical arrangements. He even composed some church music. We should recognise that in Alford we have a worthy counterblast to John Philip Sousa, himself a one-time Marine Director of Music across the other side of the Atlantic.

PLYMOUTH HOE AND OTHER TRAVELS
John Ansell 1874-1948

Of those writing light music in Britain during the first half of the present century – people like Eric Coates, Haydn Wood, Wilfrid Sanderson, Percy Fletcher, Alfred Reynolds, Montague Phillips, Albert Ketèlbey, Arthur Wood and others – some are almost forgotten, but others are remembered if only for one or two short items. One of those apparently in the former category is John Ansell, born on 26 March 1874 and who died at Marlow, on the river Thames, on 14 December 1948, although his 'nautical overture, *Plymouth Hoe* (a potpourri of popular nautical melodies rather than a truly original work) remained popular for many years with orchestras and also in a military band arrangement by the Bournemouth's Dan Godfrey and is still occasionally played – rousingly so and more than once, in Doncaster in recent years, by the Doncaster Schools' Symphonic Band. It is good to know young people still derive pleasure from the light music of yesteryear. Yet Ansell's career is of interest as it does to a degree reflect the experience of many of the other light music composers we have mentioned above.

He studied composition at the Guildhall School of Music with the Scots composer Hamish MacCunn and then – like Fletcher, Reynolds, Ketèlbey, Arthur Wood, Howard Carr and Herman Finck – pursued a career as a musical director in various London theatres. He had served his apprenticeship there, having played the viola under Sullivan's baton, and he conducted in most West End theatres at one time or another. He was particularly associated with the Playhouse, where he wrote incidental music for all productions there in his time, the Winter Garden (for seven years in the 1920s), the Alhambra, with whose orchestra he made gramophone records (also for seven years, 1913-20), the Shaftesbury and the Adelphi. He worked for four-and-a-half years (1926-30) for the BBC, which was from its beginning an encourager of most of the light music composers we discuss in this book and especially Coates, Fletcher, Reynolds and Haydn Wood; he conducted an ensemble known as the QLO Orchestra during those years and was briefly, in 1930, Assistant Conductor of the new BBC Symphony Orchestra.

Ansell's compositions include both operettas and orchestral works, some of the latter incidental music, some not. Among the operettas were *The King's Bride* (1911), *Medorah*, songs from which were published, and *Violette* (1918), which has some happy characterisation. These all achieved modest success but not more than that. We do not hear them today. According to his obituary in *The Times* (15 December 1948), Ansell's incidental music 'exhibits a soundness of construction and vein of fantasy which should ensure it the regard of discriminating audiences'. Nevertheless, it has almost all disappeared from view, though his orchestral music once enjoyed popularity both with the seaside orchestras and on the BBC. (An early *Serenade* for cello and orchestra was even premiered at the Proms in 1898). If *Plymouth Hoe* is described as a nautical overture, the slightly longer *The Windjammer* could be similarly subtitled; there was also a 'military overture', *Private Ortheris*, and another piece entitled *Tally-Ho* which might be reckoned a hunting overture. The *Overture to an Irish Comedy* was just one of a number of Ansell pieces which drew inspiration from Ireland, the others being the suite *Innisfail*, *Three Irish Pictures* and *Three Irish Dances*. Other suites included a *Children's Suite* in no fewer than ten movements, though the suite played for no longer than 25 minutes even if all the movements were done at one hearing (which in practice did not happen), a colourful *Mediterranean Suite*, in three dance-like movements representing Spain, Italy and France, and the *Suite Pastoral* in four movements.

Two dance suites were of interest: *The Shoe*, as an example of the ingenuity composers showed in devising fresh ideas and fresh titles for their light suites, which were ten a penny at that time – its five movements are entitled 'The Sabot' (Rustic Dance), 'The Ballet Shoe', 'The Court Shoe' (Passepied), 'The Sandal' (Eastern Dance) and 'The Brogue' (Strathspey) – and the four *Danses Miniatures de Ballet*, whose interest lies particularly in including no fewer than three euphoniums in the score as well as the usual wind and brass. Ansell never, in the 20-odd scores I have looked through, wrote for more than two horns and his orchestras were otherwise on the small side, maybe reflecting his experience in the theatre, but the euphonium, just one this time, also figured in the *Overture to an Irish Comedy* and the extended waltz, *The Toymaster of Nuremberg*. Other orchestral pieces by Ansell enjoyed popularity, like the lightweight entr'actes *April Blooms* and *The Elves' Wedding*, the march *Spick and Span*, the 'characteristic piece' *The Grand Vizier*, the overture *John and Sam* and the valse lente *Le Printemps*. Well-written, attractively tuneful and showing an easy, flowing style, they are sadly all forgotten except for *Plymouth Hoe*, which was mentioned even in his *Times* obituary as his best-remembered piece, although I have known people who have confused this with another overture – William Walton's so-different *Portsmouth Point*.

THE 'CORNISH RHAPSODY' MAN
Hubert Bath 1883-1945

Hubert Bath, born in Barnstaple on 6 November 1883, died at Harefield in Middlesex on 24 April 1945, just days before VE Day. He sang in the local church choir as a boy (his father, a schoolteacher, was choirmaster) and studied piano, organ and composition when he went to the RAM at the age of 17. His musical output, as we shall see, looked in several directions, but he certainly falls within our chosen field of light music, not least because his best-remembered work, the *Cornish Rhapsody* for piano and orchestra, written for the film *Love Story*, was so popular with light orchestras for so long. It was not his only film music by a long chalk; in 1929 he composed at least some of the soundtrack for the first full-length British talkie, *Blackmail*, directed by Alfred Hitchcock, and was working on the score of *The Wicked Lady* when he died. There were many others for the Gaumont British and Gainsborough (and other) studios, of which I remember particularly the 1935 Donat version of *The Thirty-Nine Steps*, *Rhodes of Africa* (1936) and *The Passing of the Third Floor Back* (1935). He conducted much for films and indeed in the concert hall.

Nor was the *Cornish Rhapsody* his only light orchestral piece. At his best Bath approached Eric Coates. Like Coates he produced several stirring marches, such as *Atlantic Charter*, with its parts for three saxophones, *Empire Builders*, *Out of the Blue* (written for an RAF Display at Hendon, and once recorded by a brass band, this was for many years the signature tune of BBC Radio's 'Sports Report'), the 'nautical march' *Admirals All*, which added two cornets and a euphonium to the usual orchestral brass of four horns, two trumpets and three trombones, and *The Nelson Touch*, performed in Doncaster and doubtless elsewhere during the 1940s. His orchestral suites ranged widely in a topographical sense: *Two Sea Pictures* and, drawing on memories of South Africa, the *African Suite* – premiered at the Henry Wood Proms in 1909 and 1915 respectively – *Two Japanese Sketches* and the *Egyptian Suite* (both the latter were published also for piano solo), the *Norwegian Suite* for small orchestra, the 'oriental suite' *Scenes from the Prophets*, *Pierrette by the Stream* and *Woodland Scenes*, all three of which were very popular, the two *Troubadour Suites*, the *Petite Suite Romantique* and a tribute to his native county, *Devonia*, whose three movements are entitled 'Prelude, Breeze at Hartland Point', 'Melodie d'amour, Lorna of Exmoor' and 'Sea Dogs of Devon', which is of course another nautical march.The stylish overture *Midshipman Easy* was also inspired by the sea and Marryat's novel of course; the *Summer Nights* waltz of 1901 achieved much popularity, while the *Princess Mary Waltz* was written for the wedding of the Princess Royal in 1923.

With G.H. Clutsam and Basil Hood he brought out an operetta, *Young England*, produced at Daly's in 1916 (an eye defect precluded his serving outside England in World War I), from which the song *Sweethearts and Wives* enjoyed great fame, and an extensive selection from which appeared on gramophone records at the time. Other stage works were in general more serious. *The Spanish Student*, after Longfellow, was written when he was studying at the Royal Academy in 1904; *Bubbole* was performed in Milan in 1920 and (retitled as *Bubbles*) by the Carl Rosa Company in Belfast in 1923 and at London's Scala Theatre the following year; and there were also *The Sire de Maletroit's Door, The Three Strangers*, after Hardy (both one-act affairs) and *Trilby*, inspired by Gerald Du Maurier's novel. In his earlier days especially Bath wrote a considerable number of short or shortish cantatas which were eagerly taken up by provincial choral societies, works such as *The Jackdaw of Rheims, Men on the Line*, for the male voices of the Great Eastern Railway, *Psyche's Departure, Look at the Clock* (described as a 'Welsh Rhapsody': 1910), *Orpheus and The Sirens, The Legend of Nerbudda* (1908), *The Wedding of Shon Maclean* (1909, written for the Leeds Festival of 1910) and *The Wake of O'Connor* (1913). The latter two were put on in my home town of Doncaster by the Doncaster Musical Society in 1911 and 1920 respectively (*O'Connor* had originally been announced for 1915). Bath even arranged *Elijah Memories*, a potted version of Mendelssohn's oratorio, and also produced smaller-scale vocal pieces, partsongs like *The Heart of the Night* (1910), *When You Sing* (1911), recitations to music, the three songs *Voices of the Air* (1911), in six parts (SAATBB), and a variety of solo songs: *Bedtime Ballads* for children, the humorous *It Was a Golfer and His Lass*, the *Three Indian Songs*, songs for the ballad opera *Polly*, revived in the 'twenties in the wake of the success of Frederic Austin's version of *The Beggar's Opera*, and several songs inspired by the sea, including *Envoi: A Sea Sketch, The Vikings' War Song, The Jolly Roger* and *Sea Memories*. As we have seen, Bath trained as a pianist at the Royal Academy – he also studied composition there with Frederick Corder – and his works include *Coquette, Italian Suite, Song of Autumn* and *Song of Summer* plus a Sonatina in F, all for piano solo, and organ pieces like *Toccatina* (1914) and *Heroic Prelude* (1928).

Bath had a genial sense of humour. He was a conductor of both Quinlan Opera (in Australia and South Africa) and Carl Rosa for short periods, he directed the GSM's Opera Class and was for a while Music Adviser to the LCC and organised its outdoor band concerts. He adjudicated band contests and composed a considerable amount for brass band himself.

Some of his output in this direction were potpourris of popular tunes but it did include *Freedom* (the test-piece at the National Championships in 1922, 1947 and 1973), which is effectively a symphony for brass condensed into a mere 12 minutes, and *Honour and Glory*, the test-piece at the same Championships in 1931. These are testing, substantial and serious works and are still played by bands – I have myself enjoyed them. He was an experienced bandsman, conducting the famed St Hilda's Band, with whom he made records.

Much of Bath's work as listed appears to show a composer, like Edward German or Sullivan maybe, who was anxious to be known for this more serious side of his output, but doomed to be remembered for more popular effusions. For every thousand who know *Cornish Rhapsody* is there even one who knows he composed a symphonic poem, *The Visions of Hannele*, written in 1913 (revised in 1920) and based on incidental music he wrote for the play *Hannele* at His Majesty's Theatre years earlier? (He was credited with chamber music too, but I have not yet discovered any.) This many-sided musical personality would be upset to think he was remembered only for *Cornish Rhapsody* but perhaps the brass band movement has saved him from that fate.

MUSICAL CASCADES
Ronald Binge 1910-1979

Ronald Binge, or Ronnie as he was generally known, was born in Derby on 15 July 1910 and was largely self-taught, though he did have early lessons in piano, organ and harmony. His first job was as composer, arranger and organist to a 'silent' cinema that had a small orchestra. After a season in Great Yarmouth, he moved to London in 1932 and played in theatre, café and dance ensembles, often on the piano-accordion. His break-through came in 1934-5 when he became the arranger for Mantovani's orchestra. After war service in the RAF (which brought him musical experience and a wife) he returned to Mantovani; the once very popular *Charmaine* was his arrangement and the even more popular (and cunningly constructed) *Elizabethan Serenade* was composed for Mantovani in 1952. It was Binge who created the 'cascading strings' sound by the use of simulated reverberation brought about by dividing the violins into several parts, each allocated a different melody note in turn. By that time Binge had gone freelance and was concentrating on composition.

His first big compositional success had been the orchestral piece *Spitfire* in 1940, composed in Blackpool while on RAF service and predating Sir William Walton's more famous tribute by at least a year. Ronnie had his own radio series with 'String Song' between 1952 and 1963 for which he wrote his own signature tune; it was only then that he turned to conducting regularly. His compositions were varied. Many were for light orchestra, novelty items like *Entry of the Robots*, the march *Briefcase and Bowler Hat*, *Red Sombrero*, in Latin American mood, the cheeky *High Stepper* (from a TV programme), *Farewell Waltz*, *Coffee Cup Chatter*, *Mischievous Mac*, *Scherzo*, written in early 19th-century style and sounding not at all unlike Schubert, *Summer Madness*, *Flash Harry*, the can-can *Faire Frou-Frou*, *Fugal Fun*, *Madrugado* ('Daybreak') which featured four saxophones as well as the usual orchestra – *Las Castahuelas*, another Spanish one, the serenade *Love in a Mist* for harp and strings, *Dance of the Snowflakes*, using the Mantovani cascade again, the prelude *The Whispering Valley*; for piano and strings, *Paramariba*, *Sailing By*, *Snakes and Ladders*, the nursery fantasy *Tales of the Three Blind Mice* (1949), *Trade Winds* (1949), a marvellous evocation of the days of sail, sets of variations on *The Carnival of Venice* (called *Venetian Carnival*: 1957), *Cockles and Mussels* (1956) and *The Keel Row, Scottish Rhapsody* (a potpourri of well-loved Scots tunes) and, probably the best known of all after the *Elizabethan*

Serenade, that charming miniature for oboe and strings *The Water Mill.*

Rather longer items, though still light in character, were *Thames Rhapsody,* written for a BBC Light Music Festival, the Concerto for alto saxophone composed for a later BBC Festival which has a gorgeously warm Romance as its slow movement (the complete Concerto is quite often performed; I heard it in Doncaster, with orchestra, only a few years ago), the *Saturday Symphony* (1966-8) and *Duel for Conductors* for brass band and orchestra (1976). *The Water Mill* was also arranged as a solo for cornet and brass band and this was not Binge's only connection with band music. Apart from *Old London* and *Trumpet Spectacular* and the novelty item for trombones and brass band *Trombonioso,* his *Cornet Carillon* of 1954 for four cornets and brass band, and yet again using the Mantovani cascade effect, was one of the most popular items ever composed for brass band (there is also a version for orchestra but this is not nearly as atmospheric).

Binge, who died in 1979, is most certainly not one of those composers remembered for just one work. *Elizabethan Serenade, Sailing By, The Water Mill, Madrugado, The Red Sombrero* and *Cornet Carillon* were popular for decades and indeed remain so. Some of his music was published for piano solo, like the *Toccata,* and *Vice Versa* (1948: both these were musical palindromes) and arrangements of *Caribbean Calypso* and *The Red Sombrero,* originally for orchestra, and the rumba serenade *Siesta,* originally for dance band. Chamber works included *The Windmill,* for oboe and piano, and *Upside Downside,* also a musical palindrome but this time for descant recorder, violin and cello, written for his young son Christopher. He even tried his hand at writing for guitar solo late in life. He composed little for voice apart from a late (1970) *Festival Te Deum,* although the *Elizabethan Serenade* was inevitably arranged, with words by Christopher Hassall, for both SATB and women's voices almost as soon as it appeared (as well as for almost every conceivable grouping of instrumental forces) and he published *Sailing By* for women's voices and one or two solo songs like *The Story of Cock Robin.* He wrote film scores, including *Desperate Moment* (1953) and *The Runaway Bus* (1954), and for some 50 American TV shows.

He served for several years on the Council of the Songwriters' Guild and then on that of the Performing Right Society. His tremendous versatility, his mastery of technique and his wealth of invention, all of which enabled him to compose miniatures of instant memorability, give him a firm, enduring and well-respected place in the pantheon of English light music.

THE 'LILAC TIME' MAN
G.H. Clutsam 1866-1951

I began researching Clutsam in 1988, the year of the Australian Bicentennial, when several Australian musicians, and especially Percy Grainger, received at least modest remembrance in concerts, but I remember seeing no mention then of the name George Howard Clutsam. Yet he was born in Sydney, New South Wales, on 26 September 1866. As a pianist, largely self-taught, he toured quite widely in the Antipodes and Asia before coming to London in 1889. For ten years he appeared as an accompanist at principal concerts in London and the provinces, accompanying his fellow Australian Melba in 1893, and then gave up playing in public to concentrate on composition. He had already made his mark in this respect as his orchestral *Carnival Scenes* received its premiere in the very first season of the Henry Wood Proms (1895). Another major orchestral item, the 'symphonic idyll' *The Lady of Shalott* (after Tennyson), was performed by the New Symphony Orchestra in London during 1909. About that time things began to happen for him on the operatic stage. He had previously (1905) written an opera, *The Queen's Jester*, and his one-acter *A Summer Night* enjoyed the accolade of a production with Beecham conducting, at His Majesty's Theatre, its first night being 23 July.

The music was praised as being colourful and imaginative. In 1912 two more operas were written: *After a Thousand Years*, a miniature affair lasting only 25 minutes, and *King Harlequin*, a four-act 'dramatic opera' which in a German translation was staged in Berlin as *Konig Harlekin*; it was based on Rudolf Lothar's *Maskenspiel*. An *Introduction and Dance* were extracted from it and performed at the Henry Wood Proms in 1913. Clutsam's 'fantastic melodrama' *The Pool* may also be listed in this connection.

At this time he was writing music criticism for *The Observer*, which he was to do for ten years (1908-18), and in later life he was Vice-Chairman of the Performing Right Society; but around the time of World War I his career turned to the more popular end of the musical theatre. *Young England*, variously described as a light opera and as a musical play, was written in collaboration with Hubert Bath (*qv*), with lyrics by Basil Hood of *Merrie England* fame, and received its first performance at Daly's Theatre in 1916, the original cast including Clara Butterworth, wife of the composer Montague Phillips (*qv*), and Harry Dearth. It was extensively excerpted on gramophone records at the time. It was followed by other Clutsam musicals, *The Little Duchess* (1922), whose most popular number was 'One Glimpse of a Face'; *Lavender*, from which 'Sunshine For You' achieved popularity; *Barbara, or the Broken Sixpence* (1932); and *Gabrielle* (1921), whose music was written jointly with Archibald Joyce, the waltz composer. A popular excerpt from the latter was 'Cowbells' and Joyce arranged a waltz from some of the operetta's themes. But Clutsam's outstanding successes in this area were in works where the music was derived from the compositions of others. *Lilac Time* was the English version of *Die Dreimadlerhaus*, a musical put together in Vienna by one Berte from tunes by Schubert. In France the musical was known as *Chanson d'Amour*, in the United States as *Blossom Time*; *Lilac Time*, in Clutsam's English version, ran for 626 performances after its premiere at the Lyric on 22 December 1922 and has often been revived. Some observers held up their hands in horror, and still do, at using (or abusing) Schubert's music in this way, but the piece has undoubted charm and I cannot remember that playing in my youth Clutsam's own piano arragements of numbers from *Lilac Time* hindered my later appreciation of Schubert: rather the reverse. Clutsam, doubtless encouraged by its success, devised another musical, *The Damask Rose* in 1929, using Chopin's music, and there have been musicals by others based on the works of Dvořák and Grieg, for example, which have enjoyed considerable success.

Clutsam, who died in London on 17 November 1951, aged 85, was also involved with the new medium of the cinema. In 'silent' days he devised for Metzler a compendium of suitable music for cinema musicians to play live to the screened pictures; and with Richard Tauber he composed music for the talkie *Heart's Desire*. By no means all of Clutsam's work was for the stage. He composed over 150 separate songs, many of them arrangements of folk and other popular tunes, others original. He was attracted to the atmosphere of the American Deep South and this inspired his most popular song, *Ma Curly Headed Babby*, which appeared in many arrangements and became particularly associated with Paul Robeson, and also others like *Creole Cradle Song, Mancipation Day; Wake up Little Darkie* and *A-Wearyin' For You*. Other songs included several 'croon songs', *By-Low-By, Gipsy Croon Song* and *Woodland Croon Song*, and ballads like *I Dreamt of a King's Fair Daughter, I Wander the Woods, If I Were a Lark, My Rose of Lorraine, Myrra* and *Sweet Be Not Proud*. More ambitious were the song-cycle *The Hesperides*, the cantata *The Quest of Rapunzel* and the two sets of *Songs of the Turkish Hills*, 12 songs in all, of which *I Know of Two Bright Eyes* became one of Clutsam's best-known songs. A few items like *The Cavaliers* and *Once There Lived a Lady Fair* were composed for chorus (SATB) and a number of his solos were arranged as partsongs.

Of his output for orchestra we have already mentioned his two most ambitious ventures. Some of the other works in this genre also reflected Clutsam's preoccupation with the southern United States, like the *Three Plantation Sketches* for small orchestra and a selection of his own *Plantation Songs* which he made for full orchestra. The suite *Green Lanes of England*, in four movements entitled 'The Joyous Wayfarer', 'The Forge' 'Noontide Lovers' and 'Gypsies', is an essay in the manner of Eric Coates and there are also a *Comedy Overture* and an intermezzo *The Blessed Damozel*, both performed at Bournemouth in 1906, and short individual movements like *April Night* and *Kopak*, both for small orchestra, the latter including also a part for a solo violin. Clutsam arranged much of his work, especially from his lighter theatre productions, for piano solo and wrote original piano pieces also; one organ work is an *Improvisation*, published by Ashdown in 1914. He was so much more than just the arranger of *Lilac Time:* his *Who's Who* entry perhaps reflected this fact as it did not mention that, his most popular success.

THE KING OF LIGHT MUSIC
Eric Coates 1886-1957

There is little need to say much in this book about Eric Coates (1886-1957) as he has already been covered so well in comparatively recent years by Geoffrey Self in *In Town Tonight*, and by the reissue of Coates' own autobiography, *Suite in Four Movements* (both published by Thames Publishing), probably because his music has for a variety of reasons survived better than that of his peers. But to write a book on British light music of this century and not include Coates would almost be to re-write *Hamlet* without the Prince. So here goes; those really wanting to know about Coates in detail are cordially referred to those two books, among others.

I saw Eric Coates once, at Sheffield City Hall on 18 April 1953, when he conducted the second half, entirely devoted to his own music, of a Hallé Orchestra concert styled 'Masterpieces of English Light Music' (few major orchestral series would risk such a programme nowadays; the first half, conducted by George Weldon, comprised Sullivan's *Di Ballo*, Edward German's *Henry VIII* dances, Percy Grainger's *Mock Morris* and *Molly on the Shore* and Haydn Wood's *Variations on a Once Popular Humorous Song*). It may be worth recalling the works he conducted on that occasion as perhaps indicative of some of those he regarded most highly. After the 'Prelude and Hornpipe' from *The Four Centuries* – surely one of the finest bits of pastiche by a British light music composer – and the delicious 'Dance of the Orange Blossoms' from *The Jester at the Wedding*, Walter Lear was the soloist in the *Saxo-Rhapsody*; which is, for all its easy fluency, still one of the finest pieces written for saxophone, and the concert ended with *By the Sleepy Lagoon* and the ever-popular *Three Elizabeths Suite*, complete. I have the happiest recollections of the concert, which is an indication – if one were needed – that Coates was a fine conductor of his own music, something borne out further by his many recordings.

Coates, unlike so many of the figures discussed in this book, had little or no connection with the theatre, either as musical director or as composer. His ballets *The Jester at the Wedding* and *The Enchanted Garden* were never staged and are to be regarded, as perhaps they always were, as concert works. The earlier *Seven Dwarfs* had little success in the theatre. Coates is reckoned primarily as an orchestral composer, his career in this direction beginning in 1911 with the first performance of the *Miniature Suite* by the Queen's Hall Orchestra – an ensemble in which

Coates played the viola – conducted by Sir Henry Wood, although there had been an earlier *Ballad* for strings, performed in Nottingham in 1904 and unpublished in Coates' lifetime but revived in recent years.

He composed a handful of chamber works and piano solos, mostly now forgotten or lost, or both (although *First Meeting* has been recorded in its original guise for viola and piano; it was published for violin and piano) and three brief choral works; but Coates' most important non-orchestral music is the corpus of 160-odd songs, mostly of the ballad type, although he published a number of settings of Shakespeare and some other 'serious' poets. Over 30 of these songs pre-dated the *Miniature Suite*, so one might justifiably say that Coates made a name with his vocal music before his orchestral work took off. His songs have done well in recorded performances over the past decade or so, particularly in a Marco Polo CD issued in 1996. He continued writing songs up to within a few years of his death in 1957, though the best-remembered of them come from the years between 1909, when his first big hit, *Stonecracker John*, appeared, and the late 1920s, which were graced by such delights as *Birdsongs at Eventide* and *Homeward to You*. As was the case with Wilfrid Sanderson (*qv*), Coates produced many songs inspired by the sea and, especially so, the West Country (eg, *A Dinder Courtship, The Widow of Penzance, By Mendip Side* and, perhaps best loved of all, the nostalgic *Green Hills o' Somerset*). But for all their shapeliness they *are* ballads; little or no attempt is made to illuminate the words, which in many cases are indeed undistinguished.

Coates was not perhaps one of the most prolific of British light music composers, except maybe as a producer of songs. Although many people connect Coates with the light concert suite, Haydn Wood actually composed more examples in that genre. It is true, however, that Coates' orchestral suites and individual movements, especially his marches, have with scattered exceptions survived better than those of any of his contemporaries. One may reasonably ask why this is so. Coates' work showed the hand of an experienced master craftsman; it may readily be deduced that he was for many years an orchestral player in one of the finest ensembles in the land. But many other British light music composers were excellent writers, too, and their work is also melodically attractive, Coates' music, however, is not merely melodically attractive: it is *memorably* melodically attractive, pointed as it is by driving rhythms. Particularly is this true of his marches, of which he produced a dozen or more which achieved enormous popularity. Some of them were adapted as signature tunes of very long-running radio programmes: *Calling All Workers* ('Music While You Work'), heard four times a day, five days a week, for many years, *Knightsbridge* ('In Town Tonight') and – not a march, but equally memorable – the valse serenade *By the Sleepy Lagoon* ('Desert Island Discs', still running). These in turn kept his music aggressively before the public. By the time he died, radio was beginning to take second place to television, but Coates also wrote title music for the small screen – like the Rediffusion March *Music Everywhere* (1948), while 'Halcyon Days', from *The Three Elizabeths*, was appropriated almost a decade after his death to introduce the amazingly popular adaptation of *The Forsyte Saga* – and indeed for the large screen. *The Dam Busters March* of 1954 has perhaps become Coates' single most popular movement, although *High Flight* (his last work, completed in December 1956; the film appeared in 1957) is scarcely less good. The main score for *The Dam Busters* is credited to Leighton Lucas (*qv*); Coates' march is primarily title music, although quotations from it elsewhere in the film may be readily discerned. Coates began his orchestral composing career in a style owing much to Edward German, who in 1911 was perhaps the major figure in British light music, but he quickly added his own thoroughly individual features, not least the incorporation of the syncopated dance-band idiom popular in the 1920s, which may be glimpsed most clearly in the last movement of *The Four Centuries* suite and in the 'phantasy' *The Three Bears*. The saxophone was particularly associated with that and other up-tempo styles and it is perhaps no accident that Coates wrote a *Rhapsody* for alto sax at a time when little concerted music had been penned for it. Coates' work, however, primarily explores the instrument's lyrical possibilities.

Truly Eric Coates remains the key figure in British light music. But why, as a Nottinghamshire man born and bred, did he leave it to Frederic Curzon to compose a *Robin Hood Suite*? One last thought: Coates had no 'identity crisis'. Edward German, Montague Phillips. Samuel Coleridge-Taylor – all these, and several others, were masters of light music while hoping, desperately in some cases, to be masters of something a little more serious. Eric Coates was happy to be 'the King of Light Music'.

COLOUR AND MELODY
Samuel Coleridge-Taylor 1875-1912

With Coleridge-Taylor, as with Edward German, Arthur Sullivan, even Montague Phillips and Haydn Wood, we have the problem of whether to regard him as a 'serious' or as a 'light' composer. On the one hand he composed a Symphony, the *Ballade* in A minor, a Violin Concerto, several cantatas, of which the *Hiawatha* trilogy became remarkably popular, but others, like *Meg Blane, Kubla Khan* and *A Tale of Old Japan*, also earned success in their day, plus much chamber music, most of it from his student days, including a Nonet, a Clarinet Quintet and a String Quartet. On the other hand, his many excursions into the fields of the light suite and the ballad surely justify us in discussing him here.

Coleridge-Taylor's early life – he was born in London on 15 August 1875 – was underprivileged. There was little money after his father, a Negro physician from Sierra Leone, deserted his (white) mother and returned to Africa. Samuel's colour was an added complication, although, viewing his life as a whole, the amount of colour prejudice against him can easily be exaggerated. He certainly did not lack for encouragement before, during and after his time at the Royal College of Music, which he entered in 1890 after early violin studies in Croydon and singing experience in a Croydon choir, and where he studied composition with Stanford. Elgar, prompted by A.J. Jaeger ('Nimrod'), recommended Coleridge-Taylor for his first major commission, at the Gloucester Three Choirs Festival, for which he wrote the *Ballade* in A minor in 1898. *Hiawatha's Wedding Feast* followed later that year and the rest of *Hiawatha* appeared within a couple of years. Both Jaeger and Elgar 'went off' Coleridge-Taylor after a few years, though it is not clear whether this was for musical or personal reasons.

Coleridge-Taylor married his wife Jessie Walmisley, a fellow RCM student, in 1899 and two children, Hiawatha and Gwendoline (Avril), were born in 1900 and 1903. Money was always a problem, so he had to take on more and more work as conductor, teacher (notably as a Professor of Composition at Trinity College, London, from 1902 and later, from 1910, in a similar position at the Guildhall School) and adjudicator. Composition did not bring in nearly enough for all he was so prolific. It is not surprising that his creative muse sagged in mid-career, say, between the years 1903 and 1908, but he did enough in his earlier and later years to leave behind him a corpus of compositions which has kept his memory as a composer alive during many of the years since he died of pneumonia, but really of overwork, on 1 September 1912 at the sadly early age of 37. The overwork probably related to his non-compositional activities.

Coleridge-Taylor's weaknesses lay perhaps in form and thematic development; his strengths were an attractive lyrical impulse, sometimes coloured by negro-based music, in which he indulged not infrequently (he was intensely proud of his negro ancestry while regarding himself in general terms as an Englishman), and colourful, professional scoring. The strengths are maybe seen at their best, while the weaknesses are of relatively little account, in his light music, of which he produced considerable quantities. As Geoffrey Self rightly says in his definitive biography *The Hiawatha Man* (Scolar, 1995), 'light music really was his true path and vocation'. Let us run the rule quickly over his output in this direction.

First there is his incidental music, initially for the Stephen Phillips plays *Herod* (1900), *Ulysses* (1902), *Nero* (1906) and *Faust* (1908) and, much more famously, for *Othello* (1911) and Alfred Noyes' *Forest of Wild Thyme*, also 1911, the latter's most popular items being the *Christmas Overture* and the three *Dream Dances*, which remained popular for years with light orchestras, although its *Scenes from an Imaginary Ballet* and *Intermezzo* are good light music also. The *Hiawatha* ballet (nothing to do with the *Hiawatha* cantata), left unfinished at his death, had to be orchestrated by Percy Fletcher, who grouped nine movements into two suites entitled *Hiawatha* and *Minnehaha*. Purely concert suites included the *Four Characteristic Waltzes* of 1898 which showed what flexibility and variety could be achieved with the same basic rhythm, *Scenes from an Everyday Romance* (1900) and, perhaps best and best known of all Coleridge-Taylor's light music, the *Petite Suite de Concert* from 1911 (to put this in chronological context, just before Coates wrote his first orchestral suite), whose elegant invention is still enjoyed by orchestras, especially that of the delicious *Demande et Reponse* often played separately. I remember the rhapsody *The Bamboula* (1910), which draws on a negro melody, subtly varied and colourfully scored, regularly appearing in light orchestral concerts 50 years ago.

Turning to vocal music, the *Bon-Bon Suite* (1908), for baritone, chorus and orchestra, is another light concert suite with the added dimension of voices, sentimental but also brilliant and gossamer-like in its invention. But time has not dealt kindly with it. Not a few of Coleridge-Taylor's solo songs, over a hundred of them altogether, were really ballads. The one I remember best – and people still sing it – is *Big Lady Moon*, the third of the *Five Fairy Ballads* of 1909. There were many others: *Thou Art Risen*

My Beloved, Life and Death, A Birthday, She Rested By the Broken Brook, Eleanore, The Gift-Rose, Sons of the Sea (a favourite of Peter Dawson), *Love's Passing* and so on. But perhaps *Onaway Awake Beloved*, from *Hiawatha's Wedding Feast*, is Coleridge-Taylor's most enduring ballad. He produced fewer choral songs, perhaps 30 in all, but several of these, like *O Mariners Out of the Sunset* and *Drake's Drum*, were popular with smaller choirs up to mid-century.

Coleridge-Taylor's smaller-scale instrumental music is often light in character. The violin was his own first instrument and his earlier essays for violin and piano included the *Two Romantic Pieces*, Opus 9 (*Lament; Merrymaking*), the *Gypsy Suite*, Opus 20 (1898), which has been orchestrated and recorded, and the *Valse Caprice* of 1898. Piano compositions included *Two Moorish Tone Pictures* (1897) and *Moorish Dance* (1904) – this was long before the 'exotic vogue' created by Ketèlbey – the *Scènes de Ballet*, the *Two Oriental Valses*, the *Forest Scenes* (1907), the *Cameos*, and the *Valse Suite: Three Fours* (1909), six waltzes, a kind of extension of the earlier *Four Characteristic Waltzes*. The latter two works were orchestrated, but by Henry Geehl (*qv*) and Norman O'Neill (*qv*) respectively. Three organ works were also published – here again, the *Three Impromptus* were arranged for orchestra by one Piercey.

Hiawatha is now rarely heard (though North Country choral societies remained faithful to it longer than most); ironically – and would Coleridge-Taylor have liked this any more than Sullivan did – his memory is kept alive by his lighter music.

WIT AND CHARM
Frederic Curzon 1899-1973

Although he was a generation, or at least a half-generation, younger than such stalwarts of the English light-music scene as Arthur Wood, Albert Ketèlbey, Wilfrid Sanderson, Percy Fletcher, Alfred Reynolds and Eric Coates, Ernest Frederic Curzon, born in London on 4 September 1899, is to be reckoned among their number as a most attractive purveyor of tuneful, beautifully scored light music, primarily for orchestra. As a boy he studied violin, cello, piano and organ, his precocity being indicated by the fact that his settings of the Magnificat and Nunc Dimittis were performed before he was 12. At 16 he was a pianist in a London theatre orchestra (what storehouses of talent those orchestras were) and at 20 he was conducting his own orchestra and composing accompaniments for silent films, then (1920) approaching their heyday as providers of light music. Curzon was also organist at Shepherd's Bush Pavilion for many years and at other places. (Surprisingly, I know of no organ music by him.) He also conducted for a time at Llandudno Pier during the Second War. He became President of the Light Music Society and died in Bournemouth on 6 December 1973.

As a composer (he became a full-time one in 1938) he was encouraged both by Sir Dan Godfrey and by Ralph Hawkes of the music publishers Boosey and Hawkes, for whom Curzon was Head of the Light Music Department. Much of his output was for orchestra, but there were songs of the ballad type like *I Bring My Love, In a Little Lane* and, published in 1951, *Someone a Little Like You*. For piano, besides arrangements of popular orchestral movements of his own, like *The Boulevardier,* the march *Ceremonial Occasion* (written in 1953, Coronation year), the *Overture Bouffe for an 18th Century Comedy;* the scherzo *Mischief* (derived from a children's ballet suite, *Charm of Youth*) and the very popular *March of the Bowmen*, he published other movements like a *Square Dance Set* (1951) and two pieces dating from 1948, *Valse Impromptu* and *Prelude: By the Lyn,* for all three of which I have discovered no orchestral counterparts. Also from 1948 was a pleasant *Elegiac Melody* for cello and piano. He worked in the theatre as a composer, producing a burlesque opera and composing music for a pantomime. His compositions were heard on 'ITMA', and he wrote fanfares for events like the Royal Tournament and the Festival of Britain in 1951.

The most substantial items among Curzon's orchestral light music were the Spanish Suite *In Malaga*, the *Robin Hood Suite*, which ends with the rousing, indeed noble, *March of the Bowmen* already mentioned and which was first performed on 18 October 1937 by the BBC Symphony Orchestra, the quarter-hour-long *Salon Suite*, the third of whose six movements is a quiet 'Period Piece in 18th-Century Manner' and the fifth a brilliant 'Clarinetto Con Moto'. Curzon's music had a characteristic sparkle, apparent especially in his overtures *Vanguard*, *Chevalier* and *Punchinello* (which latter has been recorded in both the LP and CD eras), all of which are most delightfully scored. One interesting feature of Curzon's orchestration is the presence of three (or sometimes two or even four) saxophones in many of his scores, apart from the more usual woodwind instruments. Examples are the march *Bonaventure*, the once enormously popular *The Boulevardier*, *Busybodies*, described as a duet for two trumpets (or two xylophones) and orchestra, the waltz *Cascade*, the *Dance of an Ostracised Imp* (1940), which was very frequently played at one time, *Pasquinade*, with its whiff of historical pastiche, *Serenade of a Clown*, the serenade *Simonetta*, which characterises the palm court orchestra to perfection, the march *Sons of the Soviet* and *Ringside*, where the orchestra included four saxes and a guitar.

Another interesting formation was in the *Summer Souvenir* of 1958, scored for single woodwind, accordion, harp and strings, but no brass. Few of his works were for strings alone, though one can point to the *Frolic* for strings and the *Berceuse* of 1951 for harp and strings. His one concerted piece I know of, apart from the clarinet movement from the *Salon Suite* just mentioned, is *Saltarello* for piano and orchestra, published in 1952, but this seems to me less characterful than most of Curzon. He appears to have been drawn frequently to the exotic rhythms of Spain and Hungary, although he never visited either country. One thinks of the Spanish caprice *Capriciati* (yet another score with a trio of saxophones), the pasodobles *Bravada* and *Sacramento*, the Spanish serenade *La Peineta* (1954), later arranged for mixed chorus and orchestra by Ernest Tomlinson, the czardas *La Gitana* and the gipsy caprice *Zingaresca*. I have memories of gentler pieces too, such as *Valse Joyeuse*, the valse caprice *Water Nymph*, the *Rustic Scherzo*, *Over the Hills and Far Away*, *March of the Jesters*, the serenade intermezzo *Norina* and *The Capricious Ballerina*. Several of these date from the 1950s, when Curzon was in his prime. As many of the foregoing titles show, he aimed at being witty as well as merely charming in his output, and his success in this earned him a particular niche in British light music. We should not forget him; the excellent recent CD issues have given us less excuse for doing so.

ARRANGER EXTRAORDINARY
Robert Docker 1918-1992

The death of Robert Docker on 9 May 1992, aged 73, removed one of the few notable remaining figures in the world of popular music who came to maturity during the Golden Age of British light music which ended perhaps sometime in the 1950s. Docker, who trained primarily as a violist and pianist and also as a conductor, was par excellence an arranger and a prolific one, especially for programmes like the BBC's 'Friday Night is Music Night' and Melodies for You', but also for other occasions and ensembles, including his own sextet and trio. He arranged the by now famous music for the film *Chariots of Fire* and he conducted the accompaniment when Queen Elizabeth The Queen Mother unveiled a memorial plaque to Sir Noel Coward (*qv*) in Westminster Abbey. Potpourris of popular melodies, folk-tunes, film and musical themes flowed from his busy pen. His skill in this direction was recognised in 1990 when the BBC awarded him two one-hour programmes entitled 'The Musical World of Robert Docker'. In February 1994 I attended a Doncaster concert by the Palm Court Trio led by Martin Loveday (violin) of the BBC Concert Orchestra in which Martin paid great tribute to Docker's arranging skills – his trio played a medley from *The Sound of Music* arranged by Docker which gave the familiar melodies a fresh twist.

But Docker was known as a composer (and improviser) as well as an arranger and it is for this reason that he appears in this book. Some of his works, like the *London Rhapsody* of 1974 for piano and orchestra (he was born in London) and the 'kindergarten fresco' *Ourselves When Young*, were based on popular melodies, but there were plenty of true originals, from miniatures like *Air and Jig* for violin, cello and piano, *Comet Cascade* and *Jolly Roger* for brass band and *Fairy Dance Reel, Penny Whistle Tune, Pizzicato Minuet* (1949), *West Indian Dance, Tabarinage* ('Buffoonery'), seemingly French-inspired, and *Scène du Bal*, all for orchestra. *Scènes du Ballet* (a different work, apparently, from the last-named) was a suite in the Eric Coates mould, while *Legend* and *Pastiche Variations*, both for piano and orchestra, show his affinity for, and love of, the music of Rachmaninoff, a composer he had doubtless encountered during his studies at the Royal Academy of Music. He was commissioned to write another relatively serious work, *Opus 40*, for the 40th anniversary tour of the BBC Concert Orchestra, formed in 1952 and with which he was associated for so long, and this was posthumously premiered in Ipswich in August 1992.

Born on 5 June 1918, the son of a Paddington gas worker, Docker studied piano, viola and composition at the Royal Academy. He also played organ, harpsichord and violin. The piano was his main instrument and his first job was playing it at a working men's club when he was 14 years old. Curiously he did not make his first broadcast appearance as a pianist until 1946, ten years after his first arrangement had been heard on the air. Later he formed a piano duo with Edward Rubach and this broadcast regularly.

MAN OF VERSATILITY
Percy Fletcher 1879-1932

In his centenary year (1986) and since, Eric Coates' music has had a certain amount of welcome exposure; but how many of his English contemporaries in the light music field are remembered other than perfunctorily? A signal example of this is Percy Eastman Fletcher, who was born in Derby on 12 December 1879 and died on 10 December 1932 at the early age of 52. He took lessons on violin, piano and organ, the former being his most important instrument. Like a number of his composer contemporaries, notably Arthur Wood and Alfred Reynolds, he made his living as a musical director in the London theatre world, fulfiling this position successively at the Prince of Wales, Savoy, Daly's, Drury Lane and, from 1915 until his death, His Majesty's Theatre. Soon after going to the latter he directed the very long-running *Chu Chin Chow* and was in fact responsible for much of the orchestration of Frederick Norton's score. Fletcher then composed its successor, *Cairo*, originally entitled *Mecca* and described as a 'mosaic in music and mime' which ran for 216 performances in 1921. In 1925 he brought out another musical comedy, *The Good Old Days*.

His creative activity was, however, by no means confined to the theatre. His list of compositions included ballads like *The Bells of Youth, Secret of My Heart, The Captain's Eye, The Smile of Spring, Kitty What a Pity, The Great Adventure* and *Galloping Dick*; his *Four Tennyson Lyrics* were more serious effusions among his song output. He wrote a considerable amount for chorus: *The Shafts of Cupid, The Enchanted Island*, a *Choral Rhapsody on Scottish Airs*, with orchestra (1915), *The Walrus and the Carpenter* (1910), the humorous ballad *The Deacon's Masterpiece, or the Wonderful One-hoss Shay*, also with orchestra (1911), the later (1931) *Cupid's Garland*, for male chorus, soloists and orchestra and, most popular down the years, *The Passion of Christ* (1922), one of the best of those sacred cantatas for smaller, less experienced church choirs in the style of Stainer's *The Crucifixion*; if Stainer's work owes much to Mendelssohn, Fletcher's derives something from Elgar, though it is of course no *Gerontius*. Shorter Fletcher partsongs included many for female voices only, like *The Cloud, Bees, Haste Thee Nymph*, the lullaby *Softly Sink in Slumbers Golden, O May Thou Art a Merry Time* and *The Valley of Dreams*, also carols like *Now Once Again* and *Ring Out, Wild Bells* and many settings of British and other folk melodies. Mixed-voice partsongs like *Dream Love* (1921), *Lullaby of Love*,

Haste Thee Nymph (again), *Folly's Song* (1921) and, for male voices, *The Vision of Belshazzar, A Dirge of Kisses,* the *Song of the Apple Trees* (1924) and *The Sailor's Return* were in demand for festivals.

Fletcher wrote a large number of suites for light orchestra, probably more even than Eric Coates, whose composing career was longer. We may instance *Six Cameos for a Costume Comedy* (1926), *Rustic Revels* (1918), *Sylvan Scenes, Woodland Pictures* (1920: the latter two are different despite their similar titles), *Famous Beauties* (respectively entitled Aphrodite, Versailles Palace and Cleopatra), the *Three Light Pieces* (Lubly Lulu, Fifinette and a march, Folies Bergeres), *Nautical Scenes, At Gretna Green, Three Frivolities* (ie, Dance Parade, Mam'selle Mannequin; Tango-Valse, Thé Dansant; and Galopade, Cafe Chantant), the two bagatelles, *Valsette* and *Pizzicato,* the *Parisian Sketches* of 1914 (Demoiselle Chic and Bal Masqué, of which the latter remained popular for many years), *Ballade and Bergomask* for strings only, the sprightly overture *Vanity Fair* – a title later hijacked by Anthony Collins – and many individual movements variously described as Intermezzi, Romances, Morceaux Characteristiques, Lyrical Melodies, Serenades and Waltzes.

I have heard his marches *The Crown of Chivalry* and *Spirit of Pageantry,* which have an Elgarian ambience even if they display more pomp than circumstance; other published marches were the *V.C. March,* apparently based on Frank Bridge's song *Michael O'Leary V.C.* (possibly unpublished as I have not traced a copy), a toy soldiers' march *The Toy Review* and a *Sultan's March* extracted from *Cairo.* Like Coates and Alfred Reynolds among others, Fletcher experimented in writing pastiche early music, as in the *Salon Suite in the Olden Style,* comprising Prelude, Sarabande, Minuet and Gavotte. Although the splendidly written *Folk Tune and Fiddle Dance* was scored for strings only, most of the other compositions are for full orchestra, and many Fletcher scores have a written-out part for euphonium as well as the usual orchestral woodwind and brass instruments.

In addition, the prolific Fletcher arranged suites from other composers' music. Samuel Coleridge-Taylor died in 1912 leaving his *Hiawatha Suite* and *Minnehaha Suite,* intended probably as ballet scores and having no musical connection with the choral *Hiawatha,* almost finished. Fletcher completed these and had them performed as concert works. He made a purely orchestral arrangement of Amy Woodforde-Finden's once enormously popular *Indian Love Lyrics* and made similar versions of her suites *A Lover in Damascus* and *The Pagoda of Flowers.* His fantasia for chorus and orchestra on themes from Wagner's *The Mastersingers of Nuremberg* was popular at one time; I have traced several performances in the Doncaster area either side of 1914.

Most of Fletcher's piano music was arranged from his own orchestral scores (examples are *Nautical Scenes*, *Sylvan Scenes*, *At Gretna Green* and *Bal Masque*) and a selection from *Cairo* appeared in piano form. But the *Five Lyrical Pieces*, subtitled Idylesques, the *Six Compositions*, *Four Confessions* and the early *Dreamer of Dreams* appear to be piano originals. He also put piano accompaniments to a set of *French Nursery Songs* published by Curwen. He composed quite widely for organ. An *Interlude* of 1901 is his earliest dated publication I have found, yet it is numbered as Opus 27 No 2. Later essays for organ included two from 1915, *Festival Toccata* and *Fountain Reverie*, and a *Festal Offertorium* of 1926. The *Festival Toccata*, a triumphant movement dedicated to the celebrated concert organist and composer Edwin Lemare, has been recorded by Jonathan Bielby at Wakefield Cathedral on Priory PR139. I have heard a number of Fletcher's short and simple, yet undeniably attractive, preludes on well-known hymn tunes.

In one respect at least Fletcher was a pioneer. Before 1913 brass band festival pieces were invariably operatic selections but in that year Irwell Springs Band won the National Championships at the Crystal Palace with Fletcher's specially commissioned tone poem *Labour and Love*. Other classics specially commissioned as test pieces for the brass band medium were to follow in later years, written by acknowledged major composers like Holst, Elgar, John Ireland, Bantock, Howells, Holbrooke, Bliss, Vaughan Williams, Rubbra and Gordon Jacob. Fletcher himself was asked again for the National Championships of 1926 and obliged with *An Epic Symphony*. Revived as a test piece for the National Championships of 1938 and 1951 and in 1976 in the Open Championship at Belle Vue, Manchester, this is a richly expansive piece in three movements strongly redolent of Elgar and interestingly (as one tends to think of brass band music as 'light' or even 'popular') may well be Fletcher's most serious work in any medium.

Sadly Fletcher's music (he wrote also for military band and at least one string quartet) has now all but sunk without trace. One may still occasionally hear *Bal Masqué* played by a light orchestra. Brass bands, which are mostly bastions of conservatism (and why should they not be?), revive and indeed have recorded *Labour and Love* and the *Epic Symphony* from time to time and in so doing please their audiences. And a few church choirs put on the *Passion* at Easter when they want a change from *The Crucifixion* and John Maunder's (much inferior) *Olivet to Calvary*. But we seem to have lost nearly all of that tuneful, excellently scored light orchestral music which may well have been the part of his output that he regarded most highly. Surely the best of it is worth preserving?

SPORTSMAN AND MAN OF THE THEATRE
Harold Fraser-Simson 1878 -1944

Born in London on 15 August 1872, Harold Fraser-Simson was educated at Charterhouse School and in France. For a time he worked in a shipowning firm in the City of London before turning to music. He died on 19 January 1944, following a fall at his home at Dalcross Castle near Inverness. He was a keen sportsman and indulged in golf, tennis, shooting and fishing.

As a musician he is largely remembered (when he is remembered at all) for his work in the theatre, primarily as a composer of musical comedies. His career began in the early years of this century after he had published a few songs and partsongs; the first partsong to be published was *My Sweet Sweeting*, for SATB in 1907, and Count John McCormack recorded the solo *I Sent My Love Two Roses* around that time. *Bonita*, the first of Fraser-Simson's stage shows, was produced in 1911, though he had previously had experience of amateur operatics in Sussex, where he then lived. *Bonita* enjoyed fair success, but it was its successor, *The Maid of the Mountains*, which made his reputation. It was staged first at the Prince's Theatre, Manchester, on 23 December 1916 and came to Daly's Theatre for its London run the following February, a run which was not to end until it had clocked up 1352 performances early in 1920 – second only to *Chu Chin Chow* among First War musicals. London revivals of *The Maid* came in 1921, 1930, 1942 and 1972; it was filmed in 1932. America heard it in 1918 but it proved to be less popular there. Although one generally thinks of Fraser-Simson as being responsible for its music, it is ironical that of its three big hits – *Love Will Find a Way*, *A Paradise For Two* and *A Bachelor Gay* – he composed only the first; the other two, by James Tate (*qv*), were among the numbers interpolated in the score before the London premiere. The original 'Manchester' score was entirely by Fraser-Simson.

In a sense *The Maid's* success was an embarrassment as Fraser-Simson's next musical, *A Southern Maid*, first produced in Manchester in 1917, was kept waiting for its London debut, which was not until 1920. In its Manchester run a song by the 15-year-old Eric Fogg was briefly incorporated in the score. This show enjoyed a modest success, but *Our Peg* (1919), *Missy Jo* (1921), *Head Over Heels* (Adelphi, 1923) and *Our Nell* (1924) made less of an impression. Rather better were *The Street Singer* (1924), tried out in Birmingham before coming to the Lyric for a run of 360 performances and praised for its charming music, and *Betty in Mayfair*, mounted at the Adelphi in 1925. This had only three solos against seven duets, a quartet and other ensemble numbers.

Betty in Mayfair was Fraser-Simson's last musical but it was not by any means to be his last work for the stage. A ballet, *A Venetian Wedding*, was composed in 1926; its music received a concert performance on the BBC five years later. And there was the incidental music for *The Nightingale and the Rose* (1927) and then, most notably, the music for that well-loved children's play *Toad of Toad Hall* by A.A. Milne, based on Kenneth Grahame's *The Wind in the Willows*, which opened in Liverpool in 1929 and began its London run at the Lyric at New Year 1931. It has often been revived since. Even in Grahame's original, Toad is an inveterate versifier and, according to him, composer; Milne and Fraser-Simson exploited this enjoyably.

Toad was not Fraser-Simson's only collaboration with Milne. We have already alluded to the former's (non-theatre) songs, and published titles like *I Sent My Love Two Roses*, *The Raindrop and the Rose*, *Falmouth Town* and *The Old Land* may be cited as examples. But these were to pale in popularity beside his song-settings of Milne's poems for children. No fewer than six volumes were derived just from *When We Were Very Young*, the first of Milne's four classic children's books. Fraser-Simson's slight but tuneful music so suited the poems that it came as no surprise to see those six song-books followed by five songs from *Now We Are Six* and, in 1929, no fewer than 17 *Hums of Pooh* (from *Winnie the Pooh* and *The House at Pooh Corner*) to make 67 Milne songs in all (exclusive *of Toad*). The songs when published were illustrated with E.H. Shepard's well-loved original drawings. Frederic Austin and Sir Henry Walford Davies had also been interested in setting the poems from *When We Were Very Young*; Sir Henry in fact succeeded in publishing in 1939 four songs from that book, but set for accompanied four-part choir. Generally speaking they achieved less success than Fraser-Simson's solo versions.

Further evidence of Fraser-Simson's gift for setting children's poems came with his *Teddy Bear and Other Songs*, 14 of them in all, and eight songs from *Alice in Wonderland*, which were published in 1932. All these 'mini-songs', including the Milne ones, sold well and many were recorded in the 1930s. (Robert Tear recorded some of the Milne songs in 1981). I can still recall their charm across half-a-century. Fraser-Simson's talent for composition may have been a slender one, but it was real – the point is underlined by the fact that *The Hums of Pooh* were revived and married to newly written music by Julian Slade for a successful stage presentation of *Winnie the Pooh* at the Phoenix Theatre in 1970, a quarter of a century after the death of the composer who had pioneered their musical possibilities.

FOR YOU ALONE
Henry Ernest Geehl 1881-1961

Like Ronnie Binge, Henry Ernest Geehl (1881-1961) is one who was known for his arrangements almost as much as for original compositions and who had strong associations with the brass band world. Yet his best-known original work is the song *For You Alone*, composed in 1909 and reputed to be the first song Caruso sang in English. Geehl's other songs did not quite enjoy the same popularity, though *The Mountains of Allah*, a cycle of six songs, was sung fairly frequently and *Devon Mine, The Fairy Cooks, In Sunshine and Shadow, Now Fades the Snow; Only My Love for You, In Your Arms Tonight, Sinners and Saints, The Vales of Kintore, When Spring Goes Shopping, A Yeoman's Yarn, Youth the Fiddler* and *Zinetta* were ballads somewhat above the average, while the male-voice partsong *Duty off Dunkirk* (1941) exploited a wartime incident which had caught the nation's imagination.

Geehl studied the piano in early life in Vienna (where he met Brahms) and he published a considerable amount for that instrument: a suite *The Bay of Naples*, a *Kleine Sonate* in A minor, *Harlequin and Columbine* (five movements), a *Miniature Suite: 1745*, presumably dealing with Bonnie Prince Charlie's ill-fated attempt to recover the throne, and the *Caprice Concertante* for piano and strings of 1952 were a few of the more important titles.

His orchestral works included short genre pieces like *Harlequin's Serenade, Indian Patrol*, the intermezzo *Mon Ami, The Moonlit Barcarolle*, the *Phantom Dance* (subtitled Pizzicato Morceau), *'Neath the Desert Stars* (this was surely inspired by Ketèlbey), the waltz *Legend of the Sea* and *Mazurka Russe*. More substantial were *A Comedy Overture*, premiered by the BBC Symphony Orchestra in 1937, the four *Countryside Sketches*, the suite *From the Samoan Isles, Fairyland*, premiered at the 1914 Henry J. Wood Promenade Concerts, and concertos for piano and violin.

Yet just as important in the way of performances they received were his many orchestral arrangements of songs by Chaminade, Easthope Martin, Landon Ronald and sundry others. Geehl's experience was wide. He thought first of a career as a pianist but gave this up in favour of conducting and composing. Like so many of those we discuss in this book, he conducted in theatres, between 1902 and 1908. He taught at Trinity College, London, from 1918 until the year before his death and he was a music editor for the publishers Ashdown and Enoch.

He had a particular interest in brass band music and produced many of his most significant compositions in this field at a time when few serious composers gave it a second thought. It is a well-known fact that he scored Elgar's *Severn Suite* from the composer's piano score (Geehl later arranged this for military band and, charmingly, Elgar's early *Idylle* and late *Adieu*, respectively violin/piano and piano works originally, for orchestra). The relationship over the *Severn Suite* between two rather prickly men was sometimes difficult, but a worthwhile result ensued. Geehl's own compositions for brass included a trombone solo, *Romanza*, the *Festival Overture*, *In Tudor Days*, *Normandy* (a 'Symphonic ode' in three sections: 1946), a *Sinfonietta Pastorale*, *A Happy Suite*, *James Hook* and *Thames Valley*, a suite in three movements, its first depicting a colourful regatta. *Oliver Cromwell* was a test-piece for the National Championships in 1923 and 1946 and at the Open in 1941, *On the Cornish Coast* at the Nationals in 1924 and 1948, *Robin Hood* at the Open in 1936 and 1941 and *Scena Sinfonica* at the Open in 1952. All, bar *Robin Hood*, have been recorded, together with *Threnody*, *Bolero Brillante*, *Romanza* and the *Variations on Jenny Jones*. *Oliver Cromwell* and *On The Cornish Coast* have become classics of the band repertoire, highly demanding on bandsmen even today and admirably descriptive and dramatic as tone poems, although the former, in six sections, was originally described as an overture.

SULLIVAN'S HEIR
Edward German 1862-1936

Several of the composers we discuss in this book – Hubert Bath, Montague Phillips, Haydn Wood, perhaps – had ambitions to succeed in 'serious' music but, like Sullivan before them, they were fated to be remembered, if at all, for their lighter music. Another such was Edward German, who, despite producing two symphonies and other music of symphonic stature, is remembered today primarily as the composer of the operetta *Merrie England*, one song from another operetta *(Tom Jones)* and a handful of attractive dances from various theatre works. Elgar, who, unlike all the others we have mentioned previously in this paragraph, *did* 'make it' as a serious composer (while also turning out a number of light-music masterpieces of his own), is on record as admiring German's music. One may ask whether he admired German's serious music or his lighter effusions: probably the latter. German himself, in a fit of bitterness, once told W.H. Bell, 'Let them (ie, the British public) have muck. It's all they care for'.

He was born German Edward Jones in Whitchurch (Shropshire) on 17 February 1862, the son of a Congregational Church organist and choirmaster. He showed musical ability at an early age, enjoying brass bands as well as playing church organ and domestic piano. At the age of 18 he entered the Royal Academy of Music, studying organ under Charles Steggall, violin under Alfred Burnett and composition with Ebenezer Prout. He began serious composition at this time: piano pieces, miniatures for violin and piano (including the *Bolero*), ballads, partsongs, hymn tunes, and his Opus 1 - a pizzicato piece for strings entitled *The Guitar*, performed in 1883. It was at that time he changed his name to Edward German. His first major work, a *Te Deum* for soloists, chorus and organ, earned him an award and applause when it was first performed at the St James' Hall in 1887, the year German left the Academy, where latterly he had been a sub-professor of the violin. Also from German's 'Academy period' were his first operetta, *The Two Poets* (1886), and the First Symphony, in E minor (1887, performed in 1890).

His break came in 1888, when he was appointed Musical Director of the Globe Theatre in London. Soon he had a commission to provide music for a production there of Shakespeare's *Richard III*. This was a great success and its overture, a major work, received many performances in the concert hall early in the 1890s, including one at the Leeds Festival, where it was admired by Sullivan. Other commissions followed, to write more Shakespearean incidental music, notably for *Henry VIII* (1892), then *Romeo and Juliet* (1895), *As You Like It* and *Much Ado*, and also for the non-Shakespearean plays *The Tempter* and, in 1900, Anthony Hope and Edward Rose's *English Nell*. It is significant that the most popular excerpts from all of these, and particularly of course *Henry VIII* and *Nell*, were suites of light dances, after the style of the *Gipsy Suite* introduced at the Crystal Palace in 1892. German continued to write major works, though: a Second Symphony, in A minor, was performed at Norwich in 1893 and is known by the name of that city; a *Leeds Suite*, also a substantial piece whose *Valse Gracieuse* became especially popular as a separate movement, was written for the Leeds Festival of 1895; a symphonic poem *Hamlet*; and a symphonic suite, *The Seasons*, which is as long as either of his symphonies, and which appeared in 1899.

Perhaps the crucial incident which determined that Edward German would be remembered as a light music composer came in November 1900 when Sullivan died, leaving unfinished his last operetta, *The Emerald Isle*. German, whose work Sullivan himself had admired on many occasions and indeed had suggested he was his heir, was approached to complete this. He accepted, withdrawing from an obligation to compose a violin concerto for the Leeds Festival, and *The Emerald Isle* was duly premiered in April 1901, successfully so – although it is now little heard. It remained popular with provincial societies well into the 1920s; Wilfrid Sanderson, Conductor of Doncaster Amateur Operatic Society, when asked to give his opinions on suggested operettas for 1923, said of *The Emerald Isle*, 'charming music, very pleasing, but being Irish I think it would be a mistake to give it at the present time'. Basil Hood, who had written the book for the *Isle*, quickly came up with another libretto, *Merrie England*, for German to set and it is this work more than any other which has been associated with the composer's name through its immense popularity with amateur societies.

The public received it rapturously at its premiere in 1902 and demanded more; the result was *A Princess of Kensington* (1903), which also did well at the time, although, despite a number of attractive dances, it has not survived as well as some of German's other stage works.

German's next operetta was *Tom Jones*, premiered in Manchester in April 1907, again with great success. Amusingly this took some time to reach the amateur stage in Doncaster on account of Fielding's novel, on which it is of course based, being perceived to be bawdy, but it eventually managed it after World War I. It remained popular for several decades, while never quite equalling the success of *Merrie England*; again the dances, plus of course the *Waltz Song*, were to be the most popular excerpts from it. Only one more operetta was to come from German's pen: *Fallen Fairies* (December 1909), for whom the librettist was none other than W.S. Gilbert. Gilbert and German got on together rather better than Gilbert and Sullivan had done; but their combined effort achieved much less success than most of G and S. The subject was perhaps too fanciful for audiences to properly grasp.

The decade 1901-10 may be seen in retrospect as German's 'theatre period', although he had, of course, composed incidental theatre music throughout the 1890s and in 1905 had added to that music for *The Conqueror*, a play by the Duchess of Sutherland from which once again a concert suite was extracted, comprising a *Romance*, *Satyr Dance* and *Entrance and Dance of the Children*; three songs from it were also published. Two other significant works of the first decade of the new century were the *Welsh Rhapsody*, a potpourri of Welsh tunes for the Cardiff Festival of 1904, ending with a rousing arrangement of that stirring tune *Men of Harlech* – a tune often targeted by arrangers but German's is arguably still the finest setting of all – and because of its use of traditional tunes probably to be reckoned as light music; and a charming collection of 12 songs whose lyrics came from Rudyard Kipling's children's classic, the *Just So Stories*. The decade was also notable for the development of German's work as a conductor, not only in the theatre pit but in America, where he directed the New York Symphony Orchestra in 1907.

Conducting was to absorb much of German's energy in the years up to the outbreak of World War I (and indeed after), years bedevilled by poorish health and a painful road accident. He turned down an invitation to renew his operatic partnership with Basil Hood. His creative output was restricted to songs, plus a *Coronation March* and a setting of *Veni Creator Spiritus* for the Coronation of King George V. World War I saw his making contributions to the war effort: a hymn tune, *Homage to Belgium* (1914), originally for *King Albert's Book*, a fundraising effort for Belgian refugees and published by *The Daily Telegraph*, and more settings of poems by Kipling – *Have You News of My Boy Jack?* (1916), made popular by Dame Clara Butt, and another one commemorating *The Irish Guards* (1918).

German's creative work was now almost at an end. Just two significant works were to come, both, ironically perhaps, in the serious music field. The *Theme and Six Diversions* was premiered in March 1919 and a tone poem, *The Willow Song*, inspired by Shakespeare's *Othello*, was written for the Royal Academy's Centenary Celebration Concert in 1922. Beyond these, few new compositions appeared, though German continued conducting; in the New Year Honours List of 1928 he was knighted, but perhaps even more prestigious was the award of the Royal Philharmonic Society's Gold Medal in 1934. German was 74 when he died in London on 11 November 1936.

Apart from *Merrie England*, German is remembered now for his light orchestral music; for all its assumption of an 'olde Englishe', mock-Tudor style this is certainly not 'muck', being tuneful, spontaneous and beautifully crafted. Even his more serious orchestral music – I am thinking of *The Seasons* particularly – often conveys the atmosphere of a rural countryside in dancing mood. But we should perhaps emphasise that much of his output was not orchestral. Take instrumental solos, for example. Several were for violin and piano, recalling the fact that the violin was his preferred instrument when he went to the Academy: *Bolero, Bacchanalian Dance, Souvenir, Saltarelle* and a three-movement Suite (published for flute or violin), as well as arrangements of his Shakespearean incidental music; other solos were for oboe (*Pastorale* and *Bourree*), flute (*Romance* in B flat and *Saltarello*) or clarinet (*Song Without Words*). Few think of him as a composer for piano solo, but some years ago a complete recording of German's piano music (played by Alan Cuckston) appeared, and it did not include the piano arrangements made by the composer himself of his theatre works, incidental music and operettas. German's original works for piano solo included a full-length sonata and several suites, plus individual movements, like the *Polish Dance* in E (reminiscent of Moszkowski), a *Melody* in D flat (reminiscent of Grieg), a *Valse* in A flat, *Humoresque* and a *Graceful Dance* in F. Most are pre-1900 and all are pre-1914; many look back in style to the Victorian drawing-room with echoes of Mendelssohn and all are attractive.

Edward German's best-known vocal pieces are, I suppose, *that* Waltz Song from *Tom Jones* and a handful of numbers from *Merrie England*, including the shapely *English Rose* and *O Peaceful England*. But there were plenty of 'separates'. Among the solo songs, we have mentioned Kipling's *Just So* cycle. Many of the short choral items, like *Orpheus with his Lute, Who is Sylvia?, Sweet Day So Cool* and *My Bonny Lass She Smileth*, set classical, even Shakespearean, lyrics; other choral titles included *In Praise of Neptune, The Chase, O Lovely May, Sleeping, Rolling Down to Rio* and, still to be encountered today in both SATB and male-voice-choir versions, *O Peaceful Night*. Several of these songs appeared in SATB, TTBB and two or three-part versions to maximise sales. Even some church music was published – German was perhaps here remembering his earliest beginnings, listening to music in his father's church – like the introit *Bread of Heaven On Thee We Feed* (1909), but, unlike Sullivan, Parry and Elgar, German never felt the need to compose festival oratorios, so often regarded as the best way for a British composer to make a reputation at that time. He may have been right; it worked for Elgar, but Sullivan and Parry are, and indeed were, known primarily for other works.

German was a considerable producer of solo songs. Victor Hely-Hutchinson in fact made an orchestral selection of the best-remembered titles. Mostly they were of the ballad type (and in my view to be reckoned as definitely 'light music'), like *Daffodils a-Blowing*, *Charming Chloe* (recorded by Isobel Baillie and others), *Heigh-Ho*, *London Town*, *Love the Pedlar*, *Love in all Seasons*, *Cupid at the Ferry*; *Bird of Blue*, *Love's Barcarolle*, *Sea Lullaby* and, most memorable of all, the stirring *Glorious Devon*, almost a companion piece for *The Yeomen of England* from *Merrie England*. Some, like the *Three Songs of Childhood*, *Six Lyrics* and *Three Spring Songs*, were grouped into 'cycles'. *All Friends Around the Wrekin: A Song of Shropshire* was maybe a tribute to his native county. More than most of his fellow composers he favoured Kipling's poetry. Apart from the *Just So* songs there were the popular *Big Steamers* (also set by Elgar) and *Be Well Assured* from *The Fringes of the Fleet*, which Elgar also dipped into. German's songs, solo and choral, were popular in the many competitive festivals developing in the early 20th century. Solo singers and choirs today might like to rediscover them.

In summing up German, one is tempted to overdo the comparison with Sullivan. Both yearned for success in serious music and were disappointed when this largely eluded them. For each of them a gift for tuneful invention, including an ability for writing period pastiche, was supported by superb craftsmanship. Both were knighted and both had ability as conductors (German probably more than Sullivan). But in truth their idioms were very different and one can now recognise this; Sullivan's style owes more to Italian models, German's to French. For all German's contribution to operetta, he is remembered more for his light suites – sometimes derived from those operettas, indeed, and quite often from music for the stage, although others like the *Cloverley Suite*, orchestrated by Arthur Wood, and excerpts from *Much Ado*, arranged by Stanford Robinson, were concocted by others. German's example undoubtedly inspired later British composers in the field of light music and particularly Eric Coates, whose earlier orchestral suites (before he began absorbing the contemporary up-tempo dance music into his idiom) bear more than a passing resemblance to German's. A substantial part of German's work in this direction appeared before 1900 and strictly is outside our 20th-century remit – but his influence on his successors in the light music field was at least substantial and at most seminal. He has never been overexposed on record, even recordings of *Merrie England* never having been thick on the ground; but Marco Polo have done him proud – not only the lighter music but also the more 'serious' works have been revived – so there is no excuse for us not to explore at least his orchestral output. More perhaps could be done on the vocal side, once so popular a feature of German's output, but that may hopefully materialise some day.

THE ENGLISH WALTZ KING
Archibald Joyce 1873-1963

Although he was sometimes dubbed 'The English Waltz King' or even 'The English Waldteufel' (his waltzes if anything resembled those of the Frenchman rather than the exponents of the Viennese waltz), Archibald Joyce was not quite an answer to the Strausses; the best Strauss waltzes are miniature tone-poems which make them, despite being more than a century old, attractive and significant concert pieces as well as being effective in the ballrooms of their day. Joyce's waltzes were primarily for dancing, although a number of them did find their way into the light orchestral repertoire. Nor did he only write waltzes...

But first things first. Joyce was born in London's Belgravia on 25 May 1873, the son of a band sergeant in the Grenadier Guards. In early years he was a boy chorister and studied piano and violin, playing at various dancing academies and then in sundry dance bands, including some on cruise ships. For a time he dabbled in the theatre, playing in music hall for the likes of Harry Lauder and George Robey and for a brief period was musical director at the Court Theatre Liverpool for Ellen Terry. He was, as we shall see, to return to the theatre on two occasions, but by the beginning of the 20th century he had his own dance band, flexible in number, which toured all over the country: great houses, large hotels, costume balls, receptions and garden parties. His clientele in this direction included the Royal Family. He and his players travelled thousands of miles every year.

From there it was but a step to composing for his own band, as the Strausses and many others had done. He put together some 'medley waltzes' based on popular tunes of the day; his first original waltz to attract attention was *Sweet Memories*. This was soon followed by many others, up to the 1940s at least. Although the Viennese waltz was still in vogue, Joyce, perhaps wisely, despite his published titles including *A Night in Vienna*, decided not to ape it but devise a smoother, dreamier type of dance. It is no coincidence that the word 'dream' appears in so many of his waltz titles. Indeed, *Dreaming*, which sold over a million copies in its first ten years and has been recorded some 40 times (Joyce himself recorded it with his band in 1912), was to become easily his most celebrated composition. There were also *Songe d'Automne* (Dream of Autumn), *Dreams of You, Vision d'Amour, Dream of the Ball* and other sentimental titles which were not far removed from 'dreams': *Remembrance* (1909), *Entrancing, Love's Mystery*;

Paradise, Skating on the Ice (shades of Waldteufel's most famous waltz, *Les Patineurs*), *One Night of Love, Always Gay* (surely he would not give it such a title these days), *Charming, Sweet Love and Life, Acushla*, inspired by his wife Florence, whom he married in 1919, *A Thousand Kisses, A Maiden's Blush, Let All the World Go By, I Could Dance For Ever With You, Bohemia, Fidelity; Sweet William* and *Blue*. Salome seemed to fascinate him as he produced at least three waltzes similarly titled, all shaded gently with Eastern colour: *Vision of Salome* (1909), *The Passing of Salome* (1912) and *Re-in-carnation of Salome*. *Song of the River*, dedicated to our two oldest universities, was first performed on the BBC Home Service's well-remembered *Those Were the Days* programme in 1946. *Victorious*, another late effort (1945), was dubbed a 'waltz militaire' and dedicated to Winston Churchill in celebration of the successful ending of World War II.

But although waltzes flowed from Joyce's pen almost until mid-century he was essentially an Edwardian. The great days of his dance band was the period immediately before and after World War I. (He and most of his bandsmen 'joined up' during that War). He had little sympathy with the jazz-related dance music which invaded British ballrooms after 1920 and he made no attempt – as Eric Coates so notably did – to absorb the jazz style into his own creative work. If the dancers of the 'twenties found his waltzes slightly old-fashioned, there were other outlets, such as the concert hall and even the cinema. *A Thousand Kisses* was incorporated into the 1925 Chaplin 'silent' classic *The Gold Rush*, while in 1949 *Dreaming*, with its by then archetypal Edwardian feel, was featured in the film *Trottie True*.

In the concert hall Joyce made relatively few incursions into the genre of the light suite. One example is the *Caravan Suite* of 1926, in three very episodic movements, its subject surely inspired by the exotic travelogues of Albert Ketèlbey. But there were plenty of Joyce marches. His earliest known composition, from 1884, when he was only eleven, was a march and later in life he produced *The Palace Guard, The Recruit, The Queen's Guard, Colour Sergeant, The Old Grenadier, The Coon Drum Major*, in American style, *Royal Parade, Royal Standard, Homage to the RAF*, the ceremonial march *Britannia*, and the *Prince of Wales Grand March* (1914) which incorporates Brinley Richards' *God Bless the Prince of Wales* into its trio section (Joyce's 'Prince of Wales' was of course the later King Edward VIII). A charming 'dance de ballet' *Iris*, named after his sister-in-law, who was lame, with a richly expressive melody for violas and cellos in its middle section, was surely a purely concert number. Joyce was at home with other dance rhythms besides 3/4, for example the catchy polkas *Frou-Frou* and *Colette*, the even more abandoned military two-step *Brighton Hike* (1946), an incredibly lively piece for a man of 70-odd, *Tangle Toes, Spanish Tambourine Dance, Novelty Dance, Premiere Danseuse* and many more. Published solo instrumental items included a cello solo entitled *Spanish Bolero* and a xylophone solo, *Vienna Cafe*.

As we have suggested, Joyce returned twice to the world of musical theatre. *Toto*, a 'comedy with music', with the music composed by Joyce and Merlin Morgan, opened at the Duke of York's Theatre on 19 April 1916. Each composer contributed his own tunes; Joyce's are very catchy, as may be seen from recent CDs, and doubtless Morgan's were too – at any rate a selection of the latter were recorded by Columbia on a 78. But the show did not do outstandingly well, nor did *Gabrielle* (1923), in which Joyce joined forces with G.H. Clutsam, each again contributing his own songs. Joyce published a few independent songs, apart from adding words, often of dire quality, to some of his waltzes. We can instance titles like *I'm Skipper of a Submarine, God's Greatest Gift, The Rogue of the Road, Friends Dear to Me, The Modem Girl* and, a very late (1952) number, *Dreams of Bohemia*. Even here we have the 'dream' syndrome.

Archibald Joyce died aged 89 on 22 March 1963 at Sutton in Surrey. By then his music seemed to belong to a vastly different age. But he had had many marvellous memories from theatre and dance floor. He is reputed to have been the first English waltz composer to have his compositions published on the Continent. His sales of sheet music in England were enormous. Other composers, like Sydney Baynes and Charles Ancliffe, were to follow where he had led (we also discuss them, albeit briefly, elsewhere in this book). And he could say that at least one of his compositions – *Dreaming*, of course – was known all over the world, if not to everyone by its name. His compositions generally were primarily for dancing but many of them can nevertheless take their place among the all-time classics of British light music.

MONASTERY GARDEN AND PERSIAN MARKET
The travels of Albert W. Ketèlbey 1875-1959

Albert Ketèlbey? Ah yes, the chap who wrote *In a Monastery Garden*. And wasn't there something about a Persian Market?' Ketèlbey, like most of our light music composers, is remembered for just one or two tuneful short movements – but it is surely something that he *is* remembered. In fact in the LP and CD eras he has done better than most of his light music peers for new recordings of his work.

He was born in Birmingham in August 1875, apparently under the Ketèlbey name (William Aston, thought by some to be his real name, was merely one of his later pseudonyms). He showed promise at an early age. His early teachers included Alfred Gaul, composer of cantatas popular with small provincial choirs. A piano sonata written when Ketèlbey was only 11 earned approval from no less a person than Elgar when it was performed in Worcester (though admittedly Elgar cut no great figure in the world of music in 1886). Two years later he won a scholarship to Trinity College, London – to which in later life he returned as an examiner – where he earned many awards, beating Gustav Holst into second place for one of them. He studied piano (which remained his principal instrument), organ, cello (arguably his favourite instrument), clarinet, oboe and horn; no wonder he was later to score so well. Ketèlbey wrote music during his student days and for some time afterwards which has a curious look from the composer of *In a Monastery Garden* and *Sanctuary of the Heart*: a *Caprice* for piano and orchestra, a *Concertstuck* for piano and orchestra, a Quintet for piano and wind, a *Dramatic Overture*, a *Suite de Ballet*, much solo piano music and at least one string quartet, plus *Polish Dances*, and two sets of Studies (Opp. 50, 51) for examinations at Trinity College. At the age of 16 he became organist of St John's, Wimbledon, and remained in this position while pursuing his studies at Trinity. When just 20 he toured as musical director to a light opera company and at 22 became musical director at the Vaudeville Theatre. He had previously appeared at several concert venues as a piano soloist.

His primary aim was always, however, to compose music; the problem lay in making a living out of it. The story goes that his creative genius was directed into light music when the popular cellist August van Biene offered in 1912 a prize of £50 for a cello solo to equal the amazing popularity of his own *Broken Melody*. Ketèlbey, a cellist himself, as we have seen, successfully offered his *Phantom Melody*; also in 1912 he won another prize, worth £100, in an *Evening News* competition, this time for a song. Even so he was 40 before *In a Monastery Garden* won popular acclaim in 1915; *In a Persian Market*, with its panorama of camel drivers, beggars, jugglers, snake-charmers, even a beautiful princess, followed five years later. Ketèlbey's music was always tuneful and distinctive in its colour and this enabled him in succeeding years to write a series of convincing travelogues such as *In a Chinese Temple Garden* (1925), *By the Blue Hawaiian Waters* (1927), *Italian Twilight*, originally for piano (1931), *With the Romanian Gipsies*, *Jungle Drums* (Patrol), *From a Japanese Screen*, *Algerian Scene*, *In the Camp of the Ancient Britons*, *Silver Cloud: An Indian Maiden's Song*, *The Vision of Fuji-San* and *In the Mystic Land of Egypt* (1931).

These geographical mood-pictures and other genre pieces like *Bells Across the Meadow* (1927), *In the Moonlight* (1919), *Souvenir de Tendresse*, *The Clock and the Dresden Figures* (1930), *The Sacred Hour*, *Valse Appassionata* and *Sunday Afternoon Reverie* were ideal for creating an atmosphere in the silent cinema, whether the instrumental resources available were an orchestra of 60 or just a piano. Ketèlbey's period of greatest creativity coincided (yet perhaps it is no coincidence) with the great age of live music for the silent cinema, ie, 1915-29, when up to 80% of all British professional musicians were employed in cinemas and some London cinemas had orchestras of symphonic size and instrumentation. His compositions do include scores specifically written for silent films with titles like *Dramatic Agitato*, *Amaryllis* ('is suitable for use in dainty, fickle scenes'), *Mystery*; *Agitato Furioso* ('for riots, storms, wars, etc.') and *Bacchanale de Montmartre* for 'cabaret, orgy and riotous continental scenes', but we may be sure that his more general compositions were also pressed into service by the cinema musicians of the time. Performances of his work were at their peak during silent cinema days, though as late as 1940 performing rights still brought him in nearly £3500 yearly (the amount fell after the war, though, and even more so in 'real' terms).

Ketèlbey's music was taken up by other ensembles besides cinema orchestras. It was very popular with military bands. His charmingly simple inter-mezzo-romance *Gallantry* was a recording hit for the Band of the Royal Horse Guards, while the Coldstream Guards Band later had several successes with Ketèlbey discs. He certainly provided military bands with plenty of fodder: at least one *Fanfare for a Ceremonial Occasion*, a *Fanfare for Victory* and marches like *Knights of the King*, written for the Horse Guards Band, *With Honour Crowned*, rousing stuff if a little bombastic, *Processional March*, *Heroes All* and *Royal Cavalcade* and the genre piece *A Desert Romance*.

Light (and other) orchestras took up his work, which was heard in tea-shops, seaside pavilions and on the then emergent BBC. Ketèlbey conducted his own music at Bournemouth, Margate, Harrogate and abroad, notably with the Amsterdam Concertgebouw Orchestra (he enjoyed foreign travel and spoke several foreign languages). He made several contributions to the well-stocked genre of the light suite. His own favourites apparently were *Three Fanciful Etchings* and *Suite Romantique*, but there were many others like *In a Fairy Realm, In a Holiday Mood* and *In a Lover's Garden*. I like particularly the *Cockney Suite* of 1924 whose five movements include 'State Procession', another stirring march, and the bustling finale, 'Appy 'Ampstead'. His 'descriptive overture' *Chal Romano* (A Gipsy Lad), also from 1924, has been disparagingly spoken of by some observers but I enjoyed its distinctive vigour when I heard it for the first time, played by the light music section of the Torquay Municipal Orchestra, a quarter of a century after its premiere. And so his list of works goes on: *Bow Bells, Dream Idyll, Elephants' Parade, Canzonetta,* the waltz *Fairies of the Stream, A Birthday Greeting, Love and the Dancer, The Old Belfry, Recreation Moments, Sweet Louisiana, Flowers all the Way, Sunbeams and Butterflies, Mayfair Cinderella, Remembrance* and the charming gavotte *Wedgwood Blue*. Besides *Phantom Melody* he composed one other cello solo, *My Lady Brocade*, and his *Petite Danse* pleased the flautists. His skill as an arranger was shown by his potpourris, as *A Musical Jig-Saw* and *Tangled Tunes* show, though these were less popular than similar efforts by others. Some of his arrangements were published under pseudonyms like William Aston and Anton Vodorinski. Ketèlbey's transcriptions include a six-movement suite (1916) for piano solo from Elgar's musical play *The Starlight Express* of 1915. Most of Ketèlbey's compositions were conceived for orchestra and then arranged and published for piano, in which form they sold vastly, but *Petite Caprice* (and *In a Monastery Garden*) were instances of the opposite process, and there were others. Much of his output remained piano music pure and simple. This included some *Arpeggio Studies* and much other instructional music; a considerable corpus of more serious work published under the Vodorinski pseudonym and having a distinctly Russian feel, Tchaikovsky and Rachmaninoff both coming to mind – examples are *The Pilgrims*, in three sections, *On the Volga* (a set of variations on *The Volga Boatmen* in the manner of a patrol) and *Our Village*; and light genre pieces like *Sunset Glow* (with a bell motif familiar from *Bells Across the Meadow), Golden Autumn, The Shadow of Dreams, A River Reverie* and the joyful *Song of Summer*.

We often hear the devotions of *In a Monastery Garden* and *Sanctuary of the Heart*, even the exotic rhythms of *In a Persian Market*, with vocalists, solo or choral, and an organ added to the orchestra. These additions were encouraged by Ketèlbey himself, who in addition to being a music editor for Bosworth (and Chappell and Hammond as well, at various times) and a musical director for the Columbia Record Company, made many recordings of his own works either as organist or as conductor, of ensembles like the Court Symphony Orchestra, the Casino Orchestra or his own Concert Orchestra. A few of his pieces were originally conceived for larger forces, as against having them grafted on subsequently. Columbia recorded *A Dream of Christmas*, which called for an organist, a solo vocalist, a narrator and a chorus as well as his own Concert Orchestra. He sometimes wrote just for chorus. A song for mixed voices, *Fighting for Freedom*, was written for the war effort in 1943 and his early compositions included a few church anthems. As far back as 1900 he composed a comic opera, *The Wonder Worker*, which was produced that year at the Grand Theatre in Fulham – a predecessor, *A Good Time*, was heard in 1896. His solo songs ranged from ballads like *The Heart's Awakening, I Loved You More Than I Knew, My Heart Still Clings To You, Will You Forgive?, Believe Me True, Mr. Heart-a-Dream* and *A Birthday Song*, all of which enjoyed a modest popularity, to a setting of *Blow, Blow Thou Winter Wind*, written as incidental music for a performance of Shakespeare's *As You Like It*. The song *Kilmoren* appeared in 1952, only a few years before Ketèlbey's death on 26 November 1959 at Cowes in the Isle of Wight, whither he had retired many years before to write music. Another relatively late piece is his one original contribution to brass band music (although many of his orchestral 'standards' were arranged for brass), the overture *The Adventurers*, performed and broadcast by the Fairey Aviation Works Band in 1945. This was described at the time as having two main features: 'brilliance and an effective chorale'. Most of his post-Second War works were reworkings of earlier material.

   A courteous, quiet, kindly, generous, slightly fussy man, Ketèlbey was generally popular, but he never courted the limelight, nor did he travel quite as widely as his compositions suggest. In later years he hardly ever left Cowes. He married twice, but sired no children; his principal non-musical recreation was playing billiards.

   It may be that Ketèlbey's music, several hundred separate pieces in all, emphasises emotionalism and 'effects' which in some performances go 'over the top', rather than structure and harmonic subtlety. It may well be that he was at his peak in the period 1915-30 and that his music declined in originality after the latter date. But his gift for melody and his professionalism as an orchestrator, readily acknowledged by many musicians of today and of his own day, ensured that he touched the hearts of millions. He still has this capacity, many years on, in the Age of Pop.

SONGS OF PARADISE
Reginald King 1904-1991

Reginald Claude McMahon King, born at Hampstead on 5 October 1904 into a musical family, was, like so many of the British light music composers of the inter-war period, 'made' by the emergence of the wireless – which came indeed just at the right time, when he was in his late teens. His first broadcast (of over 1400) was, however, not until 9 March 1929 (the last was in 1964). Two years before that King had formed a nine-piece orchestra to play regularly, twice daily Mondays to Fridays, at Swan and Edgar's Restaurant in the West End, which it did until 1939. King's Celebrity Trio included the cellist Douglas Cameron and the violinist Campoli, later to become so celebrated in his own right. After 1945 a new Reginald King Orchestra played first at the Spa, Whitby, then at Bridlington's Floral Hall. His gramophone recordings, for HMV, Regal, Zonophone, Filmophone, Columbia and the rare label Sterno, were legion.

He was a fine pianist and appeared with Sir Henry Wood as a soloist at the Proms soon after his time at the Royal Academy, where he studied with Harry Farjeon (King was elected a Fellow of the Academy in 1936), and remained a fine player up to the time of his death on 31 August 1991. Many of his pieces were published for the piano: genre pieces like *Beside the Lake, Evening Music* (1938), *Passing Clouds, Dreamy Willows, A Prayer at Eventide* (1938), *Song of Paradise* (which in its orchestral version was for a long time his signature tune), *Serenade For My Lady, Where Water-Lilies Dream* (1948), the intermezzo *Windflowers* (1938), *Pilgrim's Way, Rainbow Caprice, Al Fresco, Amourette, Moonlight Reverie, Tropical Moonlight* and *In the Shade of the Palms* (shades of Ketèlbey in these latter two), the more overtly rhythmic *Money Spider, Aperitif and Polka Piquante* (1949) and the romantic serenade *Julia* of 1943. His piano output also embraced more absolute works like the early Sonata in F sharp minor, performed a number of times in the 'twenties to acclaim and revived in the 'eighties (there was a Violin and Piano Sonata also), the *Four Preludes*, Opus 5 (1923), and the *Five Preludes*, Opus 7, the *Three Impressions*, Opus 3, the *Three Pieces*, Opus 4, and the acclaimed and broadcast *Fantasy* for piano and orchestra, published for two pianos. Several of the genre pieces were known in orchestral versions, often made by King himself, though Ronald Hanmer arranged *Al Fresco, Rainbow Caprice, Serenade For My Lady* and *Pilgrim's Way*, Vilem Tausky obliged for the *Polka Piquante* and Arthur Wood for *Windflowers*. In King's own orchestrations one can often discern that his music is that of a pianist, as Eric Coates' is that of an orchestral player and Alfred Reynolds' that of a man of the theatre. King's orchestral music, while not quite rivalling that of Coates in individuality and certainly not its equal in vigour, has a more than pleasing tunefulness.

The titles of some of his orchestral suites and of their individual movements could almost be Coates': *Country Life*, *Dreams in Exile* (whose movements are entitled 'Leafy Lanes of England', 'Those Far-Away Hills', and 'Heading for Home'), *In the Chilterns* (1938: 'Penn Woods in Spring', 'June Night on Marlow Reach' and 'Hunting Days'). *Rural Characters* (in four movements, depicting milkmaids, a shepherd, a harvester and a tinker) and *Youthful Days* ('Up With the Lark', 'A New Party Frock', 'Lullaby Land' and 'The First Waltz'). His overture *The Immortals*, recorded by Columbia in 1939, when its perky rhythms and rich orchestration were commented on, and the marches *Lime Grove* (the very title has BBC connotations) and *Knight of the Garter* were popular in their day; the caprice *Winter Skies* included a violin solo. Other single-movement orchestral genre pieces included the intermezzi *Daybreak*, *Love Take Me To Your Heart* and *Melody at Dusk*, the latter composed in 1938, and Ketèlbey-like descriptive morsels with evocative titles: *Dream Garden, Fair Star of Evening Green Valleys, Rising Tide, Sunset in Segovia* (this included, appropriately enough, a part for a guitar), *Phantom Fairies, Lilacs in the Rain* (1942), *Spring Meadows*, the caprice *Summer Breezes* (1936), *Sunny Serenade, The Lingering Melody, Dresden Dream, Gavotte Grotesque, Whispering Violin, Carmena, If You But Knew; A Garden in Spain* and the 'waltz serenade' *Pierrette on the Balcony*. *Meditation* and *Song of Paradise* were arranged and published for violin (or cello) and piano, the latter, plus *A Prayer at Eventide* and *Love Take Me To Your Heart*, also as songs, though King is not otherwise particularly known as a song composer.

His music is no longer fashionable and realisation of this forced his retirement in the mid 1960s, first to Devon, then to South Anston near Sheffield, but it was good to see him still composing right up to the time of his death at the age of nearly 87 and also that a few of his late compositions which reverted to the rather more serious idiom of his youth were published: Bardic Edition brought out the *Elegy* in 1989 and a *Meditation* for clarinet and piano or piano solo (1990) soon after. His last work was a quite extended *Reverie* for piano solo. He composed music over a period of 80 years. His first piano compositions were penned at the age of seven; the year after that Boosey offered to publish his *Air With Ten Variations*. People who knew him in his latter years recall him as a softly spoken, modest, courteous and kindly man. Some of these virtues – and virtues they are – are reflected in his music, which will surely always be acceptable listening.

A NOTABLE ALL-ROUNDER
Leighton Lucas 1903-1982

Leighton Lucas, born in London on 5 January 1903, is yet another figure like so many other British composers from Sullivan, Coleridge-Taylor and Elgar, through Edward German, Hubert Bath, Haydn Wood and Montague Phillips to Malcolm Arnold and Richard Rodney Bennett, who have sought – and in varying degrees obtained – recognition as serious composers but who are at least as equally at home in the lighter style. Like Ronald Binge, Lucas was largely self-taught, though later he became a Professor at the RAM. Experience with Diaghilev's Ballet Russe (1918-21) and at the Birmingham Repertory Theatre (1921-3) was followed by his conducting a performance of Rutland Boughton's opera *The Immortal Hour* in 1923. He later had further experience conducting for the ballet, and after coming out of the RAF in 1946 formed his own orchestra, which gave concerts of unfamiliar and often modern, especially French, music. He broadcast and lectured on ballet, music and the theatre. And he composed.

For the ballet he wrote: *Death in Adagio* (after Domenico Scarlatti), produced in 1938; *The Horses*, produced in 1945-6; and *Tam O'Shanter*, which remains unperformed. Film scores included those for the wartime *Target for Tonight*, *Ice Cold in Alex (The Road to Alex* from this was published separately as a stirring march) and *Yangtse Incident (The Amethyst* from this is another rousing march). Curiously, in view of this ability to write marches, he wrote the score for *The Dam Busters* (1954) but not the title march, which is of course by Eric Coates. His orchestral works were often serious in intention, though they inclined towards brevity. One thinks of the Cello Concertino (1956), the Clarinet Concerto (1957), the *Concert Champêtre* for violin, whose English premiere was at the Proms in 1956, the *Prelude, Aria and Finale* for viola d'amore (1956), the *Sinfonia Breve* for horn and eleven instruments, *A Litany* (1942) and the *Birthday Variations* (1970). But he composed his share of lighter suites like the *Ballet de la Reine*, for strings, the *Suite Française* (1940: premiered at the Proms in 1942) and *L'Europe Galante* after Campra (1939), plus various arrangements, incidental music, etc. Besides the Proms premieres, three other Lucas works were given their first performances by the BBC Symphony Orchestra: the *Sinfonia Brevis* in April 1937, *A Litany* in September 1947 and the *Chaconne* in C sharp minor in August 1949. His chamber music is often in single-movement form and many of the examples I have found are for unusual instrumental combinations: *Meditation* (1956) for cello and piano, *Aubade* for horn, bassoon and piano, *Three Dances for 3*, the latter 'three' being two harps and oboe – clearly the Goossens family – and *Disquisition* for two cellos and piano duet (1966) plus *Soliloquy* (1960) and *Tristesse*, both for viola and piano, and *Orientate* for bassoon (or cello) and piano.

For voices, Lucas wrote relatively little, though I have found a partsong *To Men*, and a madrigal, *My True Love Hath my Heart*, both for women's voices, and the SATB partsong *Sleep and Death* – the last-named two are both dated 1953; for the church he produced a Mass in G Minor (1967), available in both mixed and women's voices versions, and a *Parish Mass* (1969). However, he made his contribution to the now very important corpus of brass band music in the shape of a *Choral and Variations* (1968), which has been recorded, *Spring Song* (1962), *A Waltz Overture* (1973) and a *Symphonic Suite*. He was clearly a composer who was stimulating in his output; I recall the Leighton Lucas Orchestra's broadcast concerts back in the late 1940s and early 1950s having that same quality. Lucas died in 1982.

THE NIMBLE-FINGERED GENTLEMAN
Billy Mayerl 1902-1959

Billy Mayerl, after a period of relative eclipse following his untimely death in 1959, is experiencing a revival with both classical pianists like Eric Parkin, Susan Tomes, Phillip Dyson and Peter Jacobs and American up-tempo experts like Alex Hassan and Tony Caramia making recordings and giving much-admired recitals of his music and with two societies in this country to advocate his cause. Mayerl is best remembered for his syncopated piano solos, and wonderful entertainment they are, but, as we shall see, there was much more to him than those. He was a many-sided musical personality.

But first a biographical sketch. He was born in London on 31 May 1902, the son of a violin teacher. Billy's instrument was, however, the piano and he showed musical ability early in life, winning a scholarship to Trinity College, London, at the age of seven and playing the Grieg Concerto at the Queen's Hall at the age of nine (some sources say 12). From the age of 13 he played in various London cinemas and dance bands. He was apparently working with a hotel band in Southampton in 1921 when he was recruited for the Savoy Havana Band as its solo pianist. This made its debut in 1922 at the Coliseum and between 1923 and 1925 his work for the SHB made his name through broadcasts and recordings and gave him the security to marry his long-time sweetheart Jill Bernini, who was no mean pianist and who, although she was seven years his senior, was to outlive him by 25 years. He was the soloist in the first London concert performance of Gershwin's *Rhapsody in Blue* on 28 October 1925.

Mayerl left the Savoy in 1926; his next venture was to establish, in collaboration with Geoffrey Clayton, a Correspondence School in Modern Syncopation. This was launched early in 1926 from premises in Oxford Street. It expanded its operation and clientele, having 3000 students on its books by the beginning of 1928, with branches open in South Africa and New Zealand and later in India and Germany. Royalty were numbered among Mayerl's pupils. The School moved to the Steinway Hall in 1932. Much music was specially written by Mayerl for the School, syncopated (*Stepping Tones*) and 'straight' (*Musical Moments*). By May 1939 Billy claimed that the School had a total staff of a hundred in 117 branches worldwide and that 30,000 people had been taught altogether. World War II put a stop to its activities and, although an attempt was made to revive it in the 1950s, its operations were on a much reduced scale and the School finally closed in 1957.

During the 'twenties, Mayerl made many appearances in variety theatres both in London and the provinces. In 1926 he formed a double act with Gwen Farrar, who both sang and played the cello; this lasted until 1930 and yielded 15 gramophone records. But this was not by any means the end of Billy's connection with the stage: in fact from 1924 he had been contributing songs to West End shows, beginning with *The Punch Bowl* in that year, and he continued to do this until 1944. The first musical comedy for which he wrote the complete score was *Nippy* (Prince Edward Theatre, 1930: 137 performances), following this with the less successful *The Millionaire Kid* (Gaiety Theatre, 1931), *Sporting Love* (Gaiety, 1934: 302 performances), *Twenty-To-One* (Coliseum, 1935: 383 performances, another horse-racing musical), *Over She Goes* (Saville, 1936: 248 performances, still another horsey one and later filmed), *Crazy Days* (Shaftesbury, 1937) and *Runaway Love* (Saville, 1939, halted by the war but the subject of a Royal Command Performance in 1940).

We have already alluded to Billy Mayerl's broadcasts with the Savoy Havana Band. His radio work did not of course cease when he left the Savoy. In 1929 he even gave a radio demonstration on how to play syncopated music; in 1931 he played the first movement of Grieg's Concerto, ever a favourite work with him, with the BBC Symphony Orchestra and throughout the 1930s he was a familiar and regular artist on the wireless, mainly BBC but also Radio Luxemburg and foreign radio stations, and he appeared with many of the broadcasting orchestras of the day or in solo slots. During the war he broadcast regularly with his own band in 'Music While You Work' and in programmes for the Forces. Overwork brought a nervous breakdown in 1944, but he returned to the BBC in 1946 to broadcast, compose and make arrangements. He left in 1949 to tour Australia and New Zealand, but returned in 1951 and continued playing, arranging and composing until ill health forced his resignation in 1956. His last broadcast was on 'Desert Island Discs' in 1958, just ten months before his death on 25 March 1959.

Billy Mayerl began organising his own bands in 1926, notably for recordings with Vocalion. Later he formed his own orchestra of 26 players for *Sporting Love* at the Gaiety (1934) and for later shows. He formed a new orchestra in 1941 (the Grosvenor House Orchestra) which gave broadcasts and made records and he continued to broadcast as bandleader in the 1950s.

Mayerl was a man of boundless energy and engaging personality, short and dapper in appearance and generally equable in temperament. He packed an enormous amount into his life and this doubtless accounts for his early death, from a heart condition.

Setting aside the stage works and the many individual songs, whether for shows by others or for films like *Cheer Up*, whose hit was *There's a Star in the Sky*, or separate ones unconnected with any show, his own or anyone else's, like *Ev'ry Hour of the Day, Lullaby Baby, Resting* and *Portsmouth Road*, Mayerl composed over 150 individual original movements for piano (though many of these were orchestrated either by himself or by others like Arthur Wood, Herman Finck and Hubert Bath, who appear in this book, and Fred Adlington, Ray Noble, George Windeatt, Alan Nichols and Len Manning, who do not, or they appeared in other instrumental versions, particularly for violin and piano). A rough count suggests there were 20 suites and other multiple collections (78 movements in all), 58 individual genre pieces and 18 *Studies in Syncopation*. In addition, he brought out some 120 transcriptions of popular tunes by others (like *Limehouse Blues, Lambeth Walk, All the Things You Are, Turkey in the Straw, Phil the Fluter's Ball*, even *The Blue Danube*, of which only *Body and Soul* is still in print, though many have been recorded, especially by Eric Parkin. Many of these appeared originally in the *Billy Mayerl Club Magazine*, an offshoot of the Billy Mayerl School and which was published between 1934 and 1939; a large proportion of these transcriptions were superbly inventive and, as good transcriptions should, they add much to the original tune.

Then there are a number of purely orchestral works: the *Pastoral Suite*, performed by the BBC Symphony Orchestra pre-war and recorded on the Marco Polo label, a light-music effusion very much in the Coates manner (its opening 'Legend' is reminiscent of Quilter's *Rosamund*), the suite, *Moves in Contrast*, recorded by Mayerl himself, and the single movements *Waltz for a Lonely Heart*, beautiful and richly scored, *Beyond the Hills* and the novelty *Busybody*. One or two works were written originally for piano and orchestra – *Balearic Episode*, a concerto movement in the *Warsaw Concerto* tradition though not written for a film, and *The Forgotten Forest* of 1945, a tone-poem which Mayerl thought highly of and which for me echoes both Debussy and Rachmaninoff but sports characteristic Mayerl harmonies – while others were transcribed for that medium from piano solo originals, like the *Four Aces Suite*.

Mayerl's first attempts at composition appear to date from 1915, when he tried his hand at composing in a syncopated manner while at Trinity College, London. This was, predictably at that time, frowned on by the authorities. The piece apparently resurfaced, though doubtless considerably changed, as *Jazz Master* and was published as one of the

Pianolettes, which collection also included such other popular titles as *All-of-a-Twist*, *Eskimo Shivers* and *Jazzaristrix*. Even reckoning by the publication date, the *Pianolettes* are early works, but Billy's first published piece was the even earlier *Egyptian Suite* (1919), possibly, considering its date, inspired by Ketèlbey, though it falls well short of him in melodic inspiration. This was, however, definitely *not* a syncopated item. And so it carried on. Billy was to become known as the master of the syncopated piano solo, yet a substantial part of his output is more lyrical and in the English tradition of German and Eric Coates (though Coates imported dance-band idioms into some of his music), and sometimes, as in *The Forgotten Forest*, a substantial ten-minute piece, and perhaps the shorter tone-poem *Sennen Cove* and the earlier suite *The Legends of King Arthur*, something more serious even than that. He was a composer for all seasons.

His most famous piece, and virtually his signature tune, was *Marigold*. Many of Billy's movements bear the titles of flowers – he was a keen gardener. Not all these floral tributes are syncopated pieces, however: *Hollyhock, Marigold, Sweet William, White Heather* and *Wisteria* are, but not *Orange Blossom, Autumn Crocus, Honeysuckle, Lily Pond, Evening Primrose* or most of the movements of the four *In My Garden* suites representing the four floral seasons. Like so many of the light music composers we discuss in this book, Mayerl in his 'straight' pieces was a delightful evoker of landscapes: English ones in the *Pastoral Sketches* (1928), *Sennen Cove* (1929), *English Dance,* and *Sussex Downs* (1957), Spanish ones in *Carminetta, From a Spanish Lattice*, with its habanera middle section, and perhaps *Balearic Episode* and more exotic ones in the *Three Japanese Pictures* of 1930. Again like so many of our lighter composers, he delighted in the writing of pastiche 'early music': instances are *Minuet By Candlelight* and *Minuet for Pamela*.

Arguably the peak of Mayerl's compositional genius came in the 1930s with such numbers as *The Four Aces* suite and its pendant *The Joker* (he enjoyed cards), the lively invention of the *Aquarium Suite* and the single movements *Autumn Crocus, Mignonette, Honeysuckle, Mistletoe, Nimble-Fingered Gentleman*, the delicately imagined *Harp of the Winds, Fir-Tree, Bats in the Belfry* and the insistent *Railroad Rhythm*, not to mention all the stage shows, at least one of which, *Over She Goes*, was taken up by amateur societies and more might have been forthcoming had the American musical not taken over after 1945. But we may also point to the marvellous freshness and rhythmic vitality of the best works of the 'twenties: the *Pianolettes* (1925), already mentioned, the *Piano Exaggerations* of 1926, which include such favourites as *Jack-in-the-Box, Loose Elbows*, the bluesy *Sleepy Piano*, the *Puppets Suite* (1927) and the *Pastoral Sketches*. Nor is his post-war work, though considerably less in volume (Mayerl's health was steadily declining by that time) in any way inferior in quality. We have already alluded to *The Forgotten Forest;* other delights are *Postman's Knock, Shy Ballerina, Crystal Clear,* from 1954, *Filigree* (1955), *Funny Peculiar* (1957), *Jill-All-Alone* (1955), which refers of course to his wife, *Balearic Episode* and the *In My Garden* suites (1946-7). Indeed, many of these latter titles seem to have more depth and gravity than the exuberances of the 'twenties. He was far from written out in the 1950s and, though by then the appetite for light music generally and for Billy's music in particular was past its peak, it is a pity that his creative muse was snuffed out when he was only in his mid-fifties. His piano writing was always idiomatic and often brilliant, and my experience suggests that his piano music does not lie uneasily among piano recitals of classical music. Furthermore, although so many of his piano originals were arranged for orchestra by other hands, he could certainly orchestrate. The *Aquarium Suite,* with its parts for three saxophones, vibraphone and guitar as well as the more usual instruments, is a case in point; and at the BBC he was often called on to orchestrate the works of others. His livelier music has an infectious exuberance which surely cheers the dullest soul; his more reflective pieces have a sensitivity which in a few cases transcends the scope of light music. It is good to know the Mayerl revival is well on the way, that present-day artistes perform his works on record and in the concert room, and that several of his own recordings – and what a superb pianist he was – have been reissued.

THE 'CHU CHIN CHOW' MAN
George Frederick Norton 1869-1946

George Frederick Norton is connected in the minds of music-lovers with just one work, the musical comedy *Chu Chin Chow, A Musical Tale of the East*, produced at His Majesty's Theatre on 31 August 1916 and which ran for five years and a total of 2238 performances – then a record and one not surpassed on the English musical stage until *Salad Days* in the 'fifties. This remarkable show, based rather loosely on the story *of Ali Baba and the Forty Thieves*, was described as a combination of musical comedy and pantomime. *The Era* said Norton's music had 'a touch of the East but for the most part it was on a level with the tender melody of musical comedy' and was 'hardly inspired'. Be that as it may, many of the songs became hits and *The Cobbler's Song* in particular was in the repertoire of ballad singers for at least three or four decades. Norton himself took the role of Ali Baba in some performances, though the role was created by Oscar Asche, the librettist; Lily Brayton took the female lead. Its American production, in New York at the Manhattan Opera House, notched up 208 performances in 1917-18, with Tyrone Power and Florence Reed in the principal roles. Its first night was 22 October 1917. A revival in England in 1940 yielded a further 238 performances and there was a *Chu Chin Chow* on ice in 1953. The show was filmed in 1923 and, with George Robey, Malcolm McEachern (Mr Jetsam), Francis L. Sullivan and Anna May Wong, again in 1934. For this second film version Hubert Bath (*qv*), later to achieve fame as the composer of the *Cornish Rhapsody* from the film *Love Story*, rearranged the music.

Norton had been born in Salford on 11 October 1869 and he lived until December 1946. He studied singing with Tosti and joined the Carl Rosa Opera, but by the early 1900s he was appearing on the variety stage delivering monologues. He published many songs, most of them light in character (examples are *The Camel and The Butterfly*, *Madcap Marjorie* and *The Elephant and the Portmanteau*) and was soon being engaged to provide music for London stage shows. The first was *The Water Maidens* in 1901; he had something of a success with *Pinkie and the Fairies*, a play for children produced at His Majesty's Theatre in 1908, and he provided additional music for *Orpheus in the Underworld* (His Majesty's, December 1911), which was a version of Offenbach's *Orphée aux Enfers*. In the years before *Chu Chin Chow* really made his name as a composer, he provided the music for the Tivoli revue *What Ho! Daphne* (1913) and additional songs for *The Passing Show of 1915*. After 1916 he never quite recaptured the spark which had fired *Chu Chin Chow*. *Pamela* (1917) was coolly received, although several of the songs from it were separately published, and *The Stone of Destiny*, the score of which has been highly spoken of by some, was not staged at all. He contributed to *Flora* (1917) and *The Willow Pattern Plate*; while *Teddy Tail*, a children's fantastic musical play (1920), may be seen as a return to the mood of *Pinkie and the Fairies* of 12 years before. He was also responsible for a few independent orchestral pieces, of which we may mention the 'characteristic intermezzo' *Funeral of a Spider* and the barcarolle *La Siesta*.

At the time of his death Norton was described as being of 'a whimsical and fantastical quality of mind, loveable and a man of culture'. His gifts of telling Lancashire stories and of extemporising at the piano were recalled. For my own part, *The Robbers' Chorus* from *Chu Chin Chow* still stirs my blood 40-odd years after I heard it first.

'BANDY'
Walton O'Donnell 1887-1939

Bertram Walton O'Donnell, Irish by descent, was one of three brothers who were all, at one time or another, service bandmasters; each of them in fact served at least some time in the Royal Marines. Percy S.G. O'Donnell (1882-1945), after service as an Army bandmaster with the Black Watch and the Royal Artillery at Gibraltar, became Musical Director of the Royal Marines, Plymouth Division (1916-28), then of the Chatham Division (1928-37) and from 1937 Senior Director of Music to the Royal Marines. He succeeded his brother Walton as Conductor of the BBC Military Band in 1937 and remained with the Corporation after the BBCMB was dissolved in 1943. Rudolph, the third brother, was Bandmaster to the 7th Hussars (in which Walton served for a short period as a young man), then directed the Royal Marine Artillery Band and the RM Portsmouth Division between 1919 and 1931 before finally transferring to the RAF. (Rudolph is thought to be a unique example of a Bandmaster/Musical Director serving in all three services). Both Percy and Rudolph composed in a modest way; as examples we may note the former's *Empire Fanfare*, for trumpet, cornet, two trombones and timpani, and, from the latter, the *Celtic Waltz* and a *Fanfare on the RAF March Past*. But it was Walton who achieved most and who is remembered, albeit somewhat tenuously, today.

Born in Madras in 1887 (his father was Bandmaster of the 2nd South Wales Borderers – it is interesting to see how military banding runs in families and one thinks of the Godfreys and the Winterbottoms among other examples), he trained at the Royal Academy of Music, John Barbirolli being a contemporary. Walton's service in the Royal Marines, after a short time in the Army, was as Musical Director of the Portsmouth Division from 1917 (where he was commissioned in 1921) and then, from 1923, at Deal. His band at Deal accompanied the then Prince of Wales on a tour of Africa with such success that Walton was made a Member of the Victorian Order (he taught the Prince to play the ukelele, apparently). Walton then retired from the Marines to go to the BBC and form the Wireless Military Band ('Wireless' was later dropped in favour of 'BBC') in August 1927. This quickly became a fine ensemble (its first concert was in September 1927) and it did much to raise standards in the military, or concert, band world. Its repertoire excluded musical comedy and other light selections and 'novelty' items, but did include popular classics and a lot of what we would call light music. It was exclusively a studio ensemble and apparently never appeared in public – Walton is on record as saying that the microphone was the sternest possible taskmaster – but its basic strength of 26 players, which could be augmented as required, and its instrumental distribution were similar to service bands of the day.

A typical programme from December 1929 (normally programmes were an hour in length) comprised a fantasy from the ballet *Victoria and Merrie England* (Sullivan), a suite from the opera *The Miracle* (Humperdinck), a selection from *Turandot* (Puccini), the *Wedding Procession* from Rimsky-Korsakov's opera *Le Coq d'Or*, *Mock Morris* (Percy Grainger) and *The Flight of the Bumble Bee* (from *Tsar Saltan*, another Rimsky opera), interlaced with vocal solos from Norman Allin and Kate Winter. The Band recorded over 40 separate 78 rpm discs: overtures, including less well-known examples such as Suppe's *The Jolly Robbers* and – arranged by O'Donnell himself – Gounod's *Mirella*, marches, folk-tunes and classical arrangements, brilliant, unique ones made especially for the Band. It inspired one of the finest works ever composed for the military band medium, Gustav Holst's Prelude and Scherzo, *Hammersmith*. This was first performed in 1930 in the studio, not in public; it was also orchestrated and, so I understand from a lady who was a pupil at the time, was first tried out in a two-piano version at St Paul's Girls' School, Hammersmith, where Holst taught. Unfortunately *Hammersmith* was not recorded by O'Donnell with the BBCMB; nor was any of his own music except (in 1935) the *Crusader March*.

The band's relations with the BBC Symphony Orchestra after the latter was formed in 1930 were excellent, to the extent that the same pieces were often broadcast within a short time of each other by both band and orchestra. The band's programmes were greatly admired and enjoyed, not least by King George V. In 1937 Walton left it (and his Professorship of Harmony, Composition and Military Music at the Royal Academy) to take up a position as Head of the BBC's Northern Ireland region, which carried with it the conductorship of the Northern Ireland Orchestra. Walton was familiarly known at the BBC as 'Bandy' and he took part in many Children's Hour programmes during the 1930s. The BBCMB was, as we have said, taken over by Percy O'Donnell, who conducted it until its demise as a wartime economy measure in 1943, a move regretted by many both at the time and since. Walton was not around to see it for he died, of pneumonia, aged only 52, on 20 August 1939.

Walton O'Donnell composed much for military band. One work I heard again with renewed pleasure was his *Three Humoresques*, brilliantly inventive, harmonically adventurous for its time, and superbly scored. The titles of its three movements, 'Pride and Prejudice', 'Prevarication' and 'Petulance and Persuasion', appear to be derived from the novels of Jane Austen. The RAF Central Band played it on a record issued in 1986 and it has also been recorded by the Coldstream Guards Band. Other band classics by O'Donnell were *Theme and Variations, Two Irish Tone Sketches, Woodland Sketches* and *Songs of the Gael*; the last-named three were also arranged for orchestra. The Royal Marines Music Library at Deal still has the first two, along with the *Humoresques* and various orchestral works. *Songs of the Gael*, which I heard in Doncaster, conducted by Captain Peter Sumner (*qv*), one of O'Donnell's successors as a RM Director of Music, is an extended selection of Irish melodies and remains a big test for a military/concert band.

Walton by no means confined himself to writing for band or even to writing for wind instruments. For piano solo he published *Two Lyric Poems*, and for violin and piano *A Slumber Song*. His orchestral output, which includes works arranged from band originals and others, showed an understanding of stringed instruments to rival his virtuosity in scoring for woodwind and brass. The very lively, modestly astringent *Miniature Suite* (a Coatesian title), for strings, was popular for many years (I recall a Doncaster amateur orchestra bravely tackling it in 1966); also published were *The Irish Maiden*, based on two Irish traditional airs, a *Minuet* and the *Fragment* for strings. It would be pleasant to revive these sometime, especially the *Miniature Suite*; but we should perhaps remember Walton O'Donnell primarily for his attempts to raise the status of military band music. The late Lieutenant Colonel Sir Vivian Dunn (to whom I am greatly obliged for his recollections of O'Donnell) had no doubt that the BBC Military Band was the finest in the world in the 1930s, made up as it was of the best professional wind and brass players in London. In a private communication to me Sir Vivian recalled Walton as 'a kindly man, a good sportsman, a gentleman to his fingertips, a paragon among British musicians'. Dunn learned much from him both at the RAM and in being privileged to attend rehearsals of the BBC Military Band at Broadcasting House. He ranks O'Donnell's own music for band with that of Holst and Vaughan Williams, which is high praise indeed.

SERIOUS OR LIGHT?
The experience of Montague Phillips 1885-1969

Many of the masters of British light music in the period either side of 1900 had aspirations to be serious composers: Sullivan, most notably, Edward German, Haydn Wood, Hubert Bath, all (bar Sullivan) discussed at some length in this book and Montague Phillips, born in Tottenham on 13 November 1885. A noted boy soprano, he won a scholarship to the Royal Academy of Music, where he studied organ and composition and won several more scholarships. He worked as a church organist throughout much of his life, successively at Theydon Bois (in Essex), Christ Church, Wanstead, and Esher Parish Church. A friend of mine who sang under him in the choir at Esher recalled him as a strict disciplinarian but as also having a great sense of humour. Phillips remained closely associated with the RAM, where he was a Professor of Harmony and Composition. His extended scena for soprano, *The Song of Rosamund,* was in fact written for the RAM's centenary in 1922.

So far Phillips' life sounds like the antithesis of a composer who was to become known primarily for his works in the lighter style. It was his marriage to the light-operatic soprano Clara Butterworth, whom he met at the Academy, which helped to change this. It was for her that he wrote many of his more than a hundred songs (I have traced 102 titles). Mostly these were of the ballad type, and while they were not quite as popular as those of Sanderson, Coates and Molloy or even perhaps those of Easthope Martin or W.H. Squire, they were well enough regarded for H.M. Higgs (*qv*) to make one of his orchestral selections of some of them. Birds inspired many of Phillips' songs: *The Blackbird's Song to the Buttercup; Sing Sing Blackbird, So Sang the Thrush, Songs of a Nightingale, Though Soar the Lark* and *Sing, Joyous Bird,* the fourth of *Four Songs of Joy,* Opus 24, and certainly a joyful little imagination – possibly the Phillips song (apart from *The Fishermen of England* in *The Rebel Maid*) most likely to be encountered in performance today. Other cycles were a *Calendar of Song* (4 songs), *Dream Songs* (4), *From a Lattice Window* (5), *Old-World Dance Songs* (4 – 'Gavotte', 'Minuet', 'Sarabande' and 'Gigue'), *Sea Echoes* (3) and, from 1919, *Flowering Trees* (4).

Apart from birds, Phillips the songwriter found much inspiration in nature: *Among the Willows, Blue Bells, Butterfly Wings, Daffodil Days, The First Spring Day,* a late effort (1954), *Forest Echoes, Harvest Home, A Little Bunch of Snowdrops, My Dreamland Rose, Orchard Daffodils, Pale Yellow Rose,*

A Song of June, Sun-Flakes, Were I a Moth, When April Laughs, Wild Flowers and *Wind on the Wheat*. Other songs, which because their accompaniments were orchestrated and as such are in the BBC Library, must have been particularly popular in their day were *The Beat of a Passionate Heart, The Star, The Dawn Has a Song, Gentlemen the Toast is England* (arranged also for male-voice choir), *In the Deep, Silence of the Night, Lethe, Laburnum, Love the Jester, Nightfall at Sea, O Ship of My Delight, Open Your Window to the Morn* (also arranged for chorus, this time for three-part women's voices), *Song of the Smuggler's Lass, Starry Woods, Waiting for You* and *Wake Up! Hush'd is My Lute* was recorded during World War I. That Phillips' songs, despite their artistry and melodic interest, have survived less well than, say, the ballads of Wilfrid Sanderson and Eric Coates may possibly be explained by the suggestion that they were too good as ballads but not quite good enough to take their place alongside the art songs of Vaughan Williams, Warlock, Gurney and so on.

Phillips' best-known work was also one in which his wife had a role (Clara Butterworth also sang in two operettas in which G.H. Clutsam was involved, *Lilac Time* and *Young England*, set in the first Elizabethan era). This was the delightfully scored operetta *The Rebel Maid*, produced at the London Empire in 1921 and a stirring tale of the sea set at the time of the 'Glorious Revolution' of 1688. Because of the Coal Strike that year (1921), which caused few buses or late trains to run, it lasted a mere four months in the West End, but it became popular with amateur operatic societies up and down the country and may still be heard today. Its best-known song, *The Fishermen of England*, became a favourite concert number and is still so; a suite of dances was also extracted from the score. By contrast, Phillips' only other operetta, *The Golden Triangle*, was unsuccessful and may never have achieved performance.

Phillips' orchestral output shows the ambivalence between light and serious which we have already noted (though his obituarist in *The Times* had no doubt that he was a composer 'in the salon tradition'). It is, however, difficult to typecast a composer; many so-called 'serious' British composers like Elgar (and in our day Malcolm Arnold and Richard Rodney Bennett) have shown an outstanding gift for writing light music. Phillips produced a Symphony in C minor in 1911, two piano concertos (1907 and 1919), of which the second in E major (Opus 32) was later arranged by the composer and published in 1948 for two pianos, a *Fantasy* for violin and orchestra, Opus 16 (also published later with piano accompaniment), and a Sinfonietta (1943), broadcast in that year, all of which are serious music (other lighter Phillips works to be premiered by the BBC Symphony Orchestra were the *Surrey Suite* (1936), *A Moorland*

Idyll (1936) and the *Charles II* (1936) and *Revelry* (1937) overtures). Yet his overtures, like the sparkling *Revelry* (1937) and the descriptive *Hampton Court* (1954), a kind of pendant to the delightful *Surrey Suite* of 1936 which was arranged also for military band (in which version I have heard its first movement, and which was an affectionate portrayal of the county in which he lived), and was made up of 'Richmond Park', 'The Shadowy Pines' and 'Kingston Market', are equally clearly 'light music'.

Though Phillips expressed his horror and contempt for the jazz and other syncopated music so popular here in the 1920's (he was unlike Eric Coates in this, as the latter absorbed it most distinctively into his own style), he was on record as saying that there was a place for light music for the 'great majority of people' who lie between the 'ultra highbrows and the irredeemable lowbrows' and who 'can appreciate music which is melodious and well written but not too advanced'. It was for such people that he wrote his suites *The World in the Open Air, In May Time, Village Sketches, Dance Revels* (Mazurka, Minuet and Valse) and the *Three Country Pictures* and single movements like the *Arabesque, A Forest Melody, A Hillside Melody, Harlequin Dance, A Moorland Idyll, Summer Nocturne, Spring Rondo, Sunshine Dance* (strings only), *Violetta: Air de Ballet* and – another sparkling number I can remember across the years – the Shakespearean scherzo *Titania and her Elvish Court*. His *Empire March* was performed at a Henry Wood Prom in 1942 and *In Praise of My Country* in the shortened Prom season of 1944; these were two of several patriotic wartime effusions. Phillips' instrumental output yet again shows a similar ambivalence between serious and light. A string quartet and the Piano Concerto No 2 which he arranged for two pianos are balanced by piano arrangements of some of the light orchestral suites we have mentioned and the *Four Pieces*, Opus 28, and *Four Pieces*, Opus 29, written originally as piano solos.

That he worked as an organist for much of his life is recalled by pieces for organ like the Prelude and Fugue in G minor and arrangements of orchestral movements like *A Forest Melody*. Throughout his composing career he wrote for choirs, cantatas like *The Death of Admiral Blake* (1913), for baritone solo, chorus and orchestra, and part-songs, both for women's voices *(A Cornish Cove, Nightfall at Sea, O Ship of My Delight, A Lake and a Fairy Boat* and *The Solitary Rose)* and for mixed voices *(Dawn, Daffodils, Morning Song, Sigh No More Ladies, It Was a Lover and His Lass* and *The Vesper Bell)*. *The Empire Song*, for soloists and unison voices, doubtless stirred patriotic hearts in 1942.

Phillips died at Esher at the beginning of 1969. His more serious work never caught on; but his light work gave much pleasure and a concert programme comprising, say, *Revelry*, the *Surrey Suite* with *Hampton Court* added, *Titania*, a selection from *The Rebel Maid*, with one or two of the part-songs and a solo song or two – *Sing Joyous Bird* would be a 'must' – and rounded off with the *Empire March*, would still do so today.

BRITISH LIGHT MUSIC

Richard Addinsell   Kenneth Alford   Eric Ball

John Barry   Hubert Bath   Eric Coates

Julian Clifford (Senior)   Samuel Coleridge-Taylor   Frederic Curzon

Vivian Ellis   Robert Farnon    Percy Fletcher

Henry Geehl   Dan Godfrey II   Cecil Armstrong Gibbs

Fred Hartley    Wilfred Josephs    Albert W Ketèlbey

BRITISH LIGHT MUSIC

Billy Mayerl

Montague Phillips

Roger Quilter

William H. Reed

Alfred Reynolds

Wilfrid Sanderson

Haydn Wood

Denis Wright

Frank Wright

Reginald King and his orchestra, Floral Hall, Bridlington

Bandstand at the East Cliff Pavilion (now the King's Hall), Herne Bay.

THE GENTLE LYRICIST
Roger Quilter 1877-1953

Roger Cuthbert Quilter was born in Brighton on 1 November 1877, into a wealthy and cultured family. He grew up in Suffolk, was educated at Eton and then in 1893 went to Germany for a course of study specifically at the Hoch Conservatory, Frankfurt-am-Main, where he got to know other British musicians of the so-called 'Frankfurt School': Cyril Scott, Henry Balfour Gardiner, Percy Grainger and Norman O'Neill (all *qv*).

On returning to England in 1898, Quilter quickly became established in musical circles, particularly as a composer of solo songs. The fluent, immediately attractive idiom of these – which appears to belie Quilter's generally slow and painstaking methods of actual composition – tends to suggest the Edwardian ballad as purveyed by Wilfrid Sanderson, Eric Coates, Stephen Adams and many others, were it not that he so often set classic English texts. His Opus 1, *Four Songs of the Sea* (1900), were settings of his own words; these were followed by several settings of Herrick, the cycle *To Julia*, Opus 8, being first performed in 1905 by the great Gervase Elwes, one of many noted singers of the day to take up Quilter's songs, Shelley *(Love's Philosophy* remains popular) and many other greats of English literature. Of Quilter's early songs the Tennysonian *Now Sleeps the Crimson Petal* became especially popular, familiar in ballad concerts and in vocal interludes in light orchestral concerts. His arrangements of folk-songs and popular tunes of the past like *Over the Mountains* and *Drink to Me Only* also acquired fame, not to mention a characteristically Quilter feel. Almost his last work was an arrangement of 16 folk-songs published as *The Arnold Book* in 1947. However, it is his Shakespearean songs, in three groups at Opus 6, 23 and 30, on which much of his fame rests. Altogether he composed somewhere between 110 and 120 songs.

Whether or not Quilter's songs are sufficiently ballad-like to bring him within the purview of this book, there is no doubt that his relatively small corpus of orchestral pieces cause him to be reckoned among the Edward Germans, Eric Coateses and so on. This included a *Serenade* premiered at a Henry Wood Prom in 1907, and *A Children's Overture*, a very cleverly strung together and beautifully scored potpourri of nursery rhyme tunes, again first performed at a Promenade Concert in September 1919 and later arranged for military band by Dan Godfrey of Bournemouth fame. Some eight years before that premiere, Quilter had been invited to provide music to a children's fairy tale, *Where the Rainbow Ends*, at the Savoy

Theatre. A charming suite was extracted from this music, of which my favourite is the meltingly beautiful *Rosamund,* clearly the production of a song composer. Almost as attractive was the incidental music for Shakespeare's *As You Like It,* from 1921; the final *Country Dance* surely shows the influence of his one-time fellow student Percy Grainger. Quilter also wrote music for two ballets: *The Rake,* commissioned for inclusion in a Charles B. Cochran revue in 1925 and inspired of course by Hogarth; and *Titania.* He even had an opera, *Julia,* produced at Covent Garden in December 1936 and conducted by Albert Coates. This was not a success, probably because it was too light in style for 'grand opera' devotees but too heavy for lovers of contemporary musical comedy, and it achieved only seven performances. Publishers extracted various suites and vocal extracts from it which they issued under sundry titles including *Love at the Inn* and *Rosme,* which latter selection included a charming Concert Waltz. Among other orchestral pieces we may list the *Dickory Dock* suite for strings, the two pieces *Moonlight on the Lake* (taken from *Where the Rainbow Ends*) and *Water Nymph,* also for strings, and a *Tudor March.*

Quilter was a more than competent orchestrator and it comes as something of a surprise that his charming *Three English Dances,* Opus 11, of 1910 and premiered at the Queen's Hall in that year were actually scored by Percy Fletcher. Quilter, a fine pianist, wrote a number of arrangements of folk and popular tunes, dances and short genre pieces for that instrument, including the *Country Pieces,* two sets of studies (1910-20), the *Three Pieces,* Opus 16 (1916), of which *Dance in the Twilight* became famous, the *Two Impressions,* Opus 19, of 1920 and arrangements of *A Children's Overture, Where the Rainbow Ends* and *The Rake.* Even some 'chamber music' appeared: arrangements of his songs for violin (or cello) and piano, the *Fairy Frolic* for piano trio, and a Fantasy Quintet (1935) for piano and strings. One of his better-known numbers was for (unison or other) chorus, strings and piano, *Non Nobis Domine,* to words by Rudyard Kipling – this was written for a Pageant of Parliament in 1937 but was quickly adopted by junior choirs and soon became one of the best known (and most distinguished) of 'school' songs. It is still popular today. Quilter's partsongs are less well known than his solo songs but there are quite a few of them. Some, like *Freedom. Fairy Lullaby; Tulips* and *Come Lady Day;* are arrangements of solo songs; others, like *To Daffodils, To Daisies, Five Herrick Lyrics,* Opus 7, *Dancing on the Green, Madrigal in Satin* and *To the Virgins* are original choral pieces. Some, like *The Cradle in Bethlehem* and *Lead Us Heavenly Father,* were suitable for church use. Quilter's longest choral work was *The Sailor and His Lass,* for soprano, baritone, chorus and orchestra.

Quilter's health was never good. He was turned down for military service in World War I (though he 'did his bit' by organising concerts and recitals in hospitals). A stomach ulcer gave him great trouble and he was subject to bouts of depression, not helped by worry about his own homosexual preferences, which were then less sympathetically regarded than they are today. It is surprising that he lived into his 76th year, dying on 21 September 1953.

His musical tastes were wide; as he put it, anything 'from Bach to ragtime'. His love of English poetry is reflected in the texts that he set so ingratiatingly. He used his personal wealth, rather as did his colleague Balfour Gardiner, to pay for live performances of the works of others, including, particularly, those of Percy Grainger. In 1921 he became a founder member of the Musicians' Benevolent Fund and was to serve on its committee for the rest of his life. Quilter's music rarely if ever crossed the comparatively narrow boundaries which confined it. His muse was essentially a gentle one – not anonymous, as some have said, as one can always recognise a little-known Quilter song, even an arrangement, as being by him – and it is good to know that his songs and the *Children's Overture* remain almost as popular as ever they were. CDs, even of his his orchestral music, continue to appear and should help his reputation, as will Trevor Hold's study of the songs, *The Walled-in Garden* (Thames Publishing, 1996).

A MAN OF THE THEATRE
Alfred Reynolds 1884-1969

Reynolds, as a conductor of, and writer for, theatre orchestras has many counterparts in this book, among them Arthur Wood, Frederick Norton, G.H. Clutsam, Percy Fletcher, Hubert Bath and Edward German. He is a notable representative of the light music composers of the Coates/Phillips/Haydn Wood/Frederic Curzon era; he has appeared in the Marco Polo CD series, and a Meridian issue of his vocal and instrumental music was issued in the spring of 1996.

He was born on 15 August 1884 in Liverpool and enjoyed a happy childhood; his family ran Reynolds' Exhibition, a 'waxworks plus' which was seen as the North's answer to Madame Tussaud's. He was educated at Merchant Taylor's School, Crosby, and later in France; his musical education was similarly international in character, early study with one J.C. Walker in Liverpool being followed by a few months at the Heidelberg Conservatory and some six years in Berlin, most of them as a pupil there of Engelbert Humperdinck, the composer of *Hansel and Gretel*. His first known compositions date from this period – light waltzes like *Le Désir*, performed in Liverpool in 1906 as part of a variety bill, and *Le Vertige*, a setting *of Jubilate Deo* and possibly one of *The Song of Solomon* for Berlin's (Anglican) Church of St George in 1910, where he had become Organist and Choirmaster in 1908, and various exercises – choral and instrumental fugues, a chorale and string quartet movements – for the kindly, gently humorous Humperdinck. In 1910 Reynolds took a German company to play an enjoyable season at the Municipal Theatre in Dorpat (Tartu) in what is now Estonia, with operettas like *Die Fledermaus*, *The Count of Luxembourg* and *Der Mikado*.

Returning to England later in 1910, Reynolds found standards in opera and operetta to be less high than on the Continent, but he was lucky to obtain a job as a conductor of Philip Faraday's company touring Oscar Strauss' *The Chocolate Soldier*. Reckoned to be the youngest operatic conductor in England, he visited Liverpool, Hull, Birmingham, Scarborough, where the company had to dodge pickets of striking railwaymen, and Blackpool. In Dublin in July 1913 Reynolds married Barbara Florac, who had been understudying the part of Nadine in *The Chocolate Soldier*. Barbara later published a number of art songs which reveal a considerable talent for composition, including a setting of *It Was a Lover and His Lass* often sung by Heddle Nash. Although a daughter was born to the Reynolds in June 1914 they mostly lived apart during the 55 years of life left to Alfred (Barbara survived until 1977) but they never divorced.

After more work for Faraday early in 1914, Reynolds visited the United States later that year, narrowly missing returning to England on the ill-fated *Lusitania*. He volunteered for military service but a weak chest and proneness to pleurisy, which plagued him all his life, meant – perhaps fortunately – that he never went to France and was invalided out in 1917. This meant that he was able to continue to compose and to appear in wartime charity concerts. Some songs, notably *The Phantom Ride*, to words by his father Charles Reynolds, and *Forest Whispers* dated from the post-1910 period, but already Reynolds was becoming known for his incidental music for the theatre: *The Picture on the Wall* (1916), *There Remains a Gesture* (1920) and, most notably at this time, *The Toy Cart*, a play set in 2nd-century India and produced at the Abbey Theatre, Dublin, in 1918. Reynolds arranged a seven-movement suite, sometimes called *Vasantasena*, from this which received performances at Eastbourne, Harrogate, Bradford and Blackpool during 1919-20 and many others in later years. The music has great charm and is finely orchestrated though, as observers noted at the time, its Indian colour is negligible. But does this matter?

During the winter of 1920-21 Reynolds toured the Far East as Musical Director of the so-called Royal Opera Company, whose repertoire comprised a mixture of opera and operetta: the tour was a disaster as the pieces done were slightly old-fashioned and not attractive to the audiences there, the (local) orchestras were indifferent in quality and the company was poorly managed. The money ran out in Java and Reynolds drew on his savings to come home via Japan and Canada.

Back in England, Reynolds was busy both as conductor and composer. The incidental music for Baroness Orczy's *Leatherface* included a stirring *March of the Spears* which became a concert number and approaches Coates' best marches in quality. The orchestral *Fairy Tale* was composed for the Harrogate Municipal Orchestra in 1922. And inspired perhaps by the runaway success of *The Beggar's Opera* in Frederic Austin's version at the Lyric, Hammersmith, from 1920 onwards, he became increasingly preoccupied with refurbishing 18th-century light operas: Arne's *Love in a Village* for the Mayfair Dramatic Club (1923) and, also for the MDC originally, *Lionel and Clarissa* by Dibdin and others (1924) and Storace's *The Siege of Belgrade* (1926).

Love in a Village brought Reynolds to the notice of Nigel (later Sir Nigel) Playfair, who engaged him as Musical Director of his Lyric Theatre, Hammersmith. Reynolds remained there nine years (1923-32) and his work there in those years was notable. The Lyric was a small theatre (500 seats) and its orchestra correspondingly so: just four players (violin, viola, cello and piano), although for most specifically musical productions this was expanded to eight or nine. For the Lyric, Reynolds arranged Sheridan's *The Duenna* (music mainly by the Linleys), first produced in October 1924 to ecstatic reviews, and revived *Lionel and Clarissa* (1925) and *Love in a Village* (1928). In these Reynolds not only re-scored the accompaniments but composed many new numbers himself (nine out of 33 in *The Duenna*, ten of 27 in *Lionel and Clarissa* and eight of 30 in *Love in a Village*). Contemporary recordings were made of *Lionel and Clarissa* and, orchestrated by Sydney Baynes, the Spanish-coloured dances from *The Duenna*.

Reynolds' pen was active for the Lyric in a variety of work. This included music for plays like Molière's *Le Bourgeois Gentilhomme*, with Miles Malleson, and *The Beaux Stratagem* (the music here was mock Baroque in style, including songs), Shakespeare's *The Taming of the Shrew* (a superb overture), *Much Ado* (ditto) and *The Merchant of Venice* (including an attractive *Mascarade*), Sheridan's *The Critic*, Goldsmith's *She Stoops to Conquer* (1928: the lilting song *Ah Me, When Shall I Marry Me* become a hit) and Dryden's *Marriage à la Mode*, whose delicious ballet (Markova and Frederick Ashton participating) left the critics wanting more. A revue, *Riverside Nights*, was staged in 1926, including Arne's short comic opera *Thomas and Sally* but also much by Reynolds: an overture, the accompaniment to Wordsworth's (spoken) *The Power of Music* and the 15-minute burlesque operetta *The Policeman's Serenade*, whose charm ensured its wide appeal as a separate piece. A lighter revue, *Midnight Follies*, including songs to A.P. Herbert's words – later published, with other Herbert songs, as *She-Shanties* – a syncopated dance, *The Sirens of Southend*, and a fugue for three saxophones, was devised for Playfair as a cabaret at the Metropole Hotel. And two operettas or, to use Reynolds' term, comic operas, also appeared: the one-act *The Fountain of Youth* (1931), whose 'hit' was the atmospherically scored *Now in Her Westering Flight*, and the full-length (three-act) *Derby Day* (1932), to a book by A.P. Herbert. This was an attempt to follow in the tradition of Sullivan, but despite the colour associated with Britain's second-oldest classic horse race, including tipsters, punters, jockeys, even a chorus of 'pearly kings', and the charm of the solo songs, the music lacks Sullivan's memorability. Herbert, witty though he was, struck a less rich chord in the national consciousness than W.S. Gilbert. Nevertheless it had a fair run.

Even in Reynolds' 'Playfair years' he composed for others: incidental music, for *The Lady of the Camellias* (Garrick Theatre, 1930), in which

Tallulah Bankhead and Glen Byam Shaw appeared, Clifford Bax's *Socrates*, an austere score (though successfully adapted for concert use) for flute and harp, *The Limping Man* (Belfast, 1930, Henley's *Beau Austin* and, for Merton College, Oxford, *A New Way to Pay Old Debts*. He conducted not only for Playfair – notably Dunhill's opera *Tantivy Towers* – but for others, especially the BBC. Musical playlets, with words by Reynolds' sister Edith (such as *Shepherd's Delight, By Shrewsbury Town, Gather Ye Rosebuds* and *Sally in Our Alley*) and songs like the *She-Shanties, The Virgin's Choice, Heartsease, The Mad Shepherd, Reiver's Moon* and *You Who Have Left Me* were heard on the radio, together with selections from the incidental music we have mentioned, often conducted by Reynolds himself.

It is tempting to regard Reynolds' time at the Lyric as the climax of his work, but there was plenty to come after 1932. *1066 and All That*, a musical comedy after Sellar and Yeatman's historical spoof, was produced at the Birmingham Repertory Theatre at Christmas 1934 and later in London – 'the best theatrical joke of 1935' as *The Daily Telegraph* described it – and at the Malvern Festival of 1936. The music is, as always with Reynolds, attractive and well made if not outstandingly individual, and the piece can still (as I have myself heard) give pleasure today, especially to young performers. Reynolds remained active both in the theatre and for the BBC until well after World War II. A most attractive score was written for a production of *The Swiss Family Robinson* for Sir Barry Jackson also at the Birmingham Rep (1938). James Laver, who wrote the words, later recalled this as 'one of the happiest affairs on which I have been engaged... Alfred was the easiest possible man to collaborate with'. The music yielded a concert suite of which the 'Swiss Lullaby' and 'Ballet' are outstanding, as did Reynolds' music for *Alice in Wonderland* (1947, Stratford) and *Alice Through the Looking Glass*, the former including three characteristic dances 'Ballet of Rabbits', 'Crawl of the Caterpillars' and 'Dance of the Cards', the latter a 'Ballet of the Talking Flowers', and three more characteristic dances 'Jabberwocky', 'Parade of the King's Hobby Horses' and 'March of the Drums'. A two-act comic opera, *The Limpet in the Castle*, received its premiere in 1958 at Wombwell, South Yorkshire, in the heart of the Yorkshire coalfield (interestingly, the cast included an A. Scargill.). And there was incidental music for many other plays we have not space to mention.

The BBC particularly used Reynolds' talent for giving a facelift to old music and, in addition to reviving *The Duenna, Lionel and Clarissa* and *Love in a Village*, commissioned from him *The Dragon of Wantley* (music by J.F. Lampe and others) and Allan Ramsay's *The Gentle Shepherd. The Bookie's Opera*, for just three singers, and a return to the manner of *The Policeman's*

Serenade, was written for television. He began setting Dickens *The Village Coquettes* (Hullah's original music had been lost) but appears not to have finished it.

Reynolds wrote non-theatre songs, perhaps about forty of them in all, throughout his composing career. *Progress*, a scena to Herbert Farjeon's words, was composed in 1909; the cycle *Five Centuries of Love*, to words by Clifford Bax, the songs dated respectively 1570, 1660, 1770, 1860 and 1910 and utilising his gift for writing amusing and effective pastiche, appeared in 1946. Between those dates his output included items suitable for music-hall or cabaret like *Laughing Ann* from the *She-Shanties*, written originally for Angela Baddeley and a real showstopper, and art songs like *Have You Seen But a White Lily Grow?* (words by Ben Jonson), *At First Sight* (Ford), *A Song in Winter* (Meredith) and *March* (Wordsworth). Somewhere in between lie the duet *A Boat Beneath a Sunny Sky*, to Lewis Carroll's words, and many of his settings of A.P. Herbert, including four negro spirituals.

Instrumental concert works unconnected with the stage were few: *Overture for a Comedy* (but even this could have been used in the theatre), *A Fairy Tale* (A Nursery Nocturne), a *Regimental Slow March for the Inns of Court Regiment*, settings of Boccherini's Minuet and *Drink to Me Only* for four cellos, a jaunty *Hornpipe* for double bass, written for Victor Watson in 1927, which has been successfully revived during the past decade and published, and a *Whimsy* for bass flute and harp, possibly derived from the *Socrates* music.

Reynolds died, aged 84, at Bognor Regis on 18 October 1969. A kindly, very approachable man with a good sense of humour, he was a delightful companion and a keen clubman. His spare-time interests were given as motoring and motor-boating. He read and spoke at least eight languages. His music, vocal and instrumental, shows a fresh tunefulness which the repertoire is poorer for being without. His songs, whether originally written for plays, operas, revues or concerts, are grateful to the voice. His orchestral movements, all small in form and scale, were mostly written for a small theatre orchestra but they adapted effectively for larger ensembles. His many adaptations of 18th-century stage works may be frowned on in this purist age but in their time they helped resurrect and popularise the music of that period. They remained popular for years. He was a conductor of ability, both in the theatre and the concert hall. We should do what we can to keep his memory green.

CYRANO AND THE DOGE OF VENICE
Frederick Rosse 1867-1940

So many of the composers featured in this book are remembered for just one work, even though they produced vastly. This was certainly the case with Frederick Rosse, who was born in Jersey in 1867, and whose *Doge's March* from the incidental music he wrote for *The Merchant of Venice* long remained popular. Rosse was educated at Harrow and then abroad in Leipzig, Dresden, Brussels and Vienna. His musical career began (and largely continued) in the theatre, firstly as a singer – he took part in Sidney Jones' *The Geisha* at Daly's Theatre. From that he moved on to become chorus master at Daly's and then, again like so many of the light music composers this book passes in review, to be successively musical director at various other London theatres.

That he was a man of the theatre is reflected in most of his compositions. A musical farce *All Aboard* was produced in 1895; and incidental music was written for many plays, including *Monsieur Beaucaire* (1902 – six movements were later extracted from it to make a concert suite), *Cyrano de Bergerac* (1923), *The Three Musketeers* (whose concert suite comprises five movements), *Gabrielle* (1916), *Almond Eye* (whose concert suite also embraced five movements) and, as we have already mentioned, *The Merchant of Venice*, for the Garrick in 1905, of which the *Doge's March* is the finale of the suite. This suite, again in five movements, played for over 20 minutes, and was thus a substantial concert item. Some of these suites of incidental music were arranged by other hands, for example *Cyrano* by Charles Woodhouse and *Monsieur Beaucaire* by Ernest Bucalossi (qv) of *Grasshoppers' Dance* fame.

Not all Rosse's music was written for the theatre by any means. We may instance among this the *Suite Tragique*, the *Petite Suite Modeme* (1918) and the three *Intermezzi*, Opus 110. He also composed songs, often rather light in style, like *In the Old Countrie* and *The Refractory Monk*. His prolific, well-crafted music appears to have sunk without trace, which is a pity – even the *Doge's March*, popular enough even in the 1950s, is but little heard today, many years after his death on 20 June 1940.

DONCASTER'S PRIDE
Wilfrid Sanderson 1878-1935

Sanderson would not find a place in every compendium of British light music composers. As a composer, he did not contribute to the repertoire of the orchestral suite or light genre piece. Nor did he compose operetta, although he conducted Doncaster amateurs in it for two decades and a half. Apart from a handful of popular piano solos and one or two pieces of church music, his creative reputation rests on approximately 170 songs of the ballad type. Yet these are still popular 70 years and more after his death; and who is to say that these are not 'light music'? Such ballads were always a feature in the lighter programmes of the resort orchestras, on the BBC and even, at one time, of the Henry Wood Proms. Many figures who are undoubtedly light music composers – Coates, Haydn Wood and Montague Phillips, for example – were known as much, or almost as much, for their songs, which are mostly of the ballad type, as for their orchestral compositions. No apology is offered, or needed, for including Sanderson in these pages.

Wilfrid (not Wilfred) Ernest Sanderson, Mus.Bac. (Durham), FRCO, LRAM was born in Ipswich on 23 December 1878, the son of a Wesleyan minister. He was educated at the City of London School and, though he was originally intended for a business career, he showed musical ability early in life, conducting his first orchestra at the age of 13 and on leaving school became an articled pupil of, and later assistant to, Sir Frederick Bridge, Organist of Westminster Abbey 1882-1918, conductor, composer and academic. Sanderson remained at the Abbey for the seven years 1897-1904, his pupillage overlapping that of Edward Bairstow, and he sang in the Abbey Choir for King Edward VII's Coronation in 1902. Concurrently with that he began building up a practice as a private music teacher and he held, successively, other organist's posts in London suburban churches, notably at All Hallows', Southwark (1896-8), and St James', West Hampstead (1898-1904), which under him acquired a notable reputation for its music.

On 30 December 1903, however, he accepted the post of Organist and Choirmaster at St George's Parish Church, Doncaster, as from 1 May 1904 at a salary of £100 per annum. He remained there – except for a period of conscripted service during the latter part of World War I, when A.C.G. Jellicoe (a cousin of the Admiral) deputised – until December 1923, when he left the town, though not all its musical institutions, to live at Nutfield, near Reigate, in Surrey, apparently on account of his wife's health (he married in 1904). He travelled widely as an examiner for Trinity College in the 'twenties and 'thirties, going to South Africa in 1933. He died on 10 December 1935, amazingly, for one living in the stockbroker belt in the fourth decade of the 20th century, of typhoid. He was remembered as a tall, grey-haired (though balding in later years), distinguished-looking, bespectacled figure whose stern, even sometimes sarcastic, exterior masked a kindly, tactful and considerate nature and a jovial sense of humour. One informant recalled his once playing at a St George's evening service a 'chorale prelude' on *Yes, We have No Bananas*, a popular tune of his day. His spare-time interests included cricket, golf, tennis and motoring.

Sanderson's stipend as Organist of Doncaster Parish Church was, as we shall see, peanuts and he was not above letting church dignataries know that. Contemporary correspondence suggests that Sanderson dropped salary by moving to Doncaster, although Doncaster's teaching opportunities looked good and were so to prove. For all that, he accomplished much in the 20 years he was at the Church. He supervised a major overhaul and enlargement of its magnificent Schulze organ by Norman and Beard in 1910; Walter Parratt, Bairstow, Tertius Noble and Sanderson himself gave recitals to mark its re-opening. The choir, over 40 in number, sang excellently, discipline being good, and more modern repertoire was introduced – its peaks were perhaps the services given to mark the Coronation of 1911 and the Peace Thanksgiving in July 1919.

He had, however, many other irons in the local musical fire. As part-time music teacher at Doncaster Grammar School he had the task of arranging its annual July concert which comprised partsongs by his singing class, solo songs (often featuring his one-time pupil Topliss Green, an Old Boy, a noted professional baritone and later Director of Singing Studies at the RCM) and scenes from a Shakespeare play. July 1914's concert included Green's singing of Sanderson's *Tom a-Courting* and *Little Girl* and part of *A Midsummer Night's Dream*, for which Sanderson played Mendelssohn's music on the piano and composed a setting of *The Ouzel Cock*. A poignant occasion, in retrospect – how many of the performers were still alive in November 1918?

Sanderson had always been interested in the theatre and in 1909 he was one of the founders of Doncaster Amateur Operatic Society, which he continued to conduct until 1935, despite his residence in Surrey; at first the repertoire was Gilbert and Sullivan, then operettas by Edward German, Montague Phillips, Lionel Monckton, Ivan Caryll, Paul Rubens, Romberg, Friml and others. Between 1922 and 1931 he also conducted the rival Doncaster Thespian Amateur Operatic Society founded to perform G and S, though it, too, soon diversified into German, Lehar, Ivor Novello and Sidney Jones. Both societies are still active.

From 1912 until 1924 (with a gap between 1915 and 1919 for World War I) he conducted Doncaster Musical Society, Doncaster's leading choral and orchestral institution of the time, in works like *A Tale of Old Japan* and *Hiawatha* (Coleridge-Taylor), *King Olaf* (Elgar), *Elijah* (Mendelssohn, twice), *The Spectre's Bride* (Dvořák), *The Flag of England* (by his one-time teacher Frederick Bridge), *The Golden Legend* (Sullivan, twice), *The Dream of Gerontius* (Elgar, twice), *The Wake of O'Connor* (Hubert Bath), *Ode to the North-East Wind* (Frederic Cliffe), Brahms' *German Requiem*, *Songs of the Fleet* (Stanford, twice) and Bizet's *Carmen* in a concert performance. Major concerts were often interspersed with ballad concerts at which Sanderson's own songs were generously represented. The Society under Sanderson regularly fielded somewhere between 100 and 150 singers, a strength which the present Doncaster (and District) Choral Society would envy. Sanderson at times conducted the Leeds Symphony (later called Northern Philharmonic) Orchestra in purely orchestral concerts. The orchestras he conducted in Doncaster numbered about 24 for the operatic societies and approaching double that for the Musical Society.

We have alluded to his work as an examiner; he also adjudicated at music festivals and for a time worked for Cramer the music publisher. As a teacher he established a good connection – pupils Topliss Green and Elsa (née Elsie) Frood achieved fame as professionals. This was in Doncaster, where in 1911 his lady pupils formed a choir of 20, but he kept up his London teaching connections for maybe a decade after he had gone to Doncaster.

But he is known to posterity primarily as a composer. As a church musician his output naturally included a few pieces of church music; hymn tunes, mostly from his early youth, but including the tune *Arncliffe*, long in *The Methodist Hymn Book*, published in December 1933; the cantata-anthem *The Earth is the Lord's*, his Mus.Bac. exercise; a *Te Deum* and *Benedictus* and a *Kyrie*, all sung in Doncaster in his time; for organ, a *Reverie* played by him in a Sheffield recital in 1909 and a transcription of MacDowell's *Sea Pictures*. In more secular mode there were a choral valse song *Spring's Awakening*; and a number of instrumental miniatures, all with French titles –*Brise d'Eté*, *Three Chansonettes*, *Chanson d'Amour*, *Pirouette*, *Novelette*, *En Tournant* and *Caprice Orientate* for solo piano and *Serenata*, *Sincerité* and *Songe d'Amour*, also for violin and piano, and the *Chansonettes* and *Songe d'Amour* for piano duet. Some of these have been revived in Doncaster.

Nearly all of the 170 solo songs fall within the genre of the Edwardian ballad, but a few are rather more serious in nature, like the *Nocturnes* cycle and a setting of *Gather Ye Rosebuds*. A few had sacred texts like the early *There is a Green Hill* and *God That Makest Earth and Heaven* (premiered by Edna Thornton at a 1903 ballad concert at St James' Hall) and these could at a pinch serve as anthems. He published his first song in 1894, when he was 16 but most of the best, and best known, of them were written during his sojourn in Doncaster: titles like *Until* (1911), *Up From Somerset* (1913), *The Hills of Donegal* (1914) and *The Rose of Perfect Love* (1918). *My Dear Soul* sold 30,000 copies in a few days.

Sea songs have always been popular with British audiences, and Sanderson, recognising this, provided them with many more: *Beating up the Channel*, arranged also, possibly by the composer, for male-voice chorus, *Captain Mac*, *The Glory of the Sea*, *Where the Great Ships Ride*, the atmospheric *Harbour Night Song*, *Sea Haven*, *Sea Ways* and *Shipmates o'Mine*. Several Sanderson titles have a West Country flavour: the delicious *Devonshire Cream and Cider*, *A West Country Courting*, *Up From Somerset*, *A Dream of Plymouth Hoe*, the rousing *Drake Goes West* and the song-cycle *A Cornish Haul*. Still others derive inspiration from nature: *Easter Flowers*, *Break o'Day*, *Nightingale of June*, *Autumn Love Song*, *Little Brown Owl* and *Be Still, Blackbird*. Many of the lyrics set were by barrister Frederick E. Weatherly, who had had such a fruitful partnership with the composer 'Stephen Adams' (Michael Maybrick) (*qv*), writer of *The Holy City*, *Thorn* and *Nirvana*. *Friend o'Mine*, a chartbuster of 1913 and arguably Sanderson's most celebrated song, was offered originally to Adams, who died before he could set it; Sanderson's version was dedicated to Adams' memory – a graceful tribute.

The words of many Sanderson songs are undistinguished in a literary sense but one may argue that at least they do not get in the way of a shapely vocal line, while the idiomatic piano accompaniments helped, quite as much as the tunes, to put his work considerably above the average royalty ballad of the period and ensure its survival. The popularity of Sanderson's compositions, and specifically his songs, during the first decades of the present century is attested by the fact that he left £51,054 (£46,476 net), no mean sum in 1935. No fewer than 95 of his songs, 16 of them in four short cycles, are listed in the BBC's *Music Library Catalogue*. That they are still sung one may judge by noticing that perhaps ten of them have appeared in commercially issued or reissued gramophone records in the past two decades. (They were always popular with the gramophone from well before the days of electrical recording. As examples, Robert Radford recorded *Drake Goes West*, Charles Tree *Up From Somerset*, both in 1915, Phyllis Lett brought out *The Hills of Donegal* in the same year, Hubert Eisdell following with *Until* and Topliss Green with *The Last Call* in 1917. At least eight other songs were recorded in pre-electric days by HMV, some of them being duplicated; there was even a disc with just the accompaniment of *Until* for singers without a piano). Besides recordings, Sanderson's popularity is underlined by Sidney Baynes arranging two purely orchestral medleys of his songs, the first featuring *Drake Goes West, The Company Sergeant Major, Up From Somerest, Friend o'Mine* and *Until*.

It is surprising therefore that *The New Grove* has no entry on him (but this is to be remedied in the next edition, and that there are few references in any standard musical reference work. Denis Stevens' compendium *A History of Song* (Hutchinson, 1960) makes passing mention of him, while Sydney Northcote's *Byrd to Britten: A Survey of English Song* (Baker, 1966) patronisingly describes his work as 'reasonably competent', citing with approval *Drake Goes West, The Laughing Cavalier* and *Charm Me Asleep*. Patronage is the last thing Sanderson needs. It may be true that *Friend o'Mine*, despite its generous melodic sweep, and some other titles *(My Dear Soul, You Along o' Me, Someday at Last* and *Harlequin* come to mind) are unashamedly sentimental, with lyrics which nowadays seem naive to us. But worth preserving, surely, are *Until*, with its surging vocal line, *Drake Goes West*, with its bluff urgency and vitality (this came into its own at the outset of World War I, which broke out a few years after it was written), the forthright *Shipmates o'Mine*, the wistful nostalgia of the opening and close of *As I Sit Here*, a mood pointed deliciously by the piano accompaniment, the virile, spray-laden *Captain Mac*, the enchantingly joyous rapture and light touch of *The Valley of Laughter* (this should be in every coloratura's repertoire), the graceful simplicity of *One Morning Very Early*, the brisk urgency of *The Company Sergeant Major* (another song popular during World War I), the rich nostalgia of *The Hills of Donegal*, the ardent passion of *Lorraine* and the swinging, stirring refrains of *Devonshire Cream and Cider* and *Up From Somerset*.

One could go on. Singers, eminent and obscure, loved (and still love), Sanderson's songs for their singability, as they are easy to learn, with few, if any, awkward intervals – nor are they difficult to project to audiences which loved, and still love, memorable, recognisable melodies and straightforward lyrics. Despite the changing dictates of fashion, Sanderson will surely continue to merit, and achieve, modest revival. That we heard – and still hear – so many Sanderson songs from basses or bass-baritones is surely owed originally to Topliss Green, for whom many of them may have been written, either when Sanderson was still teaching him or slightly later, when Green was beginning to make his way in the world of professional singing, although *Lorraine* and *Hills of Donegal*, which sound best on the contralto voice, may originally have been written with Elsie Frood's voice in mind.

Musicians are usually many-sided personalities and Sanderson was more than just a popular songwriter. He was a good all-round musician – a teacher of repute, a capable, vigorous, versatile and enterprising practical performer, making valuable contributions as organist, pianist, conductor and choir trainer and finally a genuine character who enriched the musical life of Doncaster (and other places) for upwards of three decades.

CELLIST AND COMPOSER
William Henry Squire 1871-1963

William Henry Squire, born at Ross-on-Wye on 8 August 1871, was at least as well known as a cellist as he was a composer. Educated at Kingsbridge Grammar School in South Devon, he became in 1883 a Foundation Scholar at the RCM, where he studied the cello with Edward Howell and composition with Parry and Stanford. His London debut was in 1890 at the St James' Hall; he played in the Covent Garden Orchestra 1894-7 and in the Queen's Hall Orchestra 1897-1901 and toured widely as a soloist, notably with Clara Butt. He came to Doncaster in 1908 and played his own arrangements of Chopin and Offenbach (Kennerley Rumford, Clara Butt's husband, sang in the same concert Squire's song *For Me Alone*). Squire returned to Doncaster in 1910 and played his *Meditation* in C.

He taught at the RCM between 1898 and 1917 and at the Guildhall School 1911-17 and was associated with the Performing Right Society between 1926 and 1953. His last public concert appearance was in 1941 in Exeter Cathedral – he died in London on 17 March 1963, aged 91. His recording of Elgar's Cello Concerto has been reissued in recent years.

He wrote a Cello Concerto of his own and is credited with two operettas. Also putting him into the light-music sphere are his orchestral pieces – the *Serenade* for flute, clarinet and strings, Opus 15, the entr'actes *Summer Dreams, Sweet Briar* and *Slumber Song*, premiered at the Proms in 1897, 1898 and 1899 respectively, the idyll *Sylvania*, the marches *The Jolly Sailor* and *The Yeomanry Patrol* and the waltz *Lazy-Lane* – plus his instrumental miniatures and his popular ballad-type songs (his sister was a well-known soprano). The instrumental miniatures, which fused the genres of light music and instructional music and ranked high in each mode, were of course usually for cello and piano (though *Slumber Song* appeared for violin, *Sylvania* was published for piano solo in an arrangement and the attractive *Calma de Mare* was even written for a lady mandolinist). Most popular were *Danse Orientale, Harlequinade, Consolation, Larghetto* in D, *Madrigal* in G, *L'Adieu, Bourée, Danse Rustique, Gavotte, Minuet, Old Swedish Air*, the gorgeously 'Palm Court' *Prière, Tzig-Tzig*, a Hungarian czardas of considerable virtuosity, *Tarantella* and transcriptions of folksongs and of such popular songs as *Absent* (Metcalfe) and *Songs My Mother Taught Me* (Dvořák). There were many more titles and, as I have heard for myself, student cellists have still enjoyed playing them today. They go down well with audiences too.

Of Squire's songs (and these were so popular as to warrant an orchestral selection of them made by Sydney Baynes and arranged for brass band by J. Ord Hume) the most popular were *In an Old-Fashioned Town, The Toast, Mountain Lovers, Like Stars Above, A Chip of the Old Block, A Sergeant of the Line* (sung by Harry Dearth and popular in World War I), *Pals, The Corporal's Ditty, When You Come Home, If You Were Here, If I Might Only Come to You* (all of them included in the selection just mentioned), *My Prayer*, beloved of Clara Butt, *Lighterman Tom, The Moonlit Road, The Watchman, The Road that Leads to You, Three for Jack* and the duet *The Singing Lesson*. One or two of these, like *My Prayer*, were arranged as choruses.

A YORKSHIRE MUSICIAN
Arthur Wood 1875 – 1953

BBC Radio Four's *The Archers* has made the name of Arthur Wood immortal, for its signature tune, which has been played 12 times a week for more than five decades, is *Barwick Green*, the finale of a suite entitled *My Native Heath*, whose other movements are 'Knaresborough Status' (or 'Hiring Fair'), 'Ilkley Tarn' (or 'Dance of the Sprites') and 'Bolton Abbey' (Slow Melody). Although, as we shall see, much of Wood's career was spent in London, where he died on 18 January 1953, his native heath was indeed Yorkshire and the titles of many of his other compositions show that he never forgot this.

Arthur Wood was born at Heckmondwike on 24 January 1875, the son of a tailor who was a violinist in a local amateur orchestra. As a boy Arthur played the violin but the flute (and piccolo) soon became his major instruments. When the family moved to Harrogate in 1882 he received free flute lessons from Arthur Brookes of the Spa Orchestra, an orchestra Arthur Wood was soon to play in. (Brookes later emigrated and played in the Boston Symphony Orchestra). Arthur left school at the age of 12 and two years later became Organist of St Paul's Presbyterian Church in Harrogate. By the time he was 16 he was flautist, accompanist, solo pianist and deputy conductor to J. Sidney Jones, father of the composer of *The Geisha* and conductor of the Harrogate Municipal Orchestra which played four times a day in the Valley Gardens. Later he moved to the Bournemouth Municipal Orchestra and played under the baton of Dan Godfrey.

His ambition, however, was to conduct regularly and this was realised (as it was for so many of the composers herein) in London's theatreland. When he became Musical Director at Terry's Theatre in 1903 he was, at 28, the youngest MD in the metropolis. He is said to have owed this engagement to Sidney Jones (*qv*), son of his former chief at Harrogate, who was impressed by Wood's *Three Old Dances*, published in 1902. From Terry's he moved to the Apollo, where he directed Messager's *Véronique*; then to the Adelphi; the Shaftesbury, where between 1908 and 1917 he conducted *The Arcadians, The Pearl Girl, Princess Caprice* and other things; the Gaiety; His Majesty's; Daly's, where between 1922 and 1926 he was required to conduct *The Merry Widow*; the Prince of Wales'; and the Theatre Royal, Drury Lane. Wood conducted London theatre orchestras for more than three decades; in between times he toured America with *Véronique* and conducted some of the early recordings of certain of the Savoy Operas.

Wood composed prolifically. As a theatre conductor it was natural for him to try his hand at musicals of his own, like *Yvonne, Petticoat Fair* and *Fancy Fair*, the two last composed around the end of World War I. His many orchestral arrangements included selections from operettas such as Oscar Straus' *Cleopatra* and his own works in that genre; the overture to *The Arcadians* by Lionel Monckton and Howard Talbot; Elgar's early violin piece *Mot d'Amour; Greensleeves;* and, for the BBC, accompaniments to traditional songs. As was the case with Elgar, Wood's study of orchestration, which began when as a boy he copied music at 2d a sheet, was purely practical and owed nothing to academic study. He was a staff composer with Boosey & Hawkes, for whom he brought out dozens of orchestral suites and short genre pieces. Many of these recall his North Country origins: *Three Dale Dances, Three More Dale Dances, Yorkshire Moors Suite,* the Yorkshire Rhapsody *Barnsley Fair, A Lancashire Clog Dance,* the Overture *Shipley Glen,* and the miniatures *Moorland Fiddlers* and *On The Moor.* But like Albert Ketèlbey and Eric Coates he could create all kinds of mood pictures. For example, the *Three Old Dances*, which, as we have seen, helped him on his way as a conductor: their titles are True Hearts', 'Forget-me-not' and 'Gaiety'. The suite *Widow Malone* (1937) affords Irish colour and there were also the *Three Mask Dances* and the *Ballerina Suite*, not to mention trifles like *Coquetterie, Fairy Dreams, Fiddlers Three, Too Many Girls* and an *Oriental Scene*, which never quite attained the popularity of Ketèlbey's *In a Persian Market*. Wood composed a Concertino in A major for his favourite instrument, the flute, published in 1948 in a reduction for flute and piano, also a trifle, *Merriment,* for piccolo and orchestra. One item which was popular in its day, a one-step *You Can't Keep Still*, achieved publication as a solo for violin or cello.

Apart from the perennially popular *Barwick Green*, we hear little of Arthur Wood's music today, though brass bands, for whom he wrote marches like *All Clear* and *Royal Progress*, remain faithful to his transcription of the *Three Dale Dances*, in which form they sound well. (He was a respected adjudicator of band contests.) He has been dead for nearly 60 years; surely it is high time to dust down some of those orchestral suites and maybe even the Concertino for flute, so that we can see for ourselves just how good an answer to Nottingham's Eric Coates was Yorkshire's Arthur Wood.

YORKSHIRE, THE ISLE OF MAN, PICARDY AND LONDON
Haydn Wood 1882-1959

Haydn Wood was born into a musical family at Slaithwaite, West Yorkshire, in 1882. When he was only two, however, the family moved to the Isle of Man, which in later life was to be the inspiration for several of Wood's compositions: the *Manx Rhapsody (Mylecharane)*, *Manx Country Dance*, the *Manx Countryside Sketches* suite and the *Manx Overture*, all for orchestra, the Manx tone poem *Mannin Veen* (1938), which exists in versions for orchestra (I have heard this on Radio 3 and subsequently on CD and like it) and chorus and orchestra, a collection of Manx folksongs set for solo voice and piano, and a set of 21 Manx airs published for piano solo. Haydn studied the violin, latterly at the Royal College of Music with Arbos and then in Brussels; whilst at the RCM he had composition lessons with Stanford, to whom much later he was to pay tribute with his 'Stanford Rhapsody', *Westward Ho*. He won a Cobbett prize with his *Phantasie* in F major for string quartet, a substantial movement some 12 minutes long and mentioned in *Cobbett's Dictionary* as being charming and slightly influenced by Dvořák. Cobbett regretted that Wood was subsequently lost to the world of chamber music because of his indulgence in more 'ephemeral' music – presumably a reference to the 200 or more songs, mainly of the ballad type, which he began composing when he married the soprano Dorothy Court in 1909 and continued to publish for the rest of his life. *Roses of Picardy* still popular after some 100 years, is merely the best known of them. Nearly as popular is *A Brown Bird Singing*; other popular titles were *Bird of Love Divine*, *Love's Garden of Roses*, *Dear Hands That Gave Me Violets*, *O Flower Divine*, *The Island of Love* (the last four were all recorded in 1914-18), *Elizabeth of England*, *Casey the Fiddler*, *When Dawn Breaks Through*, *A Bird Sang in the Rain*, *A Leafland Lullaby*, *Daffodil Gold*, *I Want Your Heart* and *Homeward at Eventide*.

The last of Wood's songs to be published appears to have been *Give Me Your Hand* in 1957. Some of them, like *Beware*, were written as duets and some of the more popular solo songs were arranged in that form. *God Make Me Kind* and *When the Home-Bells Ring Again* appeared also in versions for solo and chorus, while *The Little Ships,* composed in 1940 as a celebration of the deliverance of Dunkirk, had a male-voice chorus *ad lib* to support the baritone soloist. Many songs had their accompaniments scored for orchestra – the BBC list at least 21 of these, many in several different keys, and a few of the best-loved, like *Roses of Picardy* and *A Brown Bird Singing*, exist in purely orchestral transcriptions and, as I have heard, even as brass band solos. As was the case with Wilfrid Sanderson and other ballad composers, a medley of Haydn Wood songs was devised for orchestra or band. His song output included a few cycles: the *Three Sea Songs*, the *Songs of June* (also three in number), *Twelve Little Songs of the Year* and *Play Time: A Cycle of (Seven) Nursery Rhymes*. (Eric Coates' list of songs also includes a number of cycles, even to the extent of featuring a group of nursery rhymes; Coates' total of songs, at about 160, is not far short of Wood's).

Roses of Picardy, Wood's most enduring and surely for him most financially profitable composition, appeared in 1916. In 1915 he had collaborated with Paul Rubens (*qv*) in a musical comedy entitled *Tina*; two years later he composed another musical, *Cash on Delivery*; and this was to be followed by others, *Clovertown* and, jointly with Jack Waller (*qv*) and Joseph Tunbridge, (*qv*) *Dear Love*. These enjoyed a modest success. For the concert hall he produced a handful of short choral works like the cantata *Lochinvar* and the *Ode to Genius*. Some of his solo songs, like *Roses of Picardy* and *With a Smile and a Song*, he arranged for chorus. Most of his instrumental pieces, whether for piano solo (like the *Prelude*, published also for organ, *Scherzo Fantastique* and *Silver Clouds*), or for his own instrument the violin (examples are *Slumber Song and Elfin Dance* and *Melodie Plaintive*) were better known in their orchestral guise. Wood, incidentally, toured for eight years as a violinist with Emma Albani's concert party.

Indeed it was for his orchestral music that Wood was perhaps most respected. This embraces everything from fanfares to concertos, which latter were for piano in D minor (published in 1947 in a version for two pianos) and for violin in B minor (likewise published, in 1932, with piano accompaniment). Although both were favourably noticed at the time (Antonio Brosa gave the premiere of the Violin Concerto in March 1933 with the BBC Symphony Orchestra) these are not heard today. Neither are the *Philharmonic Variations* of 1939 for cello and orchestra, but his orchestral rhapsodies like *The Seafarer*, based on popular sea shanties (1942), *King Orry*, *American Rhapsody* (1948), *British Rhapsody* and the *Southern Rhapsody Virginia* (1927), the overtures *Eros*, *Apollo, Life and Love*, *A May Day* and *Minerva* and the marches *Elizabeth of England* (1952: at least once recorded on LP), *March of the Patriots*, *Torch of Freedom*, *Homage March* and the *Festival March* commissioned by the BBC for their first Light Music Festival in 1949, an event I recall following with much pleasure, were all popular in their day.

An astonishing number of Wood's compositions received their premieres at the hands of the BBC Symphony Orchestra: the suite *Moods, Scherzo in the Olden Style* (1932), *Mannin Veen* (1933), the Violin Concerto (1933), the suite, *A Day in Fairyland* (1933), *Market Day* (1934), the overture *Apollo* (1935), the suite *Frescoes* (1936), *Manx Overture* (1936), *King Orry* (1938), the suite *Cities of Romance* (1937), the overture *Love and Life* (1938), the suite *East of Suez* (1939), the Variations for cello (1939), the *Minerva* overture (1941) and the *Phantasy* for strings (1945). Bands as well as orchestras took up the marches.

Like most of his contemporaries in the light music field, Wood could write good pastiche and in this direction one can point to his *Eighteenth Century Scherzo* of 1948 and possibly the *Fantasy Concerto* for strings. Besides the two major concertos already mentioned there were one or two lighter, short items for solo instrument and orchestra, like *It is Only a Tiny Garden* (for violin) and *Fleurette* (for cornet or euphonium). Wood was drawn a number of times to variation form; his early *Variations on an Original Theme* appeared in 1903, only four years after Elgar's *Enigma* and possibly inspired by it. I recall hearing at the Sheffield Philharmonic Concerts in 1953 the splendidly inventive and amusing *Variations on a Once Popular Humorous Song* – seven of them plus a finale – the song being *If You Want to Know the Time, Ask a Policeman.* He produced dozens of single-movement genre pieces: the jaunty *Sketch of a Dandy, Serenade to Youth* (1955), *Serenade at Sunset* (1940), *An Autumn Song, Harlequinade, Romany Life, Pleading Serenade, Love in Arcady, Evening Song An April Shower at Kew* (1935), *Dance of Youth* (1927), *Day Dreams; Souvenir de Valentine,* the entr'actes *Heather Bells* and *Thistledown* and many more.

In the field of the descriptive suite, which in light music terms we tend to associate more particularly with Eric Coates, Wood contributed almost a score of scores, more than Coates in fact, the earliest being entitled simply *Suite for Light Orchestra* (1929). Some of his subjects indeed parallel Coates': *London Cameos* (1947: The City, St James' Park, Buckingham Palace), the earlier *London Landmarks* (1946: Nelson's Column, Tower Hill, Horse Guards) and *Snapshots of London* (Sadlers Wells, Regent's Park, Wellington Barracks), though none of Wood's final marches in each of these suites rivalled those in Coates' *London* or *London Again* suites; or *Harvest Time (cf* Coates' *From the Countryside* or *From Meadow to Mayfair);* or *Royal Castles* (Balmoral, Caernarvon and Windsor – *cf* Coates' *Three Elizabeths);* or the ballet suite *A Day in Fairyland* from 1934 which included the popular *Dance of a Whimsical Elf (cf* Coates' *The Enchanted Garden* and *The Jester at the Wedding).* Wood, however, also sought more exotic – almost Ketèlbeyan – subjects for some of his suites:

East of Suez (1939), *Egypt*, *Cities of Romance* (1927: Budapest, Venice, Seville) and *Paris* (1935), the *Montmartre March* from which became popular as a separate item. Four of the more popular suites were *Firelight Fancies* (1949), *Frescoes* (1936), *In an Old Cathedral Town* (1934) and *Moods* (1932), the latter (exceptionally) in six movements rather than the usual three or four – the sixth, *Joyousness*, a waltz, has been recorded in the LP and CD eras. Two of Wood's suite subjects which I find particularly intriguing are *Three Famous Cinema Stars* (Valse Apache, Ivor Novello; Romance, Dolores del Rio; Humoreske, Charles Chaplin) and *Three Famous Pictures*, which preface the very famous 'Laughing Cavalier' with two movements representing pictures by Luke Fildes, one of Charles Dickens' lesser-known illustrators, 'The Village Wedding' and 'The Doctor', which to me hardly justify the description 'famous'.

The best of Haydn Wood's orchestral music rivals most of Coates' in inventive tunefulness, and his scoring, like that of all his light music colleagues of that and subsequent generations, is highly professional; Havergal Brian wrote in 1937 of an arrangement by Wood for orchestra of four Elgar songs that the orchestration had 'the true Elgarian touch'. Wood's orchestration is usually 'normal' (ie, double woodwind; the usual brass – two or four horns, two or three trumpets and three trombones; strings; and modest percussion). *The Manx Overture,* the *British Empire Fantasia* and a few shorter pieces have, however, parts for two or three saxophones and *Sketch of a Dandy* has a written-out part for an accordion.

Wood died in 1959, two years after Coates, having given pleasure to millions. He is still capable of doing that – if we let him.

THE BEST OF THE REST

ADAMS, Stephen (really Michael Maybrick) (1844-1913). Liverpool-born baritone singer and composer of many popular ballads, of which *The Holy City; Star of Bethlehem, Thora* and *Nirvana* are best remembered.

ADDISON, John (1920-) Born Cobham, Surrey. Studied RCM with Gordon Jacob (whose music his often resembles), later Professor of Composition there. Writer of chamber music in many forms, choral works and a concerto for trumpet. On the lighter side are his ballet suite *Carte Blanche*, the march *Carlton Brown of the Foreign Office* and scores for over 60 feature films, including *Reach for the Sky; Joseph Andrews, Three Men in a Boat, The Charge of the Light Brigade, I Was Monty's Double* and *A Bridge Too Far*, the two last-named notable for their marches, both adapted for the concert hall.

ADLER, Larry (1914-2001). American by birth but domiciled in London after persecution by anti-Communist extremists in the 1940s. Virtuoso harmonica player for whom Cyril Scott (*qv*), Vaughan Williams, Arthur Benjamin (*qv*), Malcolm Arnold (*qv*), etc., have written music. Himself a composer for his instrument, especially in films like *Genevieve* (1953: particularly popular), *A High Wind in Jamaica, King and Country* and *The Hook*, also of a *Theme and Variations* for harmonica and piano.

ALLITSEN, Frances (1849-1912). Professional singer, trained at Guildhall School. Composed a piano sonata, a *Cantata for the Queen* (1911), a *Suite de Ballet* and two overtures for orchestra but best remembered for her 130-odd ballad-type songs and particularly for *The Lute Player*. Some of the others are settings of German words.

ALWYN, Kenneth (Kenneth Alwyn Wetherell) (1928-). Studied RAM, then conductor, especially of ballet, before going to BBC Concert Orchestra as staff conductor 1968. Credited with a Sinfonietta for strings, TV tunes and many arrangements.

ALWYN, William (1905-85). A major symphonist who wrote music for 60 films before and after World War II and including the wartime *Desert Victory* (1943), whose stirring march was published. Other lighter music included work for radio features, *Scottish Dances, Elizabethan Dances, Festival March* (1951), *Autumn Legend* for cor anglais and strings, and the overture *Derby Day*.

AMERS, Captain H.G. (died 1936). Conductor of Eastbourne Municipal Orchestra in the 1920s and 1930s, retiring through ill-health in 1935. Compiled several novelty items, including *All on a Christmas Morning, The Wee MacGregor: A Highland Patrol* and *Bhoys of Tipperary.*

ARNELL, Richard Anthony Sayer (1917-2009). Composer of symphonies, etc; worthy of mention here for his ballets (*The Great Detective* (1953), *Punch and the Child*) and music for films, some of which has made use of electronics in an approachable way.

ARNOLD, Sir Malcolm Henry (1921-2006). A composer of nine symphonies and many concertos is surely a purveyor of 'serious' music, but in an astringent age Arnold has never been afraid to write readily recognisable tunes and, as was the case with Eric Coates, his driving rhythms are thoroughly characteristic (he and Coates began their careers in symphony orchestras). In any case, much of Arnold's large output is classifiable as light music, like his suites of *English Dances* (2), *Scottish Dances, Cornish Dances* and *Irish Dances*, his many comedy overtures, like *Beckus the Dandipratt, Tam O'Shanter* and the *Grand Grand Overture* for the first Hoffnung spectacular (1956), his prolific film music, among which we may cite *The Sound Barrier, The Belles of St Trinian's* and *Bridge on the River Kwai*, and some of his small ensemble music like the *Three Shanties* for wind quintet.

ATKINSON, Dorothy (1893-?). Composer of light suites (*Summer Sketches: Thistledown, Wild Roses, Golden Bees, Swallows*) and genre pieces like the 'valse caprice' *Moths Around a Candle, Indian Summer, Dance of the May Flies* and *Sentry Go*, also light-hearted songs (eg, *The Harvester, The Ploughman, Winklepicker Bill, When Grannie Was a Girl, O Golden Dawn, Homage* and, from a radio show entitled 'Watch Your Fancy', *Up With the Lark*).

AUSTIN, Ernest (1874-1947). Turned to music in 1907 after a business career. Much of his work was 'serious', including a symphony, the narrative tone poem (2½ hours long) *The Pilgrim's Progress*, the *Variations on The Vicar of Bray* and many choral and chamber works. On the lighter side, he composed the suite *Stella Mary Dances*, premiered at the Proms in 1918, and *Sweet Night* for small orchestra. Some of his piano music was popular in character. His large output of songs covered the whole spectrum from Shakespeare to ballads, both sentimental and hearty.

AUSTIN, Frederic (1872-1952). Brother of foregoing. At first organist and academic (both in Liverpool) but became known as a bass singer in concert (especially in *Elijah* and Delius's *Sea Drift)* and opera, for Beecham Opera Company and at Glastonbury. Professor of Singing at RAM and Artistic Director of British National Opera Company 1924. Works include many of a serious nature, like a symphony in E (1913), the rhapsody *Spring*, the choral work *Pervigilium Veneris* and many songs. On the lighter side, best remembered for his arrangments of *The Beggar's Opera*, which ran at the Lyric, Hammersmith, for 1463 performances from 1920, and its sequel *Polly*, plus the light overtures *The Rogues' Gallery* and *The Sea Venturers*, premiered at Bournemouth, and incidental music for *The Way of the World*, *The Insect Play*, etc. His son Richard Austin (1903-1989) conducted the Bournemouth Municipal Orchestra 1934-40.

AYLWARD, Florence (1862-1950). Sussex-born, studied GSM, composer of popular ballads like *Beloved it is Morn* and *How Dear You Are*.

BALL, Eric Walter John (1903-89). Bristol-born composer, arranger and conductor. From a Salvation Army family and associated for over 60 years with brass band and choral music. Involved as conductor and composer with Salvation Army until 1940s. Later editor of *The British Bandsman* and conducted at and composed for National and Open Championships. Many of his 'test' pieces are major works and other compositions were for the Salvation Army, but plenty of his pieces count as light music: the marches *October Festival, Hand and Heart, Rosslyn, Royal Salute, Sure and Steadfast* and *Torch of Freedom*, the overtures *Galatea, Homeward, Undaunted, Holiday* and *Swiss Festival*, the suites *English Country Scenes, Fowey River, Oasis Holiday Suite, Petite Suite de Ballet* and *French Suite* and three rhapsodies on negro spirituals.

BARRY, Darrol (1956-). Prolific arranger for brass and composer of light genre pieces for brass band: *Go For Gold, Nativity, Inter-City, Portrait of a City, Turkish Delight, Cassations,* and *Lullaby For Lisa.*

BARRY, John (1933-2011). Born York and a one-time pupil of Francis Jackson; prolific composer for films including several James Bond titles, also *A Doll's House, Love Among the Ruins* and *Mary Queen of Scots*, TV, theatre and the *Songs from Alice in Wonderland.*

BARSOTTI, Roger (1901-86). Born in London of Italian extraction. After experience with various military bands, became Director of Music of the

Metropolitan Police Band 1946-68. Composed prolifically for brass band and to a lesser extent for orchestra: suites like *Three Women, Carnaval du Bal* and, especially popular, *Neapolitan Suite*, waltzes, polkas and dances in Latin American rhythm, instrumental solos, popular potpourris and marches, eg, *Metropolitan, Banners of Victory, The King's Colour, The Commissioner, Motor Sport, Tenacity* and *State Trumpeters*.

BART, Lionel (really Lionel Begleiter) (1930-99). Composer and lyricist. Best- known stage show was *Oliver!* (1960), one of the most popular of all English musicals. *Fings Ain 't Wot They Used to Be* (1959), *Blitz* (1962) and *Maggie May* (1964) also did well, *Twang!* (1965), based on Robin Hood, much less so. Also responsible for many 'separate' songs.

BATH, John (1916- ?). Conducted BBC West of England Light Orchestra for a short time around 1950 before illness forced his retirement. His two best-known compositions, *Spanish Serenade* for small orchestra and *Fiddler's Fancye*, a suite of 18th-century dances for string quartet and string orchestra, date from about that period.

BAX, Sir Arnold (1883-1953). Remembered primarily for his seven symphonies, several symphonic poems and chamber music, but one must also recall his substantial contributions to light music: *Mediterranean* (1920); the *Morning Song, Maytime in Sussex* for piano and orchestra; several examples of the English comedy overture *(Festival Overture, Romantic Overture, Overture to a Picaresque Comedy; Rogue's Comedy Overture, Overture to Adventure)*; the marches *London Pageant* and the *Coronation March*, his last work; and his music for four films, two of which, *Malta G.C.* (1942) and *Oliver Twist* (1948), yielded attractive concert suites.

BAYCO, Frederick (fl 1930-70). Organist and composer of pieces like the 'pastorale' *In Olden Tymes* (for piano) and, for orchestra, *Elizabethan Masque, Inferno* and *Finger of Fear*.

BEAVER, Jack (1900-63). Educated RAM. Worked in films for Gaumont British as resident composer from 1934. Composed *Sovereign Heritage* for the National Brass Band Championships 1954.

BENJAMIN, Arthur (1893-1960). Australian-born, a 'serious' composer (of operas, orchestral and chamber music) who turned his hand to light music on a number of occasions. Best known of these is the *Jamaican Rumba* (originally for piano duet) and its companion piece, *Jamaican Song*, but we may also instance the *Light Music Suite, Red River Jig* (1945), *Caribbean Dance* (1946), the *Jamaicalypso* for two pianos (1957), *Five Negro Spirituals* (cello/piano) and the *Hyde Park Galop*, extracted from his music for the film *An Ideal Husband*. Studied piano and composition (under Stanford) at the RCM 1911 and returned there to teach piano in 1921.

BENNETT, Brian (?-). Guitarist and composer of instructional tutors; is best known for his award-winning music for the *Wexford* TV adaptations.

BENNETT, Richard Rodney, CBE (1936-2013). Superb pianist and versatile and prolific composer whose output ranges from jazz to avant-garde classical. Deserves mention in this book for his film music – for *Blind Date* (1955), a jazz-influenced score, *Far From the Madding Crowd* (1967), in classical 'Hollywood' idiom, *Nicholas and Alexandra* (1971), *Lady Caroline Lamb* (1972), *Murder on the Orient Express* (1973), whose waltz, arranged for the concert hall, has become a light music standard, and *Four Weddings and a Funeral* (1994) – and for his lighter orchestral effusions like the *Aubade, Serenade for Small Orchestra*, the *Farnham Festival Overture* (1964), in the tradition of British light overtures, and a suite arranged from *The Aviary* and *The Insect World*, originally for accompanied unison voices and suitable for children.

BERNERS, Lord (Gerald Hugh Tyrwhitt-Wilson) (1883-1950). Composer, mainly self-taught, painter, author, diplomat and eccentric. His music, all of it light in touch, included five ballets, best known being *The Triumph of Neptune* (1926) and *A Wedding Bouquet* (1936), piano solo and duet pieces, notably *Valses Bourgeoises*, and songs (one for the film *Champagne Charlie*). Berners' other film scores included *Nicholas Nickleby* (1947).

BESLY, Maurice (1888-1945). Yorkshire-born; conducted various orchestras from 1922, including the Royal Albert Hall and Scottish Orchestras and LSO. His best-known piece was the song *The Second Minuet*, one of many popular ballads. Also composed for orchestra – incidental music to *The Merchant of Venice, Arioso, Valse Romanesque, Lullaby for a Modem Infant, Portrait of a Dancer in Red*, the 'impression' *Mist in the Valley* and the suites *Chelsea China* and *Suite Romantique* – and for the piano. A schoolteacher, then in later life a solicitor and notary public and sometime Director of the PRS.

BEVAN, Frederick (1856-1939). Composer of ballads: *The Everlasting Day, The Gift Divine, The Merry Monk, The Old Soldier, The Ocean Choir, Peg Away,*

The Flight of Ages and, best known of all, *The Admiral's Broom*, popular in solo and male-choir versions (the latter arranged by Henry Geehl).

BIDGOOD, Thomas (1858-1925). Arranger of many popular selections and composer of marches (*Vimy Ridge, The Allies' Parade, The Elite, On To Victory, Sons of the Brave*) and orchestral novelties like *A Motor Ride*.

BIRCH, Montague (1884-1947). Pianist, violinist, Assistant Conductor and latterly (1940-47) Acting Conductor of the Bournemouth Municipal Orchestra. Wrote a considerable amount of light music, performed but little published, though *Intermezzo Pizzicato* was recorded in 1935, *Dance of the Nymphs* in 1933. Composed a march, *The Carabiniers*, for the Bournemouth Home Guard Band. Loyal and modest, but his 'meekness' probably worked against him.

BLACK, Stanley (1913-2002). Pianist and Conductor of BBC Dance Orchestra after World War II (1944-53); prolific arranger, also composed widely, some of it, but by no means all, in an out-and-out 'jazz' style. Titles include music for some 200 films (eg *Wonderful Life, Hindle Wakes* and *Summer Holiday*), for piano (*Busy Boy* (1946), *In a Gracious Mood, Puppet on a String*) and, for orchestra, the *Overture to a Costume Comedy* (1955) and *Fanfare for a Royal Film Performance*. Recording artiste for Decca, also conducting classical works.

BLAKE, Howard (1938-). Pianist, conductor and composer. Studied RAM with Harold Craxton and Howard Ferguson. His easy, lyrical style arguably makes him a present-day heir of the English light music tradition. Wrote concertos for clarinet, piano and violin but best known for his music for *The Snowman*, for other film music including *The Riddle of the Sands* (his splendid score for *Agatha*, about Agatha Christie's disappearance, was not used, though) and for other miniatures like the orchestral *Concert Dances*, the *Burlesca* for violin and piano, *Eight Character Pieces* and the suite *Party Pieces* for piano, plus a piano quartet and two readily tuneful trios for flute, clarinet and piano and for piano, violin and cello respectively.

BLEZARD, William (1921-2003). Studied piano and composition at RCM, London, and won Cobbett and Edward Hecht Prizes there. Wrote music for documentary films and arranged Noel Coward's music for the feature film *The Astonished Heart*. Orchestral works include *Caramba, Battersea Park Suite, Three European Dances* and *The River*, also much instrumental music, and songs for Joyce Grenfell, and many children's songs for TV. Musical director for Grenfell, Marlene Dietrich, Max Wall and Honor Blackman.

BLISS, Sir Arthur (1891-1975). His film music (*Things to Come*, 1935, a landmark, *Conquest of the Air*, 1937, *Christopher Columbus*, 1949, even a setting of *The Beggar's Opera*), marches (*The Phoenix, Welcome the Queen*), brass and military band music (*Kenilworth, Call to Adventure*) and ballets (*Checkmate, Miracle in the Gorbals*) entitle us to reckon him a significant contributor to the light music scene.

BLYTON, Carey (1932-2002). Nephew of Enid Blyton. Educated London University; music editor, lecturer and composer of numerous lighthearted pieces for orchestra (*Cinque Port, On Holiday*), choirs (*Faber's Nursery Songs* and other titles appropriate for children or amateurs), piano (*Patterns*), cello (*Pantomime*), clarinet (*Scherzo*) and guitar (*The Oceans of the Moon*); *Dracula* and *Sweeney Todd* are 'Victorian melodramas' – he has also written much for films and TV, something on which he has lectured.

BONSOR, Brian (1926-). Producer of popular arrangements and light dance movements (*Beguine, Rumba, Tango, Hoe-Down, Fiesta*), all for recorders.

BOUGHTON, Rutland (1878-1960). Composer and conductor, especially of opera; earns a place here because of the enormous popularity of 'The Faery Song' from *The Immortal Hour* (1913).

BOURGEOIS, Derek David (1941-). Born in Kingston-on-Thames; educated Magdalene College, Cambridge, and RCM. Lecturer in Music at Bristol University (1971-84) and Conductor of the National Youth Orchestra (1984-93); later director of music at St Paul's Girls School, Hammersmith. Has composed prolifically, orchestral and chamber music, church music, brass band music and songs. Much of his work is lighthearted (his 1st Concerto for Brass Band ends with a 'War March of the Ostriches'), while his *Serenade*, written for a wedding in 1968, has been arranged for various ensembles and become a popular brass band piece). Also in lighter vein are *Whirligig* and *Diversions*, both for brass, the *Barchester Suite*, based on music for a Trollope TV series, and *Rumplestiltskin's Waltz*.

BOWEN, York (1884-1961). Studied at RAM 1898-1905 and subsequently was a professor there. Developed career as solo pianist and examiner. Compositions include symphonies, concertos and extensive range of piano music, including some attractive genre pieces, a CD of which released in 1996 attracted favourable attention.

BRAHE, May H. (Mary Hanna Dickson) (1885-1956). Born and died in Australia but lived in England from 1912. Immortal as the composer of the incredibly popular and much arranged *Bless This House* (1927) and at least 100 other songs, mainly ballads, like *Down Here, I Passed By Your Window* and *A Japanese Love Song*. Some of her songs were suitable for children; a few of them were Australian folksong settings.

BRAND, Geoffrey (1926-). Studied RAM: played trumpet in RPO and at Covent Garden. Conductor, especially of wind and brass bands (notably Black Dyke), and adjudicator. Worked for BBC as radio and TV music producer 1955-67. Has published, mainly for brass, many arrangements and a number of original compositions. His son Michael has also written much for brass, arrangements and compositions, eg. *Tuba Tapestry* and, for trombone, *Rag 'n Bone*.

BRIDGE, Frank (1879-1941). Educated RCM; taught by Stanford and later taught Britten. String player and conductor. Many of his compositions, especially orchestral or chamber, are large in scale and at times advanced in idiom, but others fall within this book's scope. *Go not happy Day, E'en as a Lovely Flower* and other song titles are surely ballads; there are many light miniatures, for piano (*Three Sketches*, especially *April* and *Rosemary*, *Three Pieces*, *Four Characteristic Pieces*, *Fairy Tale Suite*, *Fireflies*), cello, viola or violin (*Moto Perpetuo, Cradle Song, Serenade, Heartsease, Melodie, Morning Song*) and chamber ensembles (*Miniatures*, 3 sets for piano trio, and, for string quartet, *Sally in Our Alley, Cherry Ripe, Sir Roger de Coverley* and the gloriously 'seasidey' *Allegro Marcato* from *Three Pieces*). Some of these were orchestrated.

BRIDGEWATER, Ernest Leslie (1893-1975). Born in Halesowen, studied at the Birmingham School of Music (with York Bowen) and was for a time MD at Shakespeare Memorial Theatre, Stratford-on-Avon. Composed music for 19 Shakespeare plays, also other plays, eg, *The Beaux Strategem, The Relapse, Tartuffe* and *Dear Octopus* and for films, notably *Train of Events*. Had a piano concerto broadcast and recorded but best known for his work for light music at the BBC, where he founded the Leslie Bridgewater Quintet (piano/strings) and in 1939-42 the BBC Salon Orchestra. Arranged much music, especially baroque items, for the Quintet; composed for small orchestra *Alla Toccata* (strings), *Rustic Suite*, the suite *Ballet in Progress*, the caprice *Prunella* (for violin and orchestra), *Harlequin, Spirit of Youth* and *Love's Awakening*.

BRODSZKY, Nicholas (1905-58). Russian-born, came to England in 1930s. Composed music for revues and many film scores, including *The Way to the Stars* (1945).

BROOKE, Byron (fl. 1925-50). Leader, then temporary Conductor (1947-8), of Bournemouth Municipal Orchestra, for whom he composed *Bourrée and Variations*, *Merry Middies*, the xylophone solos *Slippery Sticks* and *Gee Whiz*, etc.

BROWNSMITH, Reginald David (d. 1965). Remembered for his lullaby *Softly Sleeping* (1952), published in orchestral and vocal versions, also the orchestral numbers *Frills and Furbelows* and *Happy Birthday Party*.

BUCALOSSI, Ernest (1859-1933). Known primarily for his jaunty little orchestral number *Grasshoppers' Dance*, popular 50 years ago, though this was latterly only usually to be heard played by brass bands until it received a new lease of life as background to a TV milk advertisement. Other orchestral titles include the waltzes *Queen of the North*, *Primavera* and *Dear Erin*, the march *Pennon and Plume* and the genre pieces *Pensées d'Amour*, *A Hunting Scene* and *The Enchanted Valley*. Procida Bucalossi (his father) earned some fame with his operetta *Manteaux Noirs* in the 1880s, his dance arrangements of tunes from the Savoy Operas and the waltz song *Ciribiribin* (although this has mistakenly been attributed to Ernest).

BUNNING, Herbert (1863-1937). Educated Harrow and BNC Oxford. Musical Director, Lyric, Hammersmith, and Prince of Wales Theatres in the 1890s. Composed an opera, *Princess Osra* (1902), a musical play on *Robin Hood* for the Lyric (1906) and much for orchestra, including the overtures *Mistral* and *Spring and Youth*, the *Village Suite* and, premiered at the Proms, *Shepherd's Call*.

BURGESS, H.C. (d. 1940). Conductor of Weston-super-Mare Orchestra 1920-38, then of BBC Midland Orchestra; composed march *To The Clink of the Spur* and other orchestral items.

BURGON, Geoffrey (1941-2010). Deserves mention for his incidental music for the TV adaptation of *Brideshead Revisited*, the title theme of which earned as much popularity as almost any Coates melody. He has also produced, in addition to large quantities of church music and some film music (eg *Sirens*), a number of instrumental pieces, some of them in the 'lighter' category: *Four Elizabethan Dances* for brass, *Divertimento* for brass quartet, *Lullaby Aubade* and *Toccata* for trumpet and piano, and the seven piano pieces entitled *From the Insect World*. Interested in jazz. Other TV scores besides *Brideshead* include *Martin Chuzzlewit, Bleak House, Tinker, Tailor, Soldier, Spy* and *Testament of Youth*.

BURROWS, Rex (fl. 1940-60). Composer of ballads (*A Faithful Heart, My Heart Is Yours, There is no End*, etc.) and the piano suite *Hampton Court*. Early encourager of the composer Alan Ridout (1934-96).

BUSH, Geoffrey (1920-1998). Composer, in an approachable style, of two symphonies, operas, choral music and songs. Enthusiast for British music; earns mention here primarily for his comedy overture *Yorick* (1949), dedicated to the memory of Tommy Handley. Other overtures include *The Rehearsal* and *The Spanish Rivals;* his *Concerto for Light Orchestra* was composed for a BBC Light Music Festival in 1958.

BUTTERWORTH, Arthur, MBE (1923-). Manchester-born, educated RMCM. Trumpet player (Hallé Orchestra, 1955-62), teacher (Huddersfield School of Music), conductor and composer. Though output includes four symphonies, several concertos and much choral music, some of his work is light in character: *Gigues, Legend, Italian Journey* suite (Toccata, Roma; Notturno, Ravello; Tarantella, Rimini) and the ballet *Creation in the Night*, all for orchestra. Other pieces are stimulated by North Country landscapes: *The Path Across the Moor, The Quiet Tarn, Three Impressions* (reflecting facets of Northumbrian industry), and *A Dales Suite*, all for brass band, and *Lakeland Summer Night* for piano.

BUTTERWORTH, David Neil (1934-). Composer, conductor, author, broadcaster. Educated London University and GSM. Prolific composer, much of his output being in lighter forms: short choral pieces, many arrangements, pieces for brass (*Mr. Church's Toye, Four Motets*), the *Tudor Suite* for wind, *Kettlebury Hill* for oboe and strings, the *Ewell Court Suite* for piano solo and many other short instrumental solos.

BYNG, George (c.1862-1932). Born in Dublin but made his mark as a musical director in London theatres, notably at the Alhambra, for which he composed some 30 ballets. Other stage shows for which he provided music included *Guy Fawkes, The Belle of the Baltic* and *The Variety Girl*. Also wrote songs – Peter Dawson took up *My Sword and I* – and his orchestral suite *A Day in Naples* achieved popularity. Additionally he is thought to have been the 'David George' who composed light orchestral novelty pieces.

CANTELL, Frank (1901-73). Conductor of BBC West of England Light Orchestra 1950-61; prolific arranger and composer of light orchestral genre pieces.

CARR, Frank Osmond (1858-1916). Yorkshire-born conductor and composer of many pieces for the light musical theatre, including the operetta *His Excellency* (to W.S. Gilbert's words) and a ballet *Roger de Coverley* (1907).

CARR, Howard (1880-1960). Yet another who made his name conducting in London theatres. Unsurprisingly, wrote much for the stage, mostly operettas and musicals (*Shanghai, The Chinese Honeymoon*), many songs and part-songs and several popular orchestral items: the ballet suite *Carnival of the Elements*, the nautical suite *On the Briny* and the *Three Heroes* suite (O'Leary, VC, Captain Oates of Scott of the Antarctic fame and Sub- Lieutenant Warneford, VC), premiered at the Armistice in 1918, and sundry single movements like *The Jolly Roger, The Crimson Fan, Moorish Dance* and the overture *Sir Walter Raleigh*, introduced in 1940.

CARSE, Adam von Ahn (1878-1958). Born Newcastle; educated in Germany and at RAM with Frederick Corder. Later taught at Winchester College and at RAM as Professor of Harmony and Counterpoint. A prolific producer of music for young amateurs, writer of many books on various aspects of music and editor of several 18th-century orchestral works, he also contributed many additions to the light music repertory: *Norwegian Fantasia* for violin and orchestra, the overtures *Happy Heart* and *Holiday Overture*, the suites *Boulogne: A Romantic Legend* and *The Merry Milkmaids*, all for orchestra, and *Three Characteristic Pieces, Three English Pictures* and the overture *Puffing Billy* for brass band, and some instrumental pieces.

CARYLL, Ivan (really Felix Tilken) (1861-1921). Belgian-born, came to London 1882 but settled in America 1911 and died there. Composed scores for about 40 operettas or musical comedies. First success was in 1893 (*Little Christopher Columbus*). Others first produced in England were *The Shop Girl, The Circus Girl, A Runaway Girl, Our Miss Gibbs* (all collaborations with Lionel Monckton), *The Lucky Star* (1899), *The Toreador* (1901) and *The Duchess of Dantzic* (1903). Also composed many songs, dances and salon pieces for his own Light Orchestra (for which Elgar wrote *Serenade Lyrique*).

CAZABON, Albert (1883-1970). Worth a mention for his light orchestra genre movements, especially popular on the BBC just after World War II: *Three Ballet Sketches*, the entr'actes *On the Moonlight Terrace* and *Spring Morning*, the rondos *The Jester* and *Scherzando, Preludio Romantico, Columbine and Harlequin* and *Fjell Melody: Norwegian Souvenir.*

CHACKSFIELD, Frank (1914-95). Sussex-born; pianist and organist early in life but remembered as conductor, especially on radio ('Frank Chacksfield and his Orchestra' and 'The Tunesmiths'). Prolific broadcaster and recording artist and composer of light genre pieces, eg, *Hyde Park Polka, In Old Lisbon, Prelude to a Memory, Ebb Tide* and *Donkey Cart*, and film music (notably the theme from *Limelight*, while *On the Beach* made the charts in 1954).

CHARROSIN, Frederick George (died 1976). His music, mainly orchestral, achieved popularity on the BBC, particularly so after 1945. It was his colourful arrangements that were most in demand but there were plenty of 'originals', too: *Fireside Gypsies*, the intermezzo *Playbox*, the caprice *Trickery*, the paso doble *Don Carlos* and two pieces for piano (or xylophone or piccolo) with orchestra, *Snowflakes* and – a waltz – *Zita*.

CLIFFORD, Hubert (1904-59). Australian-born; conducted for BBC 1941-44; then Professor at RAM. Composed a symphony (1940) and *Serenade for Strings*. Like Hubert Bath wrote much for British films. His lighter compositions include *Five Nursery Tunes*, the *Cowes Suite*, the *Kentish Suite* ('Dover', 'Canterbury', a prelude on Orlando Gibbons' hymn-tune of that name, 'Pastoral and Folk Song', 'Swift Nicks of Gads Hill' and 'Greenwich: Pageant of the River') and *Four Sketches From 'As You Like It'*. His piece *Atomic Energy* includes parts for alto flute, E flat clarinet, heckelphone and vibraphone.

CLIFFORD, Julian (1877-1921). No relation to Hubert. Conducted resort orchestras at Harrogate, Hastings and other places. Compositions included songs, a choral ode, a piano concerto, an orchestral *Ballade*, a tone poem, *Lights Out*, the intermezzo *Fairy Fancies*, a *Meditation* and *Midge*, all for orchestra, and *Three Episodes* and *Grand Valse Caprice* for piano solo. His son, also Julian, conducted resort orchestras and on the BBC. He also composed and it is sometimes difficult now to disentangle which Julian Clifford wrote what.

COBB, Gerard F. (1838-1904). Song composer, of about 20 of Kipling's *Barrack Room Ballads*, some set more famously by others, *Cavaliers and*

Roundheads, The Scent of the Lilies, etc. An orchestral *Romanze* was performed at the Proms in 1901. Lived in Cambridge, where he was a Fellow of Trinity College.

COCKER, Norman (1889-1953). Organist of Manchester Cathedral for many years, also of Manchester's Gaumont Cinema. His jaunty *Tuba Tune* (1922) would have sounded well on each instrument.

COLES, Jack (1914-91). Sometime Conductor of the BBC Midland Light Orchestra and other ensembles. Orchestral works include the suite *A Day at the Zoo* (1950) and the genre pieces *The Girl From Cadiz, Mexican Caprice, Casbah* and *Puppet March*.

COLLINS, Anthony Vincent Benedictus (1893-1963). Hastings-born, studied RCM and played viola in LSO and Covent Garden Orchestra 1926-36. Conducted for Carl Rosa and Sadler's Wells and on many early Decca LPs. Apart from two symphonies, two violin concertos, operas, chamber music, songs and choral works, he composed for many films in USA and in this country (eg, *Odette, Derby Day, The Lady With a Lamp*) and a large quantity of light music: the overtures *The Dancing Master* and *Festival Royal*, the suites *Eire*, based on folk (or folky) tunes, *Four Styrian Dances* and *Spanish Dance Suite* and, best known of all, *Vanity Fair*, a single movement of sprightly charm, probably inspired by Thackeray's famous novel.

CORDELL, Frank (1918-80). Composer of music for films *(Damon, The Bargee, Ring of Bright Water)* and TV *(Court Martial)*; also published *Gestures* and *Patterns*, both for saxophone quartet.

CORP, Ronald (1951-). Conductor, of New London Orchestra and various choirs, broadcaster and recording artiste, notably of light music (see Discography). Compositions, mainly for chorus, include carols, *Four Elizabethan Lyrics, Laudamus* and *Jubilate Deo*.

CORRI, Clarence Collingwood (1863-1918). Member of an extensive musical family of Italian origin active in the British Isles from the 18th century. Composed dance music, songs and operettas, eg, *The Dandy Fifth: an English Military Comic Opera* (1898: especially popular), *In Gay Piccadilly* (1901) and *Lady Lavender* (c 1911).

COSTA, Raie da (1907-34). Of Portuguese origin, born in South Africa, domiciled in England, she had a sadly short life. Brilliant pianist in the 'syncopated' style – her own essays in that manner include *Razor Blades, A Toyland Holiday; Parade of the Pied Piper, Moods* and the absolutely irresistible *At the Court of Old King Cole.*

COWARD, Sir Noël (1899-1973). Famed singer and actor, playwright and (very prolific) composer. Best-known operetta was *Bitter Sweet* (1929) but *Operette, Conversation Piece* and sundry revues and musicals also did well. Composed hundreds of songs, most popular being *Poor Little Rich Girl, A Room With a View; Dance Little Lady, Mad Dogs and Englishmen* and *London Pride*. Self taught; relied on collaborators for notation and orchestration of his works, but his outstanding melodic gifts and verbal wit earn him a mention here.

COWEN, Sir Frederick Hymen (1852-1935). Born Jamaica. Conductor and composer, of major choral works, operas, six symphonies, about 300 songs, many of which are ballads, especially popular being *The Better Land* and *A Border Ballad*, and several light suites rivalling those of Edward German, though they have not survived as well. They are notable for their delicacy, eg, *The Language of Flowers, Four Old English Dances* (two sets), *In Fairyland,* as is the concert overture *The Butterfly's Ball* (1905).

CROOK, John (1852-1922). Prominent in the fields of musical theatre and Cockney song. Theatre works to which he contributed included *King Kodak, The House of Lords, Claude Duval* and, most importantly and gorgeously tunefully, *Peter Pan* (1905).

CROOKE, Sidney (fl 1940-60). Composer of popular orchestral genre pieces *(Turning Wheels, Solo Flight, Valsette, Happy-Go-Lucky; A Woodland Idyll* and a *Scherzino* for bassoon/clarinet and orchestra) and light instrumental solos. Capable pianist, with J.H. Squire Celeste Octet and other ensembles.

CROSSMAN, Gerald (1920-). Studied TCL. Played piano and accordion. Inveterate broadcaster, especially in 'Music While You Work' and player in light ensembles and elsewhere, particularly on cruise liners. His works include genre pieces like *March Espagnol, A Night in Montmartre, The Albany Waltz, La Vida Latina, Nochecita, Boulevards de Paris* and *Out of the Wood* and film music, including that for AEW Mason's detective story *The House of the Arrow.*

CURRY, David (fl 1940-60). Re-formed and then conducted a 16-piece BBC Northern Ireland Light Orchestra around 1950. Later published *Irish Pastorale* for orchestra and two books of *Irish Rhythms* for piano solo.

DANN, Horace (1896-1958). Known in his day for his sparkling concert march *Worcester Beacon*, almost worthy of Coates, played in the first BBC Light Music Festival in 1949, also *Prima Ballerina* and *Lullaby* for orchestra, piano music and songs.

DAREWSKI, Herman (1883-1947). Conductor and composer of many musicals and revues *(As You Were, Carminetta, London Paris and New York, Joy-Land, Better 'Ole*, etc.), 'separate' songs (eg, *Mary From Tipperary, The Big Brass Band, The Road to Romance)* and instrumental pieces, of which the *Coon's Wedding March* was the most popular.

DAREWSKI, Max (1894-1929). Manchester-born, conductor and composer of musicals *Tonight's the Night* (with Rubens) and *Hearts and Diamonds* and the revue *Hanky Panky*.

DAVIES, Sir Peter Maxwell (1934-). Studied in Italy and US; a schoolteacher for many years. At one time reckoned one of the avant-garde, but has also made notable contributions to the lighter genre, examples being the entertaining *Orkney Wedding and Sunrise* and that lovely piano miniature *Farewell to Stromness*. Topography has often inspired our lighter composers; has Davies' Orkneys domicile done likewise for him?

DAVIES, William (1921-2006). Organist on BBC and elsewhere; prolific arranger and composer for organ. Titles include *Organists on the March, Oranges and Lemons, Duo for Caroline*, and title music for BBC Radio's *Just William*.

DAVIS, Carl (1936-). American-born but domiciled in England. Composer of approachable and attractive work in the best British light music traditions for stage shows, including plays (such as *Beatrix*, about Beatrix Potter), ballets (eg, on Dickens' *A Christmas Carol)* and for many films, 'silent' classics like *Ben Hur, The General* and *Napoleon* and more recent ones like *King David* and *The French Lieutenant's Woman)*, also TV *(The Prince Regent, The World at War, The Far Pavilions, Our Mutual Friend, Pride and Prejudice)* and radio (*Antonio, Antony and Cleopatra)*. Collaborated with Paul McCartney on *The Liverpool Oratorio*.

DEXTER, Harry (1910-73). Born Sheffield; educated Durham University. Prolific composer and arranger, especially for students, also critic. Vocal output included anthems, educational songs and ballad-style numbers in one, two or three parts, incidental music (including the Maigret TV series), but is perhaps best remembered for his orchestral novelties – *Frankfurt Polka, Budgerigar Polka, Concetta, September Woods, Pizzicato Playtime, Waltz for a Bride*, the marches *New Town* and *Bang On* and, most popular of all, the lightly scored, charming *Siciliano*, which appeared in 1953. Founded Light Music Society 1956.

D'HARDELOT, Guy (really Helen Guy) (1858-1936). French-born, settled in England after her marriage and produced popular ballads like *Because, I Know a Lovely Garden, A Summer Song*, etc.

DIACK, John Michael (1869-1947). Remembered for his arrangements, many ballad-like songs, plus *Sing a Song of Sixpence, Little Jack Horner* and other nursery rhymes set in the style of Handel or Mozart.

DOYLE, Patrick (1953-). Studied RSAMD; has composed several theatre scores, especially for Kenneth Branagh's Renaissance Theatre Company and film music for *Henry V, Much Ado, Indochine, A Little Princess* and, most notably for the film adaptation of Jane Austen's *Sense and Sensibility*; a generally graceful and wistful score including two songs to 17th-century lyrics, and *Hamlet* (also a Branagh collaboration).

DRING, Madeleine (1923-77). Educated RCM. Writer of over 50 tasteful art songs (notably settings of Shakespeare, Herrick and Betjeman), plus entertaining cabaret and theatre songs. Her instrumental work mainly comprises tuneful miniatures for her own instrument, the piano, often inspired by dance rhythms *(Dance Suite, West Indian Dance, Mazurka, Pavane and Landler, Three French Dances, American Dance, Colour Suite*, etc), also for oboe (like the *Three Piece Suite, the Danza Gaya* and the popular *Italian Dance*; she was married to the oboist Roger Lord) and flute, eg, *Waltz, Sarabande and Tango*.

DRIVER, F. Percival (1883-?). Leicester-born, educated RAM, widely travelled as examiner. Appeared to specialise in the light genre piece for chamber ensemble (*Three Little Trios* (1927): 'The Song of the Clock', 'Harvesting Time' and the charming 'Slumber Song'; *Dainty Dance* for violin and piano) and for piano solo, eg, *All-in-a-Ring* (1936), *Four Sketches* (1926), *Little Suite*, the *Three Dance Measures* of 1926 and, revealing a talent for historical pastiche, *An Old Style Measure*. He also composed songs.

DRUMMOND, Frederick (fl. 1900-30). Renowned for his popular ballad *The Gay Highway*, beloved of Peter Dawson, and for several others: *Songs From Golden Hours, Songs of Blue Skies, Songs of Soho, Sunshine Songs, Homeland, Rosebud, Give Me Youth* and *The Call of the Road*.

DUNCAN, Trevor (1924-2006). Pseudonym of Leonard Trebilko and composer of scores for the large screen (*Joe Macbeth, The Intimate Stranger*) and for TV (*The Plane Makers*). Best known for his orchestral concert compositions in a slightly updated Coatesian idiom: the suites *Children in the Park*, pleasingly light in touch, and the *Little Suite*, whose sprightly opening March achieved wide popularity after being adopted as the signature tune to BBC TV's 1960s series of *Doctor Finlay's Casebook*, and single novelty movements like *Tomboy, Still Waters, Maniac Pursuit* and, most famously, the valse *Mignonette* and, from 1950, *High Heels*.

DUNHILL, Thomas (1877-1946). London-born, studied at RCM with Stanford. Assistant Music Master at Eton College, 1899-1908, then Professor at RCM. Composed much chamber music, many songs and much for young performers. Earns mention here for his operettas *The Enchanted Garden* (1925), *Happy Families* (1933) and most notably *Tantivy Towers*, with a horsey background, produced at the Lyric Theatre, Hammersmith, to AP Herbert's words in 1931; and also for his lighter orchestral works, which included *Dance Suite* (1919), *Waltz Suite* (1943), *Guildford Suite, Chiddingfold Suite, In Rural England, Vectis, Dances in Miniature, Fairy Suite: The Pixies, Dick Whittington Suite* and the overture *May-Time* (1945).

DUNN, Sir Vivian (1908-95). Born in India, sometime Director of Music to the Royal Marines (1931-68), also conducted many other ensembles, bands and orchestras. As a composer is worth remembering for his marches *Cockleshell Heroes* (for the 1950s film), *Globe and Laurel, The Pompey Chimes*, dedicated to Portsmouth Football Club, the *Canadian National Exhibition March, Captain General, Soldiers of the Sea* and *Commando Patrol*.

EASDALE, Brian (1909-95). Composed operas, chamber music and orchestral and choral works; earns a mention here for his film music, especially *The Red Shoes* ballet (1948), starring the young Moira Shearer, and the rousing march from *The Battle of the River Plate* (1956). Illness later in life restricted his output.

ELLIOTT, Percy (died 1932). Also wrote light music under the pseudonyms of Godfrey Newark and Walter Bush. Composed songs and, especially, light orchestral pieces much in demand in the 'silent' cinema. Some of his suites have Ketèlbey-like titles: *In Sunny Spain, Natalia: Five South African Impressions* and *'Neath Azure Skies*. Individual movements by him included *Curfew*, the intermezzo *Red Poppies*, the waltz *Youth and Spring*, the novelette for strings *Cupid in Error* and the march *Garthowen*.

ELLIOTT, Vernon Pelling (1912-96). Educated RCM; bassoonist with Sadler's Wells, Covent Garden, Philharmonia and other orchestras, also conductor; composer of music for children's TV programmes like *Ivor the Engine* (which features the bassoon prominently), *Noggin the Nog, Pogle's Wood*, etc.

ELLIS, Vivian (1903-96). Began career as concert pianist (trained at RAM under Myra Hess) but from mid-1920s passed to writing songs for London revues. Best known of his stage shows (of around 30) were *Mr Cinders* (1929), *Jill Darling* (1934), *Running Riot* (1938), *Big Ben* (1946), *Bless the Bride* (1947), *Tough at the Top* (1949) and *The Water Gipsies* (1955), the last four to A.P. Herbert's lyrics. *Bless the Bride* had most hits with *This is My Lovely Day, Ma Belle Marguerite*, etc. Also wrote for films. Composed many separate songs and orchestral pieces, including the suites *Happy Week-End* (whose finale was 'Early Morning Train') and *Holidays Abroad* (1961), which visits Switzerland, Vienna, Costa Brava, Pisa and a Paris taxi, and the single movements *Alpine Pastures* and, most famously, *Coronation Scot*, famed as a signature tune (for radio adaptations of Paul Temple) and one of the most celebrated of 'railway' pieces. It is surprising that the *Daily Telegraph*'s obituary failed to mention it.

ENGLEMAN, Harry (1912-). May be reckoned a major successor to Billy Mayerl as a syncopated pianist. Compositions in that genre include *Cannon off the Cushion, Finger Prints, Snakes and Ladders, Skittles* and *Summer Rain* for piano, also songs, eg, *Melody of Love*.

EVANS, Tolchard (1901-1978). Pianist, originally in cinemas. Composed over 1,000 songs, most popular titles being *Lady of Spain, Dreamy Devon* and *Valencia*.

EWING, Montague (1890-1957). Primarily an arranger of potpourris and a writer of light music for piano (including piano trio) and ballads. Many of his piano suites were orchestrated but mostly by other hands (eg,

Humours of Nature, Silhouettes (several sets), *Variety Suite, Fireflies, Water Colours, Guy Fawkes Night, The Wand of Harlequin)*; also produced marches like *Advance of the Tanks* and *Parade of the Home Guard*, novelty numbers and intermezzi such as *Pierrette by the Stream, Phantom Piper, Sailormen All, Dancing Clock, Through a Stained Glass Window* and *Portrait of a Toy Soldier*. His most popular song was the amusing *The Policeman's Holiday*. Also wrote songs and piano and orchestral music under the name of Sherman Myers (Myers titles include *Chasing Moonbeams* and *Moonlight on the Ganges*) and half a dozen other pseudomyms.

FARADAY, Philip Michael (fl 1900-20). Manager of touring operetta companies for which Alfred Reynolds (*qv*) conducted in 1911-12; also composer of the musical comedy *The Island* (1910) and, most successfully, of the comic opera *Amasis* (1906).

FARIS, Alexander (1921-). Conductor (for Carl Rosa, Sadler's Wells and Royal Ballet) and composer of *Sketches of Regency England*, for orchestra, an operetta (*R Loves J*) and scores for feature films (*Georgy Girl, The Quare Fellow, Rowlandson's England*) and TV (*Upstairs, Downstairs, Wings, Duchess of Duke Street*).

FARJEON, Harry (1878-1948). Born New Jersey, USA, of British parents, studied RAM with Frederick Corder, returning there as Professor 1903. Member of a notable theatrical and artistic family. Much of his large output is light, including three operettas, shorter orchestral pieces (he also wrote concertos and symphonic poems) like the *Elegy* for strings, *Idyll* and the *Hans Andersen Suite*, ballads like *An Elfin Lady* and *Vagrant Songs* and quite a lot of piano music: *Canzonetta, Elegie Heroique*, the five *Peter Pan Sketches*, the *Summer Suite* and *Pictures from Greece*, six of them altogether.

FARNON, Robert (1917-2005). Born in Toronto, Canada, but settled in British Isles since 1959 and, as well as being the composer of two symphonies, an influential figure in British light music since World War II. Trumpet player and conductor. Composed music for over 30 films (*Captain Horatio Hornblower, Road to Hong Kong, Gentlemen Marry Brunettes*, etc) and television series (eg, *Colditz*, whose march has achieved great popularity, and *Four Freedoms*). His suites include *Saxophone Triparti* (1971), *Canadian Impressions* (ten movements) and the Coatesian *Three Impressions* and *Three More Impressions*. Single movements include *Malaga, Lake of the Woods, Melody Fair, Lazy Day Country Girl*, inspired by Wordsworth, *Pleasure Drive, Seashore, Derby Day,* the marches *State Occasion, Sports Challenge* and *Concorde* and, especially popular for many years, the four pieces *Jumping Bean, A La Clare Fontaine, Portrait of a Flirt* and *Westminster Waltz.* Brass bands appreciate his *Une Vie de Matelot* and *Morning Cloud;* concerted pieces include *Rhapsody* (violin and orchestra) and *Prelude and Dance* (harmonica and orchestra). Has a UK society and a Marco Polo CD devoted to his music.

FEENEY, Philip (1954-). Worth notice here on account of his attractive ballet scores, eg, *Cinderella* (1989) and the more recent *Dracula.*

FENBY, Eric (1906-1997). Best remembered for his work for Delius, as musical amanuensis (1928-34), scholar and performer, but also a composer himself, of church music, film music (*Jamaica Inn*, 1939) and of the comedy overture *Rossini on Ilkla Moor,* written for the Scarborough Spa Orchestra in 1938.

FENOULHET, Paul (fl 1940-70). Active as conductor of the BBC's lighter orchestras in the 1950s and 60s. Many arrangements; also composer of novelty pieces like *Happidrome, The Grande Corniche* and *Top Gear* and the attractive suite *Suffolk Sketches,* whose movements include 'Flatford Mill'.

FENTON, George (1949-). Another composer for the screen, large (*Shadowlands, Gandhi* and *The Madness of King George III*) and small (the detective series *Bergerac* and *Shoestring*).

FINCK, Herman (1872-1939). English (London-born) composer of Dutch extraction. Trained at GSM, then Musical Director at the Palace Theatre 1900-20, with whose orchestra he made many recordings, Queen's Theatre, Drury Lane and at Southport. Composer of about 30 stage shows of all types musicals, operettas, revues (*Round the Map* was especially popular) and ballets – plus songs, instrumental music, mood music for the 'silent' cinema and light orchestral works: *Grand March, Pageant March, Guards Parade March, Splendour and Victory March,* the suites *My Lady Dragon Fly* and *Marie Antoinette* and genre pieces like *Dancing Daffodils, Dignity and Impudence* and, most popular of all, *In the Shadows,* originally called *Tonight.*

FOULDS, John Herbert (1880-1939). Manchester-born, played cello in Hallé Orchestra. Prolific composer; experimented with microtones and interested in Indian music (he died in India), but a substantial number of his works were light music: the 'intermezzo impromptu' *La Belle Pierrette*, *Kashmiri Boat Song*, the overtures *Le Cabaret* and *Keltic Overture* and the suites *Gaelic Melodies*, *Holiday Sketches* (Nuremburg, Bohemia, Odenwald, Coblenz), *Music Pictures* (several suites), *Suite Fantastique*, *Suite Française*, *Puppet Ballet Suite* and *Keltic Suite*, whose middle movement, 'Lament', attained great popularity.

FRANKEL, Benjamin (1906-73). Composer of eight symphonies, five string quartets, concertos, an opera and much else, often in a quite advanced idiom; he was also a light music figure – in early life he played jazz on piano and violin, and he then orchestrated and conducted West End musicals and composed film music from 1934 onwards, although sometimes this could be tough listening. His most popular piece of light music is the charming *Carriage and Pair*, from the film *So Long at the Fair*.

FRENCH, Percy (1854-1920). Irish composer of popular ballads such as *The Mountains of Mourne* and *Phil the Fluter's Ball*.

GAMLEY, Douglas (1924-98). Conductor and producer of (often lush-sounding) popular orchestrations, plus a version of *The Beggar's Opera* (published and recorded) and various original compositions, eg, *Souvenir de Granada*.

GARDINER, Henry Balfour (1877-1950). Trained in Germany (member with Grainger, Quilter and O'Neill (all *qv*) of 'Frankfurt School'); relatively small compositional output: orchestral, chamber and piano music, songs and church music. His *Shepherd Fennel's Dance* (1911), after Thomas Hardy, was once popular with light orchestras; the *Overture to a Comedy* (1906), *Humoresque* (1908) and *In Maytime* (1914) may also be listed. Used his own money to promote the compositions of his friends, especially Holst.

GAY, Noel (1898-1954), real name Reginald Moxon Armitage. Yorkshire-born; educated RCM and Christ's College, Cambridge. Went into musical theatre, writing many revues or musical comedies, eg, *The Charlot Show of 1926*, *Hold My Hand*, *Me and My Girl* (1937: included *The Lambeth Walk*), *The Little Dog Laughed* (included *Run, Rabbit Run*) and wartime shows like *Lights Up*, *Present Arms*, *The Love Racket* and *Meet Me Victoria*. Also composed many popular songs (*Round the Marble Arch*, *My Thanks to You*, etc) independent of the musical stage; others were incorporated into films.

GIBBS, Cecil Armstrong (1889-1960). Essex-born, educated Winchester and Cambridge, taught in schools and at RCM 1921-39. Adjudicator at competitive musical festivals and prolific composer of three symphonies and other orchestral music, nine string quartets and other chamber music, large-scale choral works, much piano music, works for amateur orchestras and many songs. Earns mention here for his enormously popular waltz tune *Dusk* from the *Fancy Dress Suite* of 1935, issued in countless arrangements, including a vocal one, also *Essex Suite, Miniature Dance Suite, Peacock Pie Suite, Dale and Fell Suite, Mediterranean Valse* and lighter stage pieces including the operettas *The Blue Peter* and *The Sting of Love*.

GODFREY, a musical dynasty stretching over four generations and involved with light music in military and brass bands, orchestras, etc. 'Founder' of the dynasty was Charles (I) (1790-1863), Bandmaster of Coldstream Guards (1825-63) and Musician in Ordinary to the King. Three of his five sons became military bandmasters: Daniel I (1831-1903), RAM student and later Bandmaster of Grenadier Guards (he was the first bandmaster to achieve commissioned rank) 1856-96 and then of his own band and composer of marches and popular waltzes; Adolphus Frederick ('Fred') (1837-82), RAM student, successor to his father at the Coldstreams 1863-80 and possibly the composer of the *Lucy Long* bassoon variations long popular at the Proms, although Charles I has been credited with this; and Charles II (1839-1919), also RAM student, Bandmaster of Scots Fusiliers and Royal Horse Guards, Professor at RCM and Guildhall School, adjudicator of brass bands, arranger of widely-used potpourris and composer of songs, dance music and a *Song Without Words* for orchestra. Daniel I's son, Dan II (1868-1939), was the founder and conductor for 41 years of the Bournemouth Municipal Orchestra, also a prolific arranger, especially for military band, and composer of dance music, marches and songs. His son Dan III (1893-1935) directed resort orchestras at Harrogate, Blackpool and Hastings and on the BBC and finally (1928-35) for Durban Corporation (South Africa). Charles II's three musical sons contributed much to the light music scene: Charles George (Charles III) (1866-1935) studied at RAM, directed Crystal Palace Military Band, Buxton Spa Orchestra and Scarborough Spa Orchestra; and Arthur Eugene (1868-1939), educated at St Paul's School and RAM, was musical director in various theatres including the Alhambra, Glasgow – he composed a string quartet, ballads (*A Fairy Fantasy, Stand United*), dance music and a musical comedy, *Little Miss Nobody* (1898).

There was also Herbert (1869-?), composer of the ballet *The Home of the Butterflies*.

GOEHR, Walter (1903-60). German-born, English-domiciled conductor and composer earns mention here for his conductorship of the BBC Theatre Orchestra 1945-8 and for his *Three Sketches*, and music for films (eg *Spellbound*) and radio productions.

GOMEZ, Frank (fl 1920-40). Conductor of Whitby Spa Orchestra 1923-38 and composer of light pieces including the orchestral *Climbing the Abbey Steps at Whitby*, which, as there are 199 steps, becomes progressively slower as the tired climber nears the top.

GOODWIN, Ron (1925-2003). Known particularly for his film scores for *I'm All Right Jack, Whirlpool, The Day of the Triffids*, the Agatha Christie adaptations *Murder She Said* and *The Alphabet Murders, Those Magnificent Men in their Flying Machines* and the World War II spectaculars *633 Squadron, The Battle of Britain, Where Eagles Dare* and *Force Ten from Navarone*. Several of these, like *Those Magnificent Men, The Battle of Britain* (in which film his music largely replaced Sir William Walton's, rather to Goodwin's embarrassment) and *633 Squadron*, yielded popular concert marches; other concert numbers included *City Serenade, Skiffling Strings, Venus Waltz, Minuet in Blue, Puppet Serenade, Girl with a Dream, Arabian Celebration* (commissioned by the BBC), *Prisoners of War March, Drake 400 Suite, The Armada 400 Suite* and *New Zealand Suite*.

GORDON, Gavin (1901-70). Born in Ayr, educated Rugby School and RCM, where he studied with Vaughan Williams. Actor, singer and cartoonist, also composer of songs, ballets *(A Toothsome Morsel, The Scorpions of Ysit, Regatta, The Death of Hector* and, most significantly, *The Rake's Progress*, produced at Sadler's Wells 1935 and frequently revived) and other orchestral pieces, of which the four *Caricatures* and the *Work in E Major* for strings, both parodying old dances, may be reckoned as light music.

GOURLAY, Ian (fl. 1940-70). Prolific arranger, especially for BBC light orchestras; original compositions include *The Travelling Salesman*.

GOWERS, Patrick (1936-). Composer of organ and church music, also of many scores for the Sherlock Holmes TV series.

GRAINER, Ron (1922-81). Australian-born, English-domiciled composer of the musical *Robert and Elizabeth* (1964, about the Brownings) and of film scores like *A Kind of Loving, Lock Up Your Daughters, Giants of Steam* and *The Finest Hours*, from which the *Churchill March* achieved popularity. He also wrote TV's *Doctor Who* and *Steptoe and Son* title music.

GRAINGER, Percy Aldridge (1882-1961). Australian-born, American citizen for the last half of his life, but also associated with Britain, especially collecting and arranging British folk-tunes. Impossible to do justice in 100 words to his many-sided musical personality, as pianist, arranger and composer, but he earns a place here for his short, often folky, pieces, long beloved of light orchestras – *Mock Morris, Molly on the Shore, Irish Tune from County Derry, Country Gardens, Handel in the Strand, Shepherd's Hey, Spoon River, The Immovable Do,* etc – though many are also known in piano and other 'dishings up'.

GREENWOOD, John A. (1876-1953). Protégé of William Rimmer (*qv*); conductor and tutor to major brass bands. Less prolific than Rimmer but his trombone solo *The Acrobat*, with its frequent glissandi, remains popular.

GREGSON, Edward (1945-). After early Salvation Army experience, studied RAM and since 1995 Principal of the RNCM. Despite his particular identification with music for brass and wind bands, much of his output has been 'serious', even cerebral, in character, like *Metamorphoses* for winds, *Concerto Grosso* and *Connotations* for brass band and a tuba concerto; but pieces like *Prelude for an Occasion* (brass) and *Festivo* (wind band) are in the tradition of the British comedy overture and earn him a place here. His suites for concert band *The Sword and the Crown* (1991) and *The Kings Go Forth* (1996), brilliantly scored, derive from Shakespearean incidental music.

GROOT, David de (1880-1933). Known as 'De Groot' simply; Dutch by birth but long a naturalised British subject. Directed Piccadilly Hotel Orchestra 1909-28 and sometimes larger orchestras, usually from the violin. Also composed popular tunes like *Valse Passionée* and the lilting *Piccadilly Grill Waltz*.

GUARD, Barrie (1946-). Educated GSM. TV and film composer, notably of many movements used for *The Darling Buds of May*.

GUNNING, Christopher (1944-). Born Cheltenham. Studied GSMD with Rubbra and Richard Rodney Bennett and at Durham University.

Composer of instructional instrumental music and of very attractive scores for TV, like *Yorkshire Glory*, *Agatha Christie's Poirot*, *Middlemarch*, *The Three Hostages*, *Rebecca (1997)* and *Rogue Male*.

HAINES, Herbert Thomas (died 1952). Composer of quite successful musicals around the time of World War I (*The Catch of the Season*, *Back to Blighty*; *The Talk of the Town*) and of pieces for piano or orchestra suitable for use in the 'silent' cinemas of the day: *Three Woodland Dances*, *Angela*, *Coquette*, *An Eastern Romance*, *A Shepherd's Idyll* and *Folly Dance*. His march *The London Scottish* doubtless emerged during 1914-18.

HANMER, Ronald (1917-94). Studied Blackheath Conservatory; theatre organist 1935-48, subsequently freelance orchestrator and conductor. Orchestral works include many potpourris of popular melodies; original titles are pieces like *On a Windy Day*, *Limelight Lady*, *Dot and Carry One*, the delicate *Pastorale*, long used as a radio signature tune, *Fashion Parade* and music for films. Has also written short pieces for wind instruments, with and without piano, and for brass band and smaller brass groups.

HARRISON, Julius Allan Greenway (1885-1963). Worcestershire-born, he earns a place here as one of the most important resort conductors, at Hastings 1930-40 (he made the Hastings orchestra second only to Bournemouth by the time of World War II). Much of his music is not 'light', however, as it embraces two major chamber works, a cello concerto, much sacred and other large-scale choral music (including two Masses and a Requiem), but we may point to his orchestral suites *Cornish Holiday Sketches*, *Severn Country*; *Troubadour Suite*, *Town and Country*, *Wayside Fancies* (some of whose movements are almost Coatesian in their titles) and, best of all, the *Worcestershire Suite*, several of his songs and the operetta, *A Fantasy of Flowers*.

HARTLEY, Fred (1905-80). Rhythm pianist, especially in 1930s. Widely known for his copious arrangements both before and after he became Head of Light Music at the BBC in 1946. He composed many short genre pieces for orchestra: *Alpine Festival*, *The Ball at Aberfeldy*, *Dublin Express*, *The Fair Maid of Moray*, *From the Misty Isles*, *Highland Lullaby*, *A Rose in Granada*, *Fairy Song* (in the Irish Manner), *Midnight Sun* and *Rouge et Noir*.

HARTLEY, Richard (1944-). Born Holmfirth (Yorkshire). Composer of scores for films (including the remake of *The Lady Vanishes*) and TV (eg, *Tumbledown* and – excellent pastiche – *Adam Bede*).

HARVEY, Paul (1935-). Sheffield-born; fine performer on clarinet and saxophone and prolific composer mostly for those instruments, his work usually being in lighter vein and often suitable for students.

HEAD, Michael Dewar (1900-76). Pianist and singer (often performed his songs to his own accompaniment). Songs, often ballad-like in character, include *Ave Maria, Money-O, A Blackbird Singing, A Singer, A Piper* and *The Estuary*; also produced light operas, operas for children and small-scale instrumental pieces.

HEDGCOCK, Walter (1864-1932). Born Brighton. Organist, then, from 1903, Musical Director at Crystal Palace (died shortly after playing the organ there). Composed church music, a *Suite de Ballet*, overtures and other orchestral music and ballads: *Drake's Drum, On the Road to Mandalay* (his versions of these two did not supplant rival settings), *Mighty Warriors* and *Sleep My Saviour Sleep*, recorded 1932.

HEDGES, Anthony (1931-). Educated Keble College, Oxford; taught RSAM, then (1963-95) Hull University. Prolific composer in all forms, much of his output being suitable for amateurs and and some of that maintains the traditions of British light music. The overtures *Heigham Sound, Cleveland, Holiday Overture* and, for brass, *Saturday Market* are typical light overtures; *An Ayrshire Serenade, Four Breton Sketches, British Folk Song Suite, Four Miniature Dances For My Children, Scenes from the Humber* and *Kingston Sketches* (depicting Hull) are examples of the light 'thematic' suite.

HELY-HUTCHINSON, Christian Victor (1901-47). South African-born; educated Eton and Balliol. Worked for BBC 1926-34 and 1944-7. In addition to more serious works composed *Overture to a Pantomime, South African Suite, A Carol Symphony* (really a suite and still popular) and many lighthearted songs including settings of Belloc, Lewis Carroll, Edward Lear and, most famously, a Handelian parody *Old Mother Hubbard* (also other similar parodies).

HENEKER, David, MBE (1906-2001). Born Southsea; regular army officer 1925-48. Then composer-lyricist, sometimes with others, of songs (eg, *Only Fools, She's In Love With a Soldier, Girls in Khaki*) and stage shows, notably *Make Me An Offer* (1959), *Charlie Girl* (1965), *Jorrocks* (1966), *Phil the Fluter* (1969) and, most famous of all, *Half a Sixpence* (1963).

HENMAN, Geoffrey (1896-?). Compositions, especially popular post 1945, included ballads *(The First Rose of Summer, Ploughman's Song,* etc.), stage shows (the revue *How d'You Do* and the radio musical *Mr. Barley's Abroad)* and orchestral works, suites *(High Street, My Lady's Dress* and *Open Windows)* and individual movements *(Moon Flower, Dancing Mad* and *The Charm Waltz).*

HESS, Nigel (1955-). Studied Cambridge University; with RSC 1981-5. Composer of attractive theme music for TV etc *(Hetty Wainthropp Investigates,* now popular with brass bands, *Just William, Wycliffe, Maigret, A Woman of Substance, Dangerfield).* His *Stephenson's Rocket* for wind band is an addition to the growing corpus of 'train music'; also responsible for the musical *Rats!*

HIGGS, HM (1855-1929). Known particularly for his orchestral selections of popular songs by Eric Coates, Montague Phillips, Haydn Wood (all qv) and other writers but on his own account he produced songs and orchestral compositions like the (surely Ketèlbey-inspired) suite in six movements *Life in Japan,* the *Harlequinade* suite and the musical story *In a Japanese Garden,* and the two-step *Catch Me.* He was also a music editor for Chappells.

HILLIAM, Bentley Collingwood (1890-1968). Scarborough-born. Pianist (as 'Flotsam', partnered bass singer Malcolm McEachern, 'Jetsam'), lyricist and composer, of musicals *(Beau Brummell, Princess Virtue)* and songs, both ballads and comic numbers for Flotsam and Jetsam.

HOLLINS, Alfred (1865-1942). Born in Hull and, though blind, toured worldwide as concert organist; also organist of a church in Edinburgh and professor at RNIB. Works are mainly for organ (though he published songs, anthems and piano solos) and these are mostly in lighter style, organ equivalents of what Edward German and later Eric Coates were writing for orchestra: Concert Overtures in F minor, C major and C minor, *A Song of Sunshine, Spring Song; Maytime* (a gavotte), marches, elegies, 'prayers' and sundry dances. Some of these remain popular with present-day organists.
HOPE, Peter (1930-). Well known for his many arrangements, for radio and elsewhere, of traditional tunes (for orchestra or band), whether English, American, Mexican, Italian, Russian, Scottish and, particularly, Irish. Some of his works which are not overtly arrangements rely on traditional tunes: *Irish Legend* and *The Ring of Kerry,* a suite in three movements, the first entitled 'Jaunting Car'. Has also composed a concerto for trumpet,

Playful Scherzo, Rodeo Express and songs like *The Watchet Sailor, Sweet William* and *The Unconstant Sailor.*

HOPKINS, Antony (1921-). Studied RCM; best known for his brilliant broadcasting and lecturing about music. He also composed much in a generally lighthearted, approachable vein; choral music, piano music (including three sonatas), incidental music for radio features (*Oresteia, Parkinson's Law*), for plays (*The Birds of Aristophanes,* Dorothy Sayers' *The Just Vengeance* (1946) and many Shakespeare plays) and for films (*Billy Budd, Seven Thunders, The Pickwick Papers*); his stage works include operettas for children, and several, including *Three's Company* and *Dr Musicus,* for the Intimate Opera Company, and two ballets.

HOROVITZ, Joseph (1926-). Born Vienna, came to England 1938; studied RCM (under Jacob) and in Paris. Conducted Bristol Old Vic, Ballet Russe, etc. Professor of Composition RCM from 1961. Has composed in a witty, elegant style and using jazz and popular music idioms, operas, ballets (*Les Femmes d'Alger, Alice in Wonderland*), orchestral music (*Harpsichord Jazz Concerto* and other concertos plus *Four Dances*), TV incidental music (including the theme, redolent of 1920s popular music, introducing Lord Peter Wimsey adaptations) and music for brass, eg, *Music Hall Suite* (for quintet), a euphonium concerto and the *Sinfonietta* for brass band.

HOWARTH, Elgar (1935-). Educated Manchester University and RMCM; brass band background. Much of his composing and conducting has also been for bands. Many of his band compositions, like the Cornet Concerto and *Fireworks,* are 'serious', but we can mention the early *Parade* and *Mosaic* (1956), composed for a BBC Light Music Festival, while he has penned several light novelty numbers, again for brass, under the anagrammatic pseudonym W. Hogarth Lear.

HUGHES, Ian (1958-). Essex-born conductor and composer, worth mentioning for his sumptuous score for HTV's *Poldark.*

HUME, James Ord (1864-1932). Born Edinburgh. Son of an Army bandmaster and began his career in military bands, later composer, arranger, conductor and adjudicator in the brass band world. Visited Australia and New Zealand in these capacities. Works (including arrangements) may have totalled 2000, counting those written under many pseudonyms. He was a march composer for all seasons: *BB and CF, Mount Lavinia, Lynwood, Brilliant, Edina, Diamond Jubilee, England's Queen,*

Waveney, The Prairie Flower, even *Liberty Bell,* among many others. But he also wrote cornet solos, cornet duets, two-steps, waltzes, polkas, the popular novelty numbers *The Bells of Ouseley, Danse Antique* and *Danse Romanesque,* all for band, a *Suite Bohemian, The Butterflies, Hawaiian Intermezzo* and *Melinda's Fairy Bower* for orchestra and some songs. Notoriously absent-minded but a much-loved figure.

HURST, Jan (c.1890-1967). Directed resort orchestras at Bridlington, Bath, Blackpool and Scarborough in turn between 1919 and 1952. Compositions included *The Bells of Somerset, Brighton Sea-Step* (or *South Pier Sea-Step)* and *Windermere Idyll,* all for orchestra.

IRELAND, John (1879-1962). Has several claims to be reckoned as a light music composer. *Sea Fever* and *The Holy Boy* are surely ballads; his score for the film *The Overlanders* (1946-7) was highly acclaimed; his *Epic March* inspired many during World War II; and brass bands still play his *Comedy Overture* and *Downland Suite.*

IRVING, Ernest (1877-1953). Musical Director at sundry London theatres 1900-40, then MD at Ealing Studios. Composed incidental music for Shakespeare and other plays, also for musicals and films, including *Whisky Galore.*

IVEY, Herbert (fl 1930-40). Worth mentioning for his suite *Glimpses of London* (less famous than Coates' and Haydn Wood's essays on the same subject) and the *Four Little Dances.*

JACOB, Gordon Percival Septimus, CBE (1895-1984). Composer (pupil of Stanford and Charles Wood), teacher and authority on orchestration. Reckoned a serious composer but many of his pieces are light enough to justify mention here: the *Denbigh Suite* and *Two Sketches* (English Landscape; August Bank Holiday), both for strings, the orchestral comedy overture *The Barber of Seville Goes to the Devil,* the suite *Tribute to Canterbury* and *Celebration Overture,* both for military band, and the Suite in B Major and *Prelude to Comedy* for brass band. Wrote many arrangements of popular tunes for ITMA during the Second War, a facet of his work continued in *Old Wine in New Bottles,* four English tunes arranged for winds, and other pieces.

JOHNSON, Laurie (1927-). Best known for his attractive music for military band, sometimes with a patriotic flavour: *Castles of Britain* (Caernarvon,

Dover, Edinburgh), *The Battle of Waterloo* (with narrator), *Vivat Regina* and *Royal Tour Suite*, plus the suite *Three Paintings by Lautrec*, also for military band. Stage works include the musicals *Lock up Your Daughters* (1959) and *The Four Musketeers* (1967). Film music includes that for the musical *The Good Companions* (1957), after J.B. Priestley. He also composed music for TV programmes *This is Your Life*, *The New Avengers* and *Animal Magic*.

JOHNSON, Thomas Arnold (1908-89). Lived in the Wirral, Cheshire, all his life. Studied RMCM 1928-31. Fine pianist, initially in a 'silent' cinema, then in recital and on the BBC, and composer, mainly for piano solo or duet but also of other instrumental solos and songs. Works ranged from two piano sonatas to *Whispering Zephyr*, played by Billy Mayerl (*qv*), and *Cut Glass*, used by the TV Toppers, and much instructional music and included suites based on Greyfriars School characters and others with titles like *Pantomime People* and *Punch and Judy*, *Concert Valse*, a samba, *Lady of Brazil*, and the march *Total Victory*; later scored for military band.

JOHNSTONE, Maurice (1900-76). Born in Manchester; trained at RMCM and RCM. Mainly pursued a career as a musical administrator, as secretary to Sir Thomas Beecham (1932-5) and then with the BBC 1935-60, becoming Head of North Region Music 1938-53 and Head of Music Programmes 1955- 60. His classical arrangements are still played; compositions included songs (notably *Dover Beach*) and orchestral music, best of which is the 'Cumbrian Rhapsody' *Tarn Hows*. Earns a mention here for his bustling overtures *Sea Dogs* and *Banners*, his stirring band marches *Pennine Way*, *County Palatine*, *Watling Street* and *Beaufighters*, and the *Ballade* for saxophone and small orchestra: a companion perhaps to Coates' *Saxo-Rhapsody?*

JONES, Sidney (1861-1946). London-born; as a composer of operetta, his first hit was *A Gaiety Girl* (1893), although the enormously popular *The Geisha* (Daly's, 1896) and *San Toy* (1899) made his name for posterity. George Edwardes produced all these. *The King of Cadonia* (1908) was the most popular of the later shows. Jones retired from the musical stage in 1916; altogether he wrote 12 musicals, plus the ballets *The Bugle Call* and *Cinderella*, a number of separate songs, notably the *Three Japanese Lyrics* and *Sleep*, and a few early pieces of dance music. His father was a military bandmaster and conductor of the Harrogate Municipal Orchestra; Sidney played clarinet in this orchestra and then went into conducting, notably at the Prince of Wales and Empire Theatres in London.

JOSEPHS, Wilfred (1927-97). This very prolific and eclectic composer, once a dentist, has, in addition to many choral works, instrumental sonatas, concertos and 12 symphonies, produced many works which fall within the light music category: the comedy overture *The Ants* (1959), the *Monkchester Dances*, a *Concerto for Light Orchestra*, the *Wry Rumba* for wind quintet, and music for films (eg, *Rail*) and TV (*The British Empire, The Great War, Swallows and Amazons, Cider With Rosie, The Pallisers* and *I Claudius*), some 120 scores in all.

KEEL, Frederick James (1871-1954). Baritone singer, song composer and editor of folksongs and Elizabethan songs. His compositions include many settings of Shakespearean words but plenty of ballads, nautical ones (two sets of *Salt Water Ballads*, of which *Trade Winds* became especially popular, *A Sea Burthen* and *The Ship of Rio*) and others like *Dainty Little Maiden, Entreaty, Lullaby, Remembrance* and *There Sits a Bird*.

KELLY, Bryan (1934-). Educated RCM and later studied with Nadia Boulanger. Lecturer RCM. His eclectic style is well suited to the production of light music, such as the *Provence Overture, Divertimento*, the march *Washington DC.* and the *Edinburgh Dances*, all for brass band, the attractive *Capriccio* for wind quintet, and many light orchestral pieces. These include overtures like *The Dancing Master, Latin Quarter, Sancho Panza* and *San Francisco, Comedy Film for Orchestra* and suites like *Cuban Suite* (premiered at a BBC Light Music Festival), *Calypso's Isle, Four Realms, Irish Dances, The Tempest* and *Left Bank*; he also composed instrumental solos.

KENNEDY-FRASER, Marjory, CBE (1857-1930). Daughter of a Scots folk-singer whom she also accompanied on the piano early in life. Studied Milan and Paris. Best remembered for her arrangements, vocal and instrumental, of Hebridean songs published in three sets in 1909, 1925 and 1929; many of them were collected by herself from crofters, milkmaids and the like. Lectured and wrote on the subject. Arranged other folksongs, too. Sydney Baynes (*qv*) made an orchestral selection of her song arrangements in 1923. Daughter (Patuffa) also involved in arranging Hebridean songs; *The Road to the Isles* is hers, not Marjory's.
KING, Denis (1939-). Essex-born, studied GSM. Composes for TV (*Black Beauty, Hannay, Lovejoy*) and the theatre (eg, *Privates on Parade*).

LAMBERT, Constant (1905-51). One of the best brains in 20th century British music; achieved distinction as author (of the stimulating *Music Ho!*), conductor and composer. Died, sadly young, of drink and overwork. One of the first composers to combine jazz and classical idioms convincingly. Not a prolific composer but earns a mention here for his ballet scores (most famously *Horoscope*, but also *Pomona, Romeo and Juliet* and, after Purcell, *Comus*), his film music for *Merchant Seamen* and perhaps the exquisitely scored orchestral concert movement *Aubade Heroique*.

LANCHBERY, John (1923-). Conductor, especially of ballet and opera. Composer/arranger of ballet scores, notably *La Fille mal gardée*, after Hérold, several of them for films including *The Turning Point, Nijinsky* and the delectable *Tales of Beatrix Potter*, compiled from 19th-century British music, also music for radio and TV and the suite for brass quintet *Three Girls For Five Brass*.

LANE, Philip (1950-). Associated, as music adviser, with some of Marco Polo's light music CDs. Also prolific composer of short choral pieces, Shakespearean songs, light orchestral music (*Celebration Overture, A Spa Overture, Wassail Dances, Cotswold Folk Dances*) and brass band pieces: *The Bluebell Line, Praeludium, Yodelling Brass, Little Habanera, A Spring Overture* and *Spa Suite*.

LANGFORD, Alan (1928-2011). No relation to Gordon Langford; his real name is Alan Owen. Respected for his light orchestral miniatures: *Three Amusements, Little French Suite, Trio: Three Dance Contrasts, Petite Promenade, Dance for a Square, Chanson Populaire, Chanson du Café Triste* and a *Romanza* and *Waltz*, both for strings.

LANGFORD, Gordon (1930-) (really Gordon Coleman). Conductor, pianist and producer of an enormous number of highly inventive potpourris and arrangements for chorus (including the King's Singers), orchestras and bands, especially brass bands. Has also produced many original compositions, again especially for band: *Harmonious Variations on a Theme By Handel, Sinfonietta, Prelude and Fugue*, the *Metropolis Overture, Rhapsody* for trombone and band, *Carnival Day Dance* and the marches *The Seventies Set, Merry Mancunians, Titan, Carnival Day* and *March of the Pacemakers*. Studied RAM 1947-50, played in Royal Artillery Band and with various other bands. Later involved with West End theatrical shows and with writing for films and radio.

LEE, Ernest Markham (1874-1956). Cambridge-born, later Professor at GSM, author, examiner, pianist and organist. Composed much instructional music for young pianists and many short choral pieces, also light concert suites – *Moorland and Torland, West Country Suite, Rivers of Devon* (Tamar, Dart, Torridge, Lyn), *Round the North Sea, Light Heart* – and intermezzi (eg, *Florestina*) which were quite popular; his operetta *Paris in Spring* was less successful.

LE FLEMING, Christopher Kaye (1908-85). Educated Royal School of Church Music; schoolteacher, writer and railway enthusiast; Chairman of Composer's Guild of GB 1971. Produced much choral music, sacred and secular. His instrumental works, which include *Pilford Suite, London River* and *Sutton Valence*, all orchestral suites, *Homage to Beatrix Potter* for woodwind quintet (one of several Potter-inspired works) and the piano solos *Sunday Morning* and *Bramshaw Folly* are classifiable as light music.

LEHMANN, Liza (1862-1918). Born London, daughter and wife of composers (respectively Amelia Lehmann and Herbert Bedford). Concert singer and popular song composer, especially of the cycles *Parody Pie, Alice in Wonderland, In a Persian Garden, The Daisy Chain* (12 songs), *More Daisies* (12), *Five Nonsense Songs* and *The Life of a Rose* (7). Over 150 songs altogether; other popular titles included *Cherry Ripe, There are Fairies at the Bottom of Our Garden, The Cuckoo* and *At Love's Beginning*. Also composed an operetta, *Sergeant Brue*, an opera, *The Vicar of Wakefield*, a morality play, *Everyman*, large-scale choral works and children's stories with music eg, *The Happy Prince* and *The Selfish Giant*.

LEIGH, Walter (1905-42). Studied Cambridge University and in Berlin with Hindemith, whose style he often imitated. Wrote much light music, cleverly bridging the gap between serious and popular, especially for the stage – incidental music, revues, and the light operas *Jolly Roger* and *The Pride of the Regiment*. Killed in action in Libya.

LEMARE, Edwin Harry (1865-1934). Organist of Sheffield Parish Church 1886-92, later a touring concert organist (died in America). Copious organ compositions, including major pieces like two symphonies, also lighter suites *(Summer Sketches, Twilight Sketches, Festival Suite)* and many single movements, best known of which was the *Andantino* in D flat ('Moonlight and Roses'), which, much to his disgust, he was often asked to play.

LEVY, Louis (1893-1957). Active in films from 1916 and with Gaumont and Gainsborough 1928-47 as supervisor to the music side of all their productions. Difficult to say exactly which films he composed (as against being credited with) music for; certainly that for *The Citadel* (1938) was his, also the famous signature march for the Gaumont British News and an orchestral number, *Maltese Entr'acte*.

LIDDLE, Samuel (1867-1951). Born Leeds, studied with Stanford at RCM, then worked as pianist to concert parties with Clara Butt, Plunket Greene and W.H. Squire, among others. Compositions, apart from an *Elegy* for cello and piano (? for Squire), were mainly songs of the ballad type. Butt sang his *Abide with Me*; also popular were *How Lovely are Thy Dwellings, Like As the Hart, Arabic Love Song,* sung by McCormack, *A Farewell* and an arrangement of *The Garden Where the Praties Grow*.

LITER, Monia (1906-1988). Conductor of light music ensembles, especially on the BBC, and composer of, for example, *Mediterranean Suite, Two Southern Impressions* (a bolero and a rumba), *Serenade* for harp and strings, *Jota and Rhumba, Irish Jig* and *Cossack Dance,* all for orchestra, *Scherzo Transcendent* for piano and orchestra and a *Valse Melancholique* for piano solo.

LLOYD WEBBER, Andrew (1948-). Educated RAM but musically largely self-taught. Some of his breathtakingly popular stage works, especially *Jesus Christ Superstar,* are perhaps categorisable as 'rock' or 'pop' rather than 'light' but his ability to write memorable tunes ought to earn him a place here; he has been described as the Sullivan of the late 20th century. Apart from stage hits like *Joseph and His Amazing Technicolour Dreamcoat* (originally written for a school), *Evita, Cats, Starlight Express, Phantom of the Opera* and *Sunset Boulevard,* one may mention the originally less popular *Jeeves,* book by Alan Ayckbourn, and scores for the British films *Gumshoe* (1971) and *The Odessa File* (1974). Raised to the peerage 1997.

LLOYD WEBBER, W.S. (1914-82). Director, London College of Music, and father of Andrew, whose *Requiem* (1984) was dedicated to his father's memory, and cellist Julian. W.S. was a prolific composer, especially of organ, church and other choral music, and much of his output can be classed as 'light'. Many of his songs (*The Call of the Morning, To the Wicklow Hills, I Looked Out Into the Morning, Thank God for Life, So Lovely the Rose, To Mary* and *Four Bibulous Songs*) are ballads of one type or another. Piano pieces like *Bagatelle Gracieuse, Romantic Evening, Song Without Words* and *Scherzo* recall the great days of the salon, as do the orchestral *Three Spring Miniatures* and the *Waltz* in F minor. The 1950s seem to have been a peak for him, at least in the publication of his music.

LODGE, Herbert (fl 1920-40). Conductor Margate Municipal Orchestra 1928-39 and composer/arranger of orchestral items including the intriguingly titled *Tunelandia*.

LONGSTAFFE, Ernest (1888-1958). Best remembered for his foot-tapping ballad *When the Sergeant Major's on Parade*; other song tributes to men in uniform include *The Captain of the Fire Brigade*, *Here Come the Guards*, *The Leader of the Town Brass Band*, *The Recruit*, *Home Guards*, (this appeared also in instrumental guise), *Where's the Sergeant?* and *What's the Matter with PC Brown?* There were other songs, also musical monologues, stage works like the musical *His Girl* and the revue *Up With the Lark*, and a march, *Palace of Varieties*. Margaret Longstaffe, surely a relative (? wife or sister), composed the *NFS March* in 1944.

LOUGHBOROUGH, Raymond H. (died 1967). Song composer of the 'superior ballad' type, most popular titles being *At Sundown*, *The Lover and the Song* and *The Homing Ship*. Like so many English ballad composers, many of his songs indeed have a feel of the sea: *My Haven*, the four-song sequence *Old Ships* and, inspired by Dunkirk, *The Little Ships*. Like Alfred Reynolds and H. Lane Wilson (both *qv*), among others, he arranged many 18th century English songs. His orchestral works – *Jevington Suite*, *Passing Shadows*, *Sea Dreams*, *Summer Noon* – were orchestrated by people like Baynes, Arthur Wood and H.M. Higgs (all *qv*) and may have been piano originals; he produced a few light genre pieces for chamber ensemble, eg, *Mirage* and *Song of Sunset*.

LUBBOCK, Mark (1898-1986). Educated Eton and in Vienna, served in Great War; conducted theatrical touring companies, then worked at BBC 1933-44. Wrote many musical plays (*The King Can Do No Wrong* was the first 'opera' to be specially composed and broadcast for radio); his songs achieved popularity (*A Smuggler's Song*, *The Whispering Poplar*, *Lullaby River*), as did his orchestral novelties – *Saltarello*, *Moon Lullaby* and, especially often played in its day, the cheerful *Polka Dots*.

MACBETH, Allen (1856-1910). Greenock-born, studied at the Leipzig Conservatory, then conducted the Glasgow Choral Union, held organists' positions in Scotland and directed the Glasgow Atheneum Music School. A light music composer? Yes; for in amongst his chamber music and cantatas we find an operetta, *The Duke's Doctor*, incidental music for *Bruce, Lord of the Isles* (a play after Scott) and a considerable number of 'Grand Hotel'-type orchestral minatures, of which we can instance *Heart's Ease*,

Romantic Melody and, most celebrated of all, the much arranged *Forget-me-Not*.

MACEWAN, Désirée (1902-c.1970). Syncopated pianist in the Billy Mayerl manner; her composition *Sweet Lavender* is reminiscent of Mayerl both in title and idiom. More seriously, her orchestral poem *Clam Var* was premiered at the Proms 1921 and her *Summertime Fancies* for piano solo was published.

MACKERRAS, Sir Alan Charles McLaurin (1925-2011). American-born; domiciled first in Australia, then in Britain since the 1950s. Conductor, especially at Sadler's Wells/ENO and of BBC Concert Orchestra 1954-6. Inventive arranger of ballet scores based on Sullivan (*Pineapple Poll*) and Verdi (*The Lady and the Fool*) and composer of music for various BBC radio productions.

MACLEAN, Alexander Morvaren ('Alick') (1872-1936). Affectionately called 'the God of Scarborough', he conducted that resort's Spa Orchestra with brilliant success between 1911 and 1935. He was perhaps the finest resort conductor after Bournemouth's Dan Godfrey. His compositions in general hardly reflected this, as his major works included an oratorio and no fewer than nine operas, some of them produced in Germany. On the lighter side, we can however point to his incidental music for plays like *Cyrano de Bergerac* and *The Jest* and his contributions to the musical farce *The White Silk Dress*. Father (Charles Donald MacLean, 1843-1916) was also a prolific composer of *inter alia*, light orchestral works.

MACLEAN, Quentin Stuart Morvaren (1896-1962). Son of foregoing. Organist at various London churches and theatres, notably the Trocadero and the Elephant & Castle, where he recorded in the 1930s. Later went to USA. Compositions included *Babbling*, *Rondolet* and *Parade of the Sunbeams*, equally charming in its original organ version and an orchestral arrangement.

MANTOVANI, Annunzio Paolo (1905-80), known usually just as 'Mantovani'. Born in Venice, settled in London from 1921. Violinist (father played under Toscanini at La Scala), composer and conductor. Led Hotel Metropole Orchestra 1925, later went into broadcasting and recording in a big way. He introduced the 'cascading strings' motif, though its invention should be credited to Ronald Binge (*qv*). Became the King of 'Mood Music' post-1945. Compositions included *Red Sails in the Sunset*,

Serenade in the Night, Poem to the Moon, September Nocturne, Bullfrog and – especially celebrated – *Charmaine,* mostly for orchestra. *Moulin Rouge* became a UK chart hit in 1953.

MARTIN, Frederick John Easthope (1882-1925). Born in Stourport; studied with Coleridge-Taylor (*qv*) at Trinity College, London. Suffered poor health and had to spend much time on the French Riviera. Best-known composition was *Evensong,* variously arranged; other instrumental works included *Souvenirs* for piano, *Castanets* (violin/piano) and *Two Eastern Dances* for orchestra, premiered at the Proms. Most of his output was for the voice, including some church music and many ballad-style songs. He, like Squire, Sanderson and Molloy, had an orchestral selection of his ballads made by Henry Geehl (*qv*). Many were grouped into cycles like *Songs of the Hedgerow; Songs of Syria* and *Songs of the Fair* (3 sets), from which *Come to the Fair* is still popular; other separate titles included *One and Twenty* and *Who Goes a-Walking?*

MAY, Simon (1944-). Educated Cambridge University, then taught at Kingston GS. Composed a musical *Smike* (after Dickens' *Nicholas Nickleby*) and credited with a vast amount of TV music, eg, for *Eastenders, Trainer* and *Howard's Way.*

McCALL, J. Peter (really Peter Dawson) (1882-1961). Baritone singer, born Adelaide, Australia, came to England 1902; prominent in opera, concert and on record. Most famous composition was the ballad *Boots;* but there were many other similar ones, eg, *Deep-Sea Mariner, The Jolly Roger, The Pirate Goes West, Route Marchin', Song of the Drum* and *The Lord is King;* from the titles one can almost hear Dawson singing them. Dawson used other pseudonyms for his compositions.

MEALE, John Arthur (1880-1932). Born Slaithwaite (Yorks); Musical Director at Central Hall, Westminster 1912-32. Composed anthems and songs and many organ pieces in an 'orchestral' style which are light in character: *Fountain Melody, In Peril on the Sea, The Magic Harp, At Sunrise, A Storm at Sea, A Night at Sea, Twilight* and *A Summer Idyll.*

MELACHRINO, George (1909-65). London-born, into a musical family; studied at Trinity College, London. Showed remarkable versatility, playing violin, viola, saxophone and clarinet and singing with various 1930s dance bands. Army service in World War II, during which he conducted and formed the Orchestra in Khaki and the British Band of the Allied

Expeditionary Force (1944). After the war created the 'Melachrino Sound' (close harmony string writing) with his own orchestra, which played and popularised many new light music compositions, not least Melachrino's own: *Winter Sunshine, Ode to Strings* ('Waltz in Water Colours'), the busy *Woodland Revel* and the *Starlight Roof Waltz*, from a revue of 1947. Also composed songs and music for many feature films, including the notorious *No Orchids for Miss Blandish*. Prolific recording artist: made 100 78s, over 50 LPs.

MENGES, Herbert (1902-72). To be reckoned a holiday orchestra conductor because he founded and directed the Brighton (later Southern) Philharmonic Orchestra 1925-72, though he conducted orchestras elsewhere, especially in London theatres like the Old Vic and Sadler's Wells. Composed music for Shakespeare plays put on at the former theatre and a delicate score for Gordon Daviot's popular play *Richard of Bordeaux*. His songs included ballads such as *Buckland Bells* and *The Little Seamstress*. Studied RCM with Vaughan Williams and Holst.

MILLER, George (1877-1960). Conductor of various military bands, especially Grenadier Guards 1922-42. His grand march *Galatea* was popular.

MOLLOY, James (1837-1909). Irish-born composer of operettas, Irish folksong arrangements and ballads, including *Love's Old Sweet Song, The Postilion, Voices, Darby and Joan, Bantry Bay* and *The Kerry Dance*. Sydney Baynes (*qv*) made an orchestral selection of his best-remembered songs.

MONCKTON, Lionel John Alexander (1861-1924). Educated at Charterhouse and Oxford University. Called to the Bar 1885, then wrote dramatic and music criticism for the *Pall Mall Gazette* and the *Daily Telegraph*. Composing career in the theatre began with a single song used in the George Edwardes burlesque *Cinder-Ella* (1891). Continued to compose for Edwardes, at first often in collaboration with Ivan Caryll (eg, in *The Circus Girl, A Runaway Girl* and *Our Miss Gibbs*), then often with Howard Talbot, especially in *The Arcadians* (1909) and *The Mousme* (1912). *The Country Girl* (1902) and *The Quaker Girl* (1910), amongst others, appear to be more or less entirely his own work; these two and *The Arcadians* have remained popular with amateurs into our own day. His gift for writing striking melodies like *Soldiers in the Park* ('Listen to the Band'), coupled with the virtue of self-criticism, made his work stand out in the Edwardian theatre. Altogether contributed to over 20 musicals. Married to Gertie Millar, for whom he wrote some of his best numbers.

MONTGOMERY, Robert Bruce (1921-78). Educated Merchant Taylors' School and Oxford University. Many of his approachable, even romantic, compositions were for voice(s), but we include him here on the strength of his 38 film scores (including three of the Richard Gordon 'Doctor' films, also *Escapade* and *Eye Witness*) and his ballad opera *John Barleycorn* (1965). Also wrote ingenious and entertaining detective stories under the name Edmund Crispin; most have musical references, two allude to film music.

MORLEY, Angela (1924-2009). Remembered for her attractive orchestral piece *A Canadian in Mayfair* (1953: the 'Canadian' is Robert Farnon: *qv*). Later went to USA and wrote much for the large and small screen. Her big screen hit was the lovely music for *Watership Down* (1978). Also composed under the name Wally Stott.

MOSS, Katie (1881-1947). Violinist, pianist and singer, deserves mention as the composer of *The Floral Dance*, a 'chart hit' of 1911 and at times since and one of the most popular ballads of all time, said to have been written immediately after a visit to Helston in Cornwall. Other ballad titles included *The Morris Dancers*, *Come Away Moonlight*, *Out of the Silence* and the five-song cycle *Dreams of Youth*.

MULDOWNEY, Dominic (1952-). Once a pupil of Harrison Birtwistle and regarded as an avant-garde composer, but has written much attractive music in lighter vein, a ballet, *The Brontes*, and scores for dramatic productions – especially at the National Theatre – and TV, an example being his music for Jane Austen's *Emma*, part composed, part selected from contemporary sources.

MULLINAR, Michael (1895-1973). Composer of the 'superior ballad' type. Unfortunately for him, some of his song-titles became better known in versions by others: *I Will Go With My Father a-Ploughing* (1951), *The Smuggler's Song* and *To Daffodils*. Other titles worth reviving are *Cotswold Love*, *The Seas are Quiet* and *Cider*. Interested in music for children – wrote cantata *The Princess and the Swineherd*, the nursery rhyme arrangement *Pippin Hill* and a piano suite, *Grimms' Fairy Tales* – and in folksong, in which field he made many arrangements. Also pianist and arranger, eg of Vaughan Williams' *Greensleeves*.

MURRAY, Alan (1890-1952). Active until well after World War II as a composer of ballads (*Too Tired to Sleep*, *The Wandering Player*, *Love is the*

Star and, easily the most popular, *I'll Walk Beside You)* and instrumental miniatures like *I Had a Dream*.

MYDDLETON, William Herbert (died 1917). Arranger of popular orchestral and band potpourris on traditional tunes *(The Leek, The Rose, By the Swanee River, Down South)*. Also composed, for piano *(Eventide)* and songs (eg, *Lorna Doone)*.

MYERS, Stanley (1930-93). American-born but English-domiciled. Known for his *Cavatina*, very popular in vocal and instrumental (especially guitar solo) versions, originally from the film *The Deer Hunter*, and for much other powerful incidental film music, eg, for *Castaway; Kaleidoscope, The Lightship* and *Lady Chatterley's Lover*.

NELSON, Havelock (1917-). Educated Trinity College, Dublin, and Royal Irish Academy. After wartime RAF service joined the BBC in Belfast 1943, where he conducted the BBC Northern Ireland Light Orchestra and other ensembles. Prolific composer of orchestral works, a ballet, a choral suite, many songs and partsongs, *Three Irish Diversions* for piano, *Cameos* for clarinet and incidental music for radio and TV plays and films. Forced to retire in 1977 on reaching BBC retiring age of 60 (how absurd), he then went to Trinidad to direct a local opera company.

NEWMAN, Eldridge (died 1940). Conductor of the Folkestone Municipal Orchestra 1928-39 and composer of the ballet suite *Les Lutins* and a *Dorset Suite* whose finale, 'The Old Josser's Dance', achieved popularity.

NEWSOME, Roy (1930-). Yorkshire-born, from a brass band family. Conductor (eg, of Slaithwaite, Black Dyke, Stanshawe, Besses O' Th' Barn and Fairey Bands and the National Youth Band of Great Britain), adjudicator, broadcaster, lecturer (in Band Studies) at Salford College of Technology and composer for brass. His works include the concert overture *The Legend of the Chateau de Chillon*, the *BBC March*, *Westward Suite*, *Suite for Switzerland*, *Two London Sketches*, single movements like *North West Passage, Roller Coaster, Father Neptune, Sylvia* and *Hat Trick* and solos for cornet, soprano cornet and E flat bass (*Bass in the Ballroom* is quite popular, possibly because bass solos are relatively few).

NICHOLLS, Frederick (fl 1920-40). Composer of superior ballads (*Tears, Idle Tears, Eldorado, Foreign Lands, Our Ship, Blow Bugle Blow*) and instrumental miniatures like the piano solos *Meadow Dance* and *Dancing Midges*.

NICHOLLS, Horatio (really Lawrence Wright) (1888-1964). Composer under various names of an enormous number of popular songs, eg, *Down Forget-Me-Not-Lane, Among My Souvenirs, Back to Those Happy Days, That Old Fashioned Mother of Mine, When the Guards Are on Parade, Babette, Blue Eyes* and *Amy* in honour of the aviator Amy Johnson) and of instrumental pieces like the waltzes *Omaha, Delilah, Fate* and *Peace,* the novelty entr'acte *Clodhoppers' Dance* and the march *Golden Mile.* Other Wright pseudonyms were Gene Williams and Betsy O'Hogan, under which latter name the popular *Old Father Thames* appeared.

NOBLE, Harold (fl 1935-80). Mainly associated with music for voices (eg, radio opera *The Lake of Menleuth, Variations on Polly Put the Kettle On* for chorus and orchestra, *Laughing Song, King Charles, The Hills* for tenor and women's chorus, the very popular *Do You Remember an Inn, Miranda?,* much church music and many arrangements of folksongs) but also composed the elegy for brass *Tintern Abbey;* the *Arietta* for horn and piano, and *The Blue Train,* published for piano solo, etc.

NOBLE, John (1936-2006). Formerly lecturer at Doncaster College. First compositions were for the Doncaster College Repertory Players' Children's Theatre shows; these led during the 1970s to concert works, including sonatas for clarinet, saxophone and recorder, a saxophone quartet and, in lighter form, the *Cats' Suite* for clarinet and piano, a suite for two clarinets and piano, *Fiesta* for piano duet and *Fairy Dances* for recorder and piano written for a concert on one Friday 13th, in 13-bar phrases with a 13-note 'motto'.

NOVELLO, Ivor (really David Ivor Davies) (1893-1951). Actor, playwright and composer. Born Cardiff, son of music teacher and composer Clara Novello Davies. Played piano, sang in Magdalen College Choir as a boy. Published first song at 17; *Keep the Home Fires Burning* and *Till the Boys Come Home* were hits of 1914-18. First musical comedy produced 1916; later co-operated with lyricists P.G. Wodehouse (*The Golden Moth,* 1921) and Christopher Hassall (all his most famous shows, from 1935 onwards – *Glamorous Night, Careless Rapture, Crest of the Wave, The Dancing Years, Arc de Triomphe, Perchance to Dream, King's Rhapsody*). A superb melodist, mention of whom we can scarcely leave out of this book.

O'NEILL, Norman Houstoun (1875-1934). One of the 'Frankfurt School' of composers, along with Quilter, Balfour Gardiner and Percy Grainger (all *qv*). Produced over 50 scores of incidental music for plays from

Shakespeare to J.M. Barrie (the 'Prelude and Call' from *Mary Rose* became popular) and Maeterlinck (dances from *The Blue Bird* were done at the Proms), also ballets and many non-theatre orchestral compositions – *Two Shakespearean Sketches*, *Variations on an Irish Air*, the suited *Fairy Tale* and the overtures *In Springtime* and *In Autumn* – plus songs and piano music. Died, following a street accident, in the same year as Elgar, Holst and Delius.

ORNADEL, Cyril (1924-2011). Conductor, arranger and composer of musicals (*Pickwick*, *Treasure Island*, *Ann Veronica* and *Great Expectations*) and orchestral miniatures (*Sunday Afternoon*). He also composed film scores.

PALMER, Cedric King (1913-99). A native of Sussex, but long London domiciled and educated at RAM and TCL, he has excelled as composer, pianist, violinist, cellist, oboist, singer, lecturer, author and conductor (of the King Palmer Light Orchestra and other ensembles). His potpourris of Sousa marches and Offenbach galops are among the most popular of his many arrangements, but he also produced much original work, for stage shows (*Gay Romance*, 1937, and *The Snow Queen*, for instance), films (*Cockney Kids' Adventure*), piano solo, and orchestra – suites (*Down a Country Lane*, *Out of Doors*, *Eight Period Pieces*), genre movements (*Paddle Steamer*, *Frivolity*, *Hackney Carriage*, *Country Market*), 'activity music' suitable for radio and film titles (he is credited with 300 recorded pieces of 'mood music') and marches (*With Pomp and Pride*, *Kingsway* and *March of the Astronauts*).

PARAMOR, Norrie (1914-79). Conductor of various light orchestras, including BBC Midland Radio Orchestra from 1972, arranger and composer of film scores and mood music. Wrote music for the Richard Gordon film *Doctor in Distress*. Most famous for his arrangement of *Z Cars* theme music.

PARKER, Alan (1944-). Educated RAM; guitarist, composer of a mass and scores for 20 films (*Jaws 3D*) and 75 TV features, including the 1996 BBC spectacular *Rhodes*, *Minder* and *Angels*.

PARKER, Clifton (1905-89). Largely self-educated. Writer of music for many films, including *HMS Defiant*, *Mystery Submarine*, *The Blue Lagoon*, *The Wooden Horse* and, most famously, *Sink the Bismarck* (1960), whose rousing march was separately published. But he also composed for the theatre – the musical *The Glass Slipper*, incidental music for *Othello*, unison songs for *As You Like It* and various short dramatic pieces – songs, piano and other instrumental music and much for orchestra: the light suites *The Land of Nod* and *Phantasy Suite*, pieces in Latin American mood and the popular seascape *Western Approaches*.

PARR-DAVIES, Harry (1914-55). Remembered as a writer of memorable songs, sometimes published separately but mostly inserted in films (*Shipyard Sally, We're Going to be Rich, Lassie for Lancashire* and *The Show Goes On*) or forming part of stage shows like *Lisbon Story* (1943: *Pedro the Fisherman* was the hit of this), *Jenny Jones, Her Excellency, The Glorious Days* and *Dear Miss Phoebe* (1951), famous for *I Leave My Heart in an English Garden*.

PATTERSON, Paul Leslie (1947-). Chesterfield-born, studied RAM, then with Richard Rodney Bennett. Latterly lecturer RAM. Interested in electronic music, but like Bennett a versatile composer, his output embracing many forms from serial to light. In this latter category we can instance the *Comedy for Five Winds* for wind quintet, *The Royal Eurostar* and *Eurostar Fanfares* (1994) for brass (has also composed much for brass band, but often in a 'modern-experimental' style) and some film music.

PEARSON, Johnny (died 2001). Devotees of *All Creatures Great and Small* will be familiar with his delightful title tune music; almost as famous is his other TV tune, 'Sleepy Shore' from *Owen MD*.

PEEL, Gerald Graham (1878-1937). Born in Manchester and died in Bournemouth. Studied at Harrow and (with Ernest Walker) Oxford. Apart from a few piano pieces, his compositions are all songs, of which he wrote about a hundred, exclusive of folksong settings. (He had studied singing with George Henschel). These songs hover in idiom between ballad and art-song; most famous is *In Summertime on Bredon*, one of four Housman *Shropshire Lad* settings. Other cycles included two for children and *The Country Lover;* 'singles' popular in their day were *The Early Morning, Flow Down, Cold Rivulet* and *The Lute Player* (although Frances Allitsen's setting has survived better). Peel's generously lyrical gift deserves better of posterity.

PENN, Arthur A. (1875-1941). Composed comic operas around the end of World War I (*The Lass of Limerick Town*, 1917; *Captain Crossbones*, 1918; and *Mam'zelle Taps*, 1919) but by far his best known song was

Smilin' Through, written for an eponymous stage show in 1919 and much later incorporated into two similarly named Hollywood talkies. Other ballad titles included *The Honeysuckle and the Bee* and *Gingham Green*.

PHELOUNG, Barrington (1954-). Australian-born, studied RCM, now lecturer there. Conductor; composed music for *Inspector Morse*, *Nostradamus*, *Days of Majesty* and many other TV features in approachable and attractive style, also concertos for guitar, cello, etc.

PITT, Percy (1869-1932). London-born, German-trained. Conductor, especially of opera (Covent Garden; BNOC), then Musical Adviser to infant BBC until 1930. Prolific composer – his music is highly competent, but often lacking in individuality: ballads, instrumental solos and orchestral music, including, on the lighter side, the *Coronation March* (1896), *Air de Ballet*, *Suite de Ballet* (1901), *Three Old English Dances* (1903), *Serenade* (1910), *Aria* for strings (1913) and the *Sakura* ballet suite (1914), all premiered at the Proms.

POSFORD, George (really Benjamin George Ashwell) (1906-76). Folkestone-born composer of musicals, like *Good Night Vienna* (probably the most popular), *Balalaika*, *Gay Hussar* and *Magyar Melody*, and of orchestral pieces like *Transatlantic Rhapsody*, *Broadcasting House*, *Sundown Serenade* and *Song of the Clyde*; also composed for radio and films.

POWELL, Thomas James (1897-1965), Welsh brass band conductor and composer of the *Snowdon Fantasy* and numerous marches: *The Spaceman*, *The Contestor* and several featuring Welsh castles, Caernarvon, Cardiff, Caerphilly and (most often played) Coch.

PRICE, Richard Maldwyn (1890-1952). A native of Welshpool and the first D.Mus (Wales) after study at the University College of Wales at Aberystwyth. Organist, choirmaster and schoolmaster; his compostions included sacred choral works, string quartets and, for brass band, *Owain Glyndwr* and *Henry V*, which were adopted as test-pieces at the Open Championships in 1938 and 1941 respectively. Much of his orchestral music is light in character: *Bijou Suite*, *Cambrian Suite* (for strings), *Gwalia Suite*, *Recreative Suite*, jolly overtures *(Concert Overture, English Overture, A Little Overture)* and individual genre pieces such as *Air de Ballet*, *Bolero*, *Concert Valse* and *Fantasy on Captain Morgan's War Song*.

RABINOWITZ, Harry, MBE (1916-). Born in Johannesburg, educated at Witwatersrand University and GSM. Went to BBC in 1953 after experience in West End theatres; in radio 1953-60, BBC Television 1960-68, then with ITV 1968-77 before going freelance. Directed some of the BBC's lighter orchestras but also had experience with the LSO, LPO, RPO, Philharmonia Orchestra, RLPO, Boston Pops and LAPO. Composed film, TV and radio music *(Love For Lydia, Thomas and Sarah)*. A good pianist; his *Strolling Player* was published for piano solo.

RAPLEY, Felton (1907-76). Another prolific arranger, he also composed widely: church music, unison songs suitable for children, solos for piano and organ (he excelled as a performer on both instruments) and many pieces for orchestra in a generally light style. These included an overture, *Down the Solent, A Highland Vision, An Irish Legend, Twilight Meditation, Evening in Capri, Elegy for Strings, String Prelude* and the march *Metropolis*.

RAWLINSON, Harold (1891-1978). One of the lesser-known followers of Eric Coates and Haydn Wood in writing light orchestral suites and genre pieces, though like them he also produced popular songs such as *Dear Susan, The Philosopher* and *Heigho Youth*. Orchestral suites included *In the Days of Chivalry* (a suite of troubadour songs), a lyric suite for strings, *The Open Road* (Song of the Open Road, Song on the Hills, By the Camp Fire) and an overture and two suites of incidental music to *The Maid of Orleans*. Popular single movements were *In a Kentish Garden, Serenade* and *Aubade*.

RAWSTHORNE, Alan (1905-71). Earns a place here primarily because of his work around the time of World War II, when he composed music for 22 films (including *The Cruel Sea)*, four plays and radio features, also arrangements of popular French songs; his attractive light suite *The Creel*, for four hands, one piano, dates from 1950; and the *Street Corner* overture (1944) is one of the best in the tradition of British light comedy overtures. In 1964 he composed a *Suite for Brass Band*. A later example was the *Overture for Farnham* (1967). Interestingly he found musical inspiration in T.S. Eliot's *Practical Cats* in 1954, decades before Andrew Lloyd Webber (*qv*); his music for the ballet *Madame Chrysanthème* (1955) is attractive.

READE, Paul (1943-). Studied at the RAM. Composer of very approachable ballet scores including *Byron*, premiered 1996, and the earlier *Hobson's Choice*, also of instructional music, incidental music for TV (*Jane Eyre*, from which a suite was published, *Great Expectations, Great Railway Journeys* and *A Tale of Two Cities*), instrumental miniatures (Aspects *of a Landscape* for oboe, 1987), a saxophone quartet, *Waltz* for strings, etc.

REDMAN, Reginald (1892-1972). Studied at Guildhall School and joined the BBC, where in the 1940s formed the West Country Studio Orchestra which was confined by its size largely to light music. A prolific composer of concertos, an opera, a cantata, tone poems, many songs and chamber music his lighter effusions included the suites *Marston Court, From a Moorish Village* and the folky *West Country Suite,* a *Rhapsody on Somerset Folk Songs* and the charming *Away on the Hills* for strings.

REED, William H. (1876-1942). Studied RAM, violinist (friendly with Elgar, about whom he wrote two books) and conductor. Composer of a symphony, a violin concerto, symphonic poems and chamber music, also of much music for students and, most popular in their day, pieces which may be reckoned as light music: the overtures *Merry Andrew* and *Touchstone,* the suites *Scenes from the Ballet, Aesop's Fables, Down in the West Country; Suite Venitienne* and *Miniature Suite* and individual genre pieces like *The Lincoln Imp, Shockheaded Peter, Will o'the Wisp, Valse Brillante* and *Valse Elegante.*

REED, William Leonard (1910-2002). Educated RCM; lecturer, for British Council, and teacher. Composer in a wide variety of forms, some of them light in character – musicals, eg, *The Vanishing Island* (1955), *Annie* (1967) and *Love All* (1978), orchestral pieces like the *Concert Overture* of 1950, *Mountain House Suite, Festive March, Three Dance Movements, Idyll* and *Scherzo,* also piano music (*Three Surrey Impressions* and *Four Child Portraits*).

REILLY, Tommy MBE (1919-2000). Canadian-born harmonica player; settled in England 1935. Michael Spivakovsky wrote a concerto for him (1951); he gave the premiere of *Prelude and Dance* by Robert Farnon (*qv*) in 1966. Composer of incidental music for radio, TV and films and short concert pieces for harmonica (the *Serenade* has been recorded).

REYNOLDS, Wynford Hubert (1899-1958). Directed the Felixstowe Spa Orchestra in the 1930s and broadcast with this and the Raeburn Orchestra. Composed his own signature tune, *Spa Song* (also known as *Cocktail of Happiness*), a waltz *Morning Glory* and the novelties *Stringing Along* and *Twinkletoes.* Some of his compositions were published under the name Hugh Raeburn.

RICHARDS, Goff (1944-). Educated RCM, taught in schools and at Salford College of Technology before going freelance. Conducted brass and wind bands and choirs; prolific arranger for choirs and bands – compositions, mostly for band, include *The Aeronauts, Oceans, Cornish Fantasia*, the *Jaguar* march, *Continental Caprice* and the *Saddleworth Festival Overture*.

RICHARDSON, Clive (1908-98). Born in Paris of English parents, studied RAM. Composed mostly for orchestra, though his works include a number of songs, much film music, the 'hymn of praise' *Salute to Industry*, for chorus and orchestra, and a tantalising instrumental piece, *Three Flemish Folk Tunes* for two harps and oboe (obviously for the Goossens family). Especially remembered for his relaxed short orchestral genre piece *Beachcomber* (1949) and the *London Fantasia* for piano and orchestra, a depiction of the Battle of Britain, but also worthy of mention are *Continental Galop, White Cliffs, Running off the Rails* and two signature tunes, *Melody on the Move* and *Tom Marches On*, the 'ITMA' march, one of many musical contributions to that programme by him.

RIEGO, Teresa del (1876-1968). Born of Spanish parents in London. Studied London and Paris; sang many times in public, especially in charity concerts during both world wars (she was widowed in the first one). Composed over 300 works, mainly solo songs of the ballad type, most famous of which was *Homing*, which appeared in 1917. Other titles popular in their day were *O Dry Those Tears, Harvest, Thank God for a Garden, The Reason, Slave Song* and *Sink Red Sun*. She set French, German and Spanish words as well as English; some of her songs were suitable for children. Her gift of melody set her above the average among ballad composers.

RIMMER, William (1862-1936). From a brass band family. Conducted major brass bands up to 1910, also prolific composer of brass band music – many marches (*Knight of the Road, The Australasian, Slaidburn, The Cross of Honour, Viva Birkinshaw, Punchinello* and *The Cossack* are only a few), instrumental solos *(Silver Showers, Hailstorm* and *Cleopatra)*, the *Rule Britannia* overture and many arrangements of classical orchestral works. Rimmer's own orchestral compositions *(Southport Belles* march, *The Bells of St Malo* and *Wedding Bells)* have survived less well than his brass band works, which are still played, as are those of William's nephew, Drake Rimmer.

ROBERTON, Sir Hugh Stevenson (1874-1952). Founder and conductor of Glasgow Orpheus Choir 1901-51), also adjudicator. Produced an enormous number of choral arrangements of popular tunes and many original choral compositions, including the perennial favourite, *All in the April Evening*.

ROBINSON, Eric, OBE (1908-74). Brother of Stanford (*qv*). Educated RCM, orchestral player. After war service went into TV 1947, conducting and presenting 'Music For You' and other programmes. His compositions include *Novelloitis* and *Television Chimes*, both for orchestra.

ROBINSON, Stanford, OBE (1904-84). Leeds-born conductor, of BBC Theatre and BBC Opera Orchestras between 1932 and 1952 and of various other orchestras on a freelance basis. Also arranger of traditional and popular melodies and operatic selections (eg, a set of *Savoy Dances* from G & S) and composer of original ballads (*To You Eternally*; *A Prairie Lullaby*), choral pieces (*The Three Crows*), a *Rondo* for two pianos, the *Valse Serenade* for orchestra, incidental music, etc.

ROE, Betty (1930-). Trained RAM, London; has worked as singer, musical director, coach, adjudicator, examiner, etc. Composer of chamber operas and much choral and solo vocal music, mostly serious but including books of cabaret-style songs and numerous musicals and entertainments for children, nearly all written in collaboration with librettist Marian Lines.

RONALD, Sir Landon (really Landon Ronald Russell) (1873-1938). Studied RCM. Conductor, especially of New Symphony (Royal Albert Hall) and Scottish Orchestras, pioneer recording artiste and Principal of GSM 1910-38. Wrote 300 songs, many of the ballad type (*Down in the Forest, O Lovely Night* and *June Rhapsody* were the most popular), an operetta, *A Capital Joke*, two ballets and incidental music to *The Garden of Allah*, a concert suite from which was aired at the Proms in 1920.

ROSE, David (1910-90). London-born, settled in America as a boy but his orchestral pieces *Holiday for Strings* (1942), *Big Ben* and *Dance of the Spanish Onion* were popular with British, as well as American, light orchestras.

ROSSBOROUGH, Patricia (1902-92). Virtuoso pianist in the syncopated style, who made many records between the wars and may fairly be ranked with Billy Mayerl (*qv*) and Raie da Costa (*qv*). Published three piano solos: *Darts and Doubles*, *Hong Kong Haggis*, both 'syncopated', and *Irish Country Dance*, more folky.

ROWLEY, Alec (1892-1958). London-born and trained at RAM; pianist, organist, teacher, writer and composer. His compositions were legion and very approachable – a large proportion of them had a teaching element, others were classical, notably two piano concertos, two piano sonatas, two organ symphonies and a string quartet. But many of them count as light music – miniature concertos for piano, violin, cello and organ, suites in the Eric Coates mould like *Three Arcadian Pictures*, *English Dance Suite*, *Country Idylls* and *Nautical Suite*, all for orchestra, similar effusions for small chamber ensembles and piano (eg, *Aquarium*, *Chinese Suite* and *Three Centuries* – cf Coates' orchestral *Four Centuries*) and some of his many songs, both solo and choral. Died on the tennis court.

RUBENS, Alfred Paul (1875-1917). Lyricist and composer of works for the theatre. The longest-running musical comedies for which he wrote at least some of the music were *The Toreador* (1901), *Miss Hook of Holland* (1907), *Tonight's the Night* (1914) and *Betty* (1915). Of these, *Miss Hook of Holland* was the one particularly taken up by British amateur societies.

RUSSELL, Kennedy (died 1954). A writer of popular songs, like *As You Pass By*, *Young Tom o'Devon*, *The Church Bells of England*, *At Santa Barbara* and *Gypsy Dan*; other songs were incorporated into film, revue and operetta. For orchestra he wrote the genre pieces *Tinkabelle* and *Old Romance*; pianists enjoyed his *Little Clockwork Fairy* and the light suite *The Wooing of the Snowflakes*.

RUTTER, John (1945-). Educated Highgate School and Clare College, Cambridge, where he became Director of Music 1975-9. Conductor and composer of approachable and very tuneful larger-scale choral pieces (*Gloria*, *Requiem*, *Magnificat*) and shorter anthems, services, carols – both originals and arrangements, all spicy and attractive, usually with orchestra accompaniments – folksong settings etc., also a folk-based *Suite for Strings* and the *Suite Antique* for flute and strings.

SCOTT, Cyril Meir (1879-1970). Member of 'Frankfurt School' of composers. Wrote much chamber music, concertos and operas but his piano miniatures *Lotus Land*, *Water Wagtail* and *Danse Negre* became very popular light classics.

SCOTT-WOOD, George (1903-78). Glasgow-born; a classical pianist in his youth but went into popular music in the 1920s. Director of Light Music for Parlophone 1930-39. An exponent of the piano-accordion, both as a soloist and in various bands he formed. Light orchestral compositions include *Penny Farthing Polka*, *The Flying Scotsman*, *Dainty Debutante*, *London Caprice*, *Holiday for Accordions*, *Shy Serenade* (his signature tune) and a suite *Carnival of Bacchus*, representing four drinks, Amontillado (a Spanish-flavoured number), Moselle, Tokay (a czardas) and Champagne (a galop).

SEMPRINI, Alberto (usually called 'Semprini', simply) (1908-90). Of Anglo-Italian parentage; popular in concert and on radio. Produced many arrangements for piano or piano and orchestra; original compositions included *Variations on a Boogie* for piano solo, songs, and the *Mediterranean Concerto*, used as the signature tune for his radio feature 'Semprini Serenade'.

SHADWELL, Charles (1898-1979). Sometime Conductor of BBC Dance Orchestra post 1945. His many compositions included the march *Down With the Curtain*, and the genre pieces *Will o' the Wisp*, *Sunset* and *Lulworth Cove*.

SHARP, Cecil (1859-1924). Educated Uppingham and Clare College, Cambridge. Collected, in UK and US, nearly 5,000 British folk-song and dance tunes, 1,118 of which were published, 501 with accompaniments, and supplied incidental music for Shakespeare's *A Midsummer Night's Dream* (1914).

SHARPE, Trevor L. (1921-2010). Military band Director of Music; many arrangements – band compositions include *Ceremonial Occasion*, *Fanfare and Soliloquy* and *Prelude to a Festival*.

SIEBERT, Edrich (really Stanley Smith-Masters) (1903-1984). Largely self-taught; with military bands until 1946. Subsequently prolific composer, especially for brass (though for military band and orchestra also), of novelty pieces (*Bees-a-Buzzin'*, *Delaware Waltz* and the galop *Over the Sticks*, adopted as a radio signature tune), marches (*Follow the Band*, *The Queen's Guard*, *The Queen's Trumpeters*, *Vermont*, *Portsmouth Chimes*), suites (*Brass Band Sketches*) and countless arrangements.

SLADE, Julian (1930-2006). Actor, then (1953) Musical Director with Bristol Old Vic, for whom he wrote (all the music and many of the lyrics) his most enduring musical show, *Salad Days* (1954: 2283 performances, later revived and televised), which is wonderfully fresh in its invention. *Free as Air* (1957) also achieved considerable success, *Follow That Girl* (1960), *Hooray For Daisy!* (1960), *Wildest Dreams* (1961), *Vanity Fair* (1962), *Nutmeg and Ginger* (1963) and *Trelawny* (1972) less so. As a Cambridge undergraduate composed his first two musicals for the Cambridge ADC – later provided musical versions of *The Duenna* (Sheridan) and *The Comedy of Errors* (Shakespeare) and music for a stage version of A.A. Milne's *Winnie The Pooh*.

SLANEY, Ivor (1921-98). Composer of tuneful pieces for orchestra like *Three Irish Reels*, the suite *Three Village Greens*, *Sighing Waltz*, *Reveille for a Toy Soldier*, *Whistling Wallaby*, *Georgian Rumba*, *Mice on the Move*, *An Edwardian Entr'acte* and *Three Irish Jigs*.

SMYTH, Ethel (1858-1944). Feminist and arguably still the finest British woman composer. *The Boatswain's Mate* is a comic opera, *Entente Cordiale* an operetta – the intermezzo *Two Interlinked French Folk Melodies* from the latter was once a popular light orchestral number.

SOMERVILLE, Reginald (1867-1949). A man of the theatre as he composed the operas *David Garrick* (1920: to his own text) and *Antonio*. More popular than either was the operetta *The Mountaineers* (1909), for which he also wrote some of the lyrics. His compositions also included ballads (*Songs of Friendship, Only, The Amber Necklace, When Dreams Come True*) and light orchestral items: *Four Fancies, Three Light Pieces, Sabot Dance, Souvenir d'Autrefois, The Honey Bee* and *The Knight Errant*.

SPAIN-DUNK, Susan (1880-1962). Daughter of a Folkestone alderman; violinist and viola player, educated RAM. Composed much chamber music admired by Cobbett and conducted her own works at the Henry Wood Proms in the four seasons 1924-7: *Suite for strings, Idyll, Romantic Piece* (flute and strings), the overture *Kentish Downs* and the symphonic poem *Elaine*. Mostly her orchestral works fall within the light category: the overtures *The Farmer's Boy* and *Andred's Weald*, conducted by her in the Royal Artillery Theatre, Woolwich, *The Water Lily Pool* for flute, harp and strings, *Two Scottish Pieces* ('By St Mary's Loch' and 'Kerrera'), *Four Spanish Dances*, the fantasia *Weald of Kent* and the rousing concert march *Kentonia*. Many of these titles show how faithful she was to her native county.

SPARKE, Philip (1951-). Composer of bright, tuneful music for bands, both 'wind symphonic' (*Gaudium*) and brass: overtures *The Prizewinners, A*

Tameside Overture, A London Overture, Concert Prelude, Jubilee Overture, suites – *A Celtic Suite, A Malvern Suite, Fanfare, Romance and Finale, Music for a Festival* – individual movements (*Orient Express, Skyrider, Pantomime, Endeavour, Fantasy* for euphonium and band, *Aubade* ditto, *Song For Ina* ditto, etc), also many arrangements.

SPOLIANSKY, Mischa (1898-1984). Russian-born, settled in England in 1930s. Composed the musical *Who's Taking Liberty* (1939) and scores for many 'thirties and 'forties films, including *Sanders of the River* and *King Solomon's Mines*.

SQUIRE, J.H. (1880-1956). No relation of W.H. Squire (*qv*), cellist and conductor. Formed J.H. Squire Celeste Octet (piano, celeste, strings) 1913, which gave over 500 broadcasts between 1923 and the 1950s and made many records, especially for Columbia. Composed *An Irish Love Song, The Piccaninnies' Picnic, An Ant's Antics, Moonbeams and Shadows* and other genre pieces.

STEADMAN ALLEN, Raymond Victor (Ray) (1922-). BMus. Durham. Responsible for many hundreds of fine arrangements and compositions for voices and/or brass band, mostly for the Salvation Army: the tone poem *The Holy War,* many brass works based on sacred songs, *Daystar,* the 'Victorian snapshot' *On Ratcliff Highway* and *Seascapes,* all for brass band, the trombone quartet *Sparkling Slides* and the choral *Children's Suite*.

STERNDALE BENNETT, T.C. (died 1944). Descended from composer-conductor William Sterndale Bennett (1816-75). Earned a reputation for his ballads, mainly humorous – *What-Nots* (3 sets), *Slow Coach, The Carol Singers* and, most famously, *Leanin',* whose accompaniment was orchestrated by Sydney Baynes and Stanford Robinson (both *qv*) among others. Other songs were interpolated into stage shows as diverse as the revue *Back to Blighty* and Shakespeare's *Measure for Measure*.

STRACHEY, Jack (1894-1972). At his peak in the 1940s and 1950s. Composed for musicals (*Belinda Fair,* 1949, *Dear Little Billie, Lady Luck*) and revues (*New Faces, The Punch Bowl, Shake Your Feet* and *Spread it Abroad,* from which came his biggest hit, the song *These Foolish Things*). Other popular songs included *Tramway Queen, The Old Bells of Bow, A Boy, a Girl and the Moon* and *Good Queen Bess.* For orchestra he produced *In Party Mood, Ascot Parade, Mayfair Parade,* the waltz *Pink Champagne,* the beguine *Starlight Cruise,* and the marches *Knights of Malta* (1942),

Shaftesbury Avenue, Theatreland and *Overture and Beginners*, the latter three reflecting his preoccupation with the theatre.

STUART, Leslie (really Thomas Barrett). (1864-1928). Born Southport. Achieved success with *Floradora* (1899, several times revived) and, less so, with other shows. Also composed about 65 popular songs, including *Soldiers of the Queen, The Bandolero, Little Dolly Daydream* and *Lily of Laguna*.

SUMNER, Capt Peter, MBE (1929-2000). Joined Royal Marines 1944 and rose to be Director of Music, C in C Fleet Band. Subsequently worked for Doncaster Metropolitan Borough Council in its Peripatetic Music Service, retiring in 1993, though remained active in music locally. His arrangements, for bands and, when he became Conductor of the South Yorkshire Police Male Voice Choir in 1976, voices, are wide-ranging; his original compositions include marches *(Zeebrugge, Ready Aye Ready*, both with bugles, the latter for the Sea Cadets, *The Blue Light*, dedicated to the police, and *Sergeant of Marines)*, the suite *Celebration* (for band or orchestra), inspired by the 800th Anniversary of Doncaster's first charter in 1994, featuring historical pastiche (using actual troubadour melodies) and ending with a march worthy of Coates, and the single movements *Barcelona* (a paso doble), *Alpine Frolic* and a moving, Elgar-inspired, *Soliloquy*. An oboist, he composed the oboe solo *Water Nymph*.

SUTHERLAND, Iain (? -). Conductor, arranger of traditional and popular tunes, especially for 'Friday Night is Music Night', and composer, eg, of the *Three Castles Suite*.

SWANN, Donald (1923-94). Born Llanelli of Russian parents. Composed much church music, carols, art songs (to words by Tolkien, Betjeman, and C. Day Lewis), an opera *(Perelandra,* words C.S. Lewis) and lighter works for the stage, including *Lyric Revue* (1951), *Penny Plain* and *At the Drop of a Hat* (1956), but is best remembered for his brilliantly memorable light songs, especially those to Michael Flanders' lyrics: *The Slow Train, Rhinoceros Song, Elephant Song, Warthog Song, The Gas Man Cometh, I'm a Gnu* and, most famous of all and long associated with baritone Ian Wallace, *The Hippopotamus Song* ('Mud').

TALBOT, Howard (really Richard Lansdale Munkittrick) (1865-1928). American-born but educated and domiciled in London. Wrote, at least in part, some 17 musicals, three of which, *A Chinese Honeymoon* (1901), *The*

Arcadians (1909) and *The Boy* (1917), the latter two co-composed with Lionel Monckton (*qv*), with whom he often collaborated, ran for over 800 performances each.

TAPP, Frank (1884-1953). An almost forgotten figure in British light music but his work was frequently played in its day. Titles include the *Waltz Idyll* (à la Viennoise) of 1938 for piano and *A Wayside Melody*, *Woodland Echoes*, *Waltz Suite* and the topographical *English Landmarks Suite* (a waltz, 'Ascot', 'Tintern Abbey' and the march 'Whitehall') and the overture *Beachy Head*, all for orchestra. Directed Bath Pump Room Orchestra 1910-19.

TATE, James W. (1875-1922). Best known for two songs *A Bachelor Gay* and *Paradise for Two* interpolated into *The Maid of the Mountains* by Harold Fraser-Simson (*qv*) for its London run. Also composed musicals and revues of his own, eg, *Round in Fifty*, *The Beauty Spot* and *The Peep Show*; and separate songs like *A Broken Doll*, *Every Little While* and *Come Over the Garden Wall*. Not to be confused with Arthur Frank Tate (1880-1950), composer of *Somewhere a Voice is Calling*, *Love's Devotion* and other popular songs between c.1910 and 1935.

TAUBER, Richard (really Ernst Seiffert) (1892-1948). Well-loved Austrian-born tenor, famous for his interpretations of Mozart and later Lehár (notably *You Are My Heart's Delight* in *The Land of Smiles*), also conductor. Naturalised British subject 1940; composed the score for the musical *Old Chelsea*, produced in 1943, which included the hit *My Heart and I*.

TAUSKY, Vilem (1910-2004). Born in Moravia; English-domiciled since World War II. Conductor, especially of opera. Latterly he was Britain's oldest working conductor. Compositions include a string quartet, cello sonata, concertos for oboe and percussion and several of a light character: the orchestral suite *From Our Village*, the festival march *Men of Tomorrow*, the scherzo *Soho*, various arrangements of British and Czech folk melodies, a *Ballade* for cello and piano, and two overtures for brass band – *Concert Overture* and *Cakes and Ale*.

TEMPLE, Gordon (fl 1900-10). A popular Edwardian ballad composer and surely Irish-born with titles like *The Old Green Isle*, *Sweet Vale of Avoca* and *In Sweet Killarney*; but undoubtedly his best-known song is *Trooper Johnny Ludlow*; a hit of 1907. No relation of Hope Temple.

TEMPLE, Hope (really Dotie Davies) (1859-1938). Irish born, of English parents, and later the wife of André Messager, the French operetta composer (although they did not long live together). Wrote songs from the age of 14, mainly sentimental ballads with titles like *An Old Garden, My Lady's Bower, Fond Heart Farewell, Memories, Thoughts and Tears, In Sweet September* and *God's Lily.* Fond of riding; an injury whilst on horseback ruined her intended career as a pianist.

TEMPLETON, Alec (really Andrew) (1909-63). Welsh-born though a USA citizen from 1941. Blind; he earns a place here on account of his popular parody *Bach Goes to Town*, originally for piano but arranged for orchestral and other combinations. Composed concertos and songs but his shorter lyrical instrumental pieces have survived best: *Siciliana* for violin, *Scherzo Caprice* for oboe, *Pocket Size Sonata* for clarinet and, for piano, *Blue Brass* and *Drowsy Blues*, both in syncopated style, and *Toccata*.

THIMAN, Eric Harding (1900-75). Born Ashford, Kent; largely self-taught but later himself taught at RAM and London University. Prolific composer of music for choirs (mainly short pieces), piano solo, organ solo (he was Organist at the City Temple) and chamber ensembles, much of it suitable for young amateurs. His songs include many ballads (*I Travel the Road, Snowbird, I'm in Cupid's Garden, My Sheep Dog and I*) and *Merry Old Canute* for C.B. Cochran's *1926 Revue*; his orchestral music was light in character and included the suites *Fittleworth Fair, Highland Scenes, Two Irish Melodies, Two Irish Pieces* and the march *Stirling Castle*.

THWAITES, Penelope Mary (1944-). Pianist, brought up in Australia, but English domiciled for many years. Advocate for Australian music, especially Percy Grainger (*qv*), also composer of lighthearted songs and piano pieces, many suitable for young performers.

TOMLINSON, Ernest, MBE (1924-). Lancashire-born, studied Manchester University and RMCM. In RAF during World War II. Worked as an arranger and as an organist in London before forming Ernest Tomlinson Light Orchestra and Singers (1955) and then Northern Concert Orchestra (1969). In that year also founded an electronic music studio, but his orchestral compositions especially follow in the Eric Coates tradition with titles like *Festival Suite, Lyrical Suite, A Mediterranean Suite,* two suites of *English Folk Dances, Three Pastoral Dances* and *English Pageant.* His *Little Serenade* became a radio signature tune (as did *Dick's Maggot* from the first *English Folk Dance* suite) and many other attractive single movements gained popularity. *A Comedy Overture* and the *Merseyside Overture* followed in the English tradition of the bright, light overture. *Sinfonia 62* and *Symphony 65* both opposed a symphony orchestra and a jazz band. His prolific list of compositions includes concerted pieces for French horn and for five saxophones, one opera, film music, choral music, organ music and brass band music, but he has still found time to chair the Composers' Guild of Great Britain and the Light Music Society and, from 1966, be a Director of the Performing Right Society.

TOMLINSON, Fred (1927-), brother of Ernest (*qv*), choirboy at Manchester Cathedral, then King's College, Cambridge, subsequently took BA degree at Leeds University. Worked for over 30 years as singer, arranger, chorus master, etc, for TV and radio; was particularly associated with the TV series 'Monty Python' and 'The Two Ronnies'. Original work includes choral and orchestral *Chaucer Suite*. Leading expert on the music of Peter Warlock.

TORCH, Sidney, MBE (1908-90). (Really Sidney Torchinsky) Theatre organist pre-1939, then Conductor of RAF Concert Orchestra during the war and subsequently conducted BBC Concert Orchestra in 'Friday Night is Music Night' 1953-72. Prolific arranger and composer of light orchestral music: *Barbecue*, *Duel for Drummers*, *Going for a Ride*, *Shooting Star*, *Cornflakes*, *Bicycle Belles*, *Meandering*, *Romany Rhapsody* and, most famously, the *Trapeze Waltz* of 1963. Wrote *London Transport Suite* for the BBC's Light Music Festival of 1958.

TOSTI, Sir Francesco Paolo (1846-1916). Italian composer and singing teacher, settled in London, where he taught the Royal Family and was knighted. Composed many ballad-type songs in English (*Good-Bye*), French and Italian.

TOWNS, Colin (1948-). Highly respected composer for films (*Full Circle*) and TV (*Cadfael*, *Pie in the Sky*, *The Buccaneers*, *Beatrix Potter*, etc.).

TOYE, Geoffrey (1889-1942). Born Winchester, trained at RCM. Conductor, of D'Oyly Carte Opera (for which he rearranged *Ruddigore* and compiled a new overture, 1921), at Sadler's Wells and other theatres and for Royal Philharmonic Society. Composed operas, for stage and radio, choral music and the ballets *Douanes* and *The Haunted Ballroom* (1935), the ghostly waltz from which was long a popular light orchestral number.

TRANCHELL, Peter (1922-93). Associated with Cambridge as student and later (at Gonville & Caius College) don. Remembered for his opera *The Mayor of Casterbridge* (Cambridge, 1951); also composed anthems, a cantata and, on the lighter side, a series of vocal 'entertainments', instrumental miniatures and, also produced at Cambridge (in 1954), the musical comedy *Zuleika*, after Max Beerbohm.

TROTÈRE, Henry (really Henry Trotter) (1855-1912). Composer of once-popular ballads like *The Deathless Army, My Old Shako, I Did Not Know* and *In Old Madrid*, also dance music.

VINTER, Gilbert (1909-69). Born in Lincoln. Trained at Kneller Hall and RAM. Served in RAF in World War II; afterwards Conductor of BBC Midland Light Orchestra, then of BBC Concert Orchestra and his own Concert Band. Prolific composer for light orchestra – medleys of traditional melodies, *Portuguese Party*; the light overtures *Mr Know-All* and *Overture to a New Venture*, the *Song-Dance Suite, The Playful Pachyderm* and *Reverie*, both for bassoon and orchestra (he was a bassoonist), and *Hunter's Moon* for horn and orchestra – chamber ensembles (*Miniatures* for wind quintet), military band (eg, *The Chantyman* and *The Cobbers March*) and brass band, for which he composed several major works used as test-pieces. Although some feel his thematic invention lacks individuality, his music is well constructed and superbly orchestrated.

WALLER, Jack (1885-1957). Composer, actor and theatre manager. Composed musicals produced in London between the wars, usually in conjunction with Joseph Tunbridge: *Please Teacher, Yes Madam, Princess Charming, Virginia,* etc.

WALTON, Sir William (1902-83). One of the leading 'serious' British composers of this century, it is surprising how much of his output is categorisable as light: *Façade*, at least its orchestral, ballet version; his contributions to the English comedy overture – *Portsmouth Point, Scapino, Johannesburg Festival* and *Capriccio Burlesco*; his Coronation marches *Crown Imperial* and *Orb and Sceptre*, carrying on the *Pomp and Circumstance* tradition; the *Partita*; and his considerable corpus of film music, whether Shakespearean (*As You Like It, Henry V, Hamlet, Richard III*) or inspired by World War II (*The First of the Few, The Foreman Went to France, The Battle of Britain*, etc).

WARNER, Ken (1902-88) (really Onslow Boyden Waldo Warner). Son of violist and composer H. Waldo Warner; educated GSM, played in dance bands including Peter Yorke's. Joined BBC 1940, playing in or 'fixing' various light orchestras. Prolific arranger and composer of mood music and light genre pieces, most popular of which was *Scrub Brother, Scrub*, referring to a violinist drawing the bow back and forth over a string.

WATTERS, Cyril (1907-84). Produced many instrumental arrangements and composed for brass (concert march *By Royal Command* and *A Cotswold Lullaby* for band and *Pastoral Theme* for brass quartet), military band (march *A Blaze of Light*) and orchestra, genre pieces like *Willow Waltz, Piccadilly Spree, Bargain Basement, Valse Coquette, Polka Piquante, Amorette, Heidelberg Polka, Plain Sailing* and *Rio Rhythm*, mostly from the 1950s. Before 1939 known as a syncopated pianist in the Billy Mayerl style; compositions in this direction include *Butterfingers* (1937).

WETHERELL, Eric David (1925-). Born Tynemouth; educated Queen's College, Oxford, and RCM. Played horn in various orchestras during the 1950s, then repetiteur, Royal Opera House, Covent Garden (1960), Assistant Musical Director Welsh National Opera (1963) and Conductor, BBC Northern Ireland Orchestra (1976-81). Lives in Bristol. Orchestral works, apart from arrangements and music for films and TV, include the overture *Beau Nash, Bristol Quay* and the suites *Welsh Dresser* and (strings only) *Airs and Graces*, all in the English light music tradition.

WHELEN, Christopher (1927-93). Worth mention here for his tuneful music for radio features (including plays and operas), films and stage plays from the 1950s onwards.

WHITE, Edward (1910-94). Self-taught; violinist, saxophonist and clarinettist with various dance ensembles. Served RAF World War II; also involved in broadcasting. Composed much 'mood music' after the war; three of his genre pieces became especially popular – *Caprice for Strings, Runaway Rocking Horse* and, for many years the signature tune of BBC Radio's 'Uncle Mac's Children's Favourites', the cheeky *Puffin' Billy* nearly as popular as *Coronation Scot* by Vivian Ellis (*qv*) as a piece of 'railway music'. Other titles included *The Clockwork Clown, Fairy on the Fiddles, Idle Jack, Yodelling Strings* and *City Prelude* – evocative titles and, generally speaking, evocative music.

WHITE, Maude Valérie (1855-1937). Born Dieppe of British parents. Studied Heidelberg, Paris and RAM (with Macfarren). Apart from a few instrumental solos, a ballet and some choral music, her output comprises 300 songs, many of them of the 'drawing-room ballad' variety *(Until, The Devout Lover, The Exile, How Do I Love Thee, The Sea Hath its Pearls, There's a Bower of Roses)* but also including settings of Browning, Herrick, Tennyson, Shakespeare and, especially popular, Byron's *So We'll Go No More A-Roving*, still to be heard. An excellent linguist, she also published songs in German, French, Italian, Norwegian and Spanish.

WHITLOCK, Percy (1903-46). Organist in Kent and at Bournemouth (St Stephen's Parish Church, and, between 1932 and 1946, the Pavilion). Composed music for church and organ (much of the organ music is lightish in character); also wrote for orchestra, mainly for the Bournemouth Municipal Orchestra, some of it under the pseudonym Kenneth Lark: the *Wessex Suite* (Waltz, Revels in Hogsnorton; The Blue Poole; March, Rustic Cavalry), *Holiday Suite* (Waltz, In the Ballroom; Spade and Bucket Polka; Civic March), the concert overture *The Feast of St Benedict*, *Balloon Ballet*, *Ballet of the Wood Creatures* and the marches *Dignity and Impudence* and *The Phoebe* the latter named after a World War II cruiser.

WIGGINS, William Bramwell (Bram) (1921-). Educated TCL, RAM. Trumpet player LSO and Philharmonia, then music master Stowe School. Compositions, for brass band, include *Celebration Overture* and the suites *Mardi Gras* and *Mediterranean Holiday*.

WILLCOCKS, George Henry (1899-1962). Military bandsman, eventually MD Irish Guards 1938-49. After retirement went into brass banding as conductor. Compositions included marches *Fordson Major, Guards Armoured Division, Consul* and *Palace Forecourt*.

WILLIAMS, Charles (1893-1978). His two best-remembered tunes come from the mid to late 1940s: *The Dream of Olwen* from the film *While I Live* (1948), one of some one hundred films he wrote music for (others were *Kipps, The Young Mr Pitt* and *The Apartment;* he was resident composer to Gaumont British 1933-39); and *The Devil's Galop*, signature tune of the radio serial 'Dick Barton, Special Agent'. Violinist and conductor, of the Queen's Hall Light Orchestra and his own Concert Orchestra, he composed a large number of catchy orchestral single movements. Some, like *The Nursery Clock, Rhythm on Rails, Sleepy Marionette* and *Model Railway;* suggest a preoccupation with mechanical objects. Other popular titles were *Jealous Lover, The Starlings, Girls in Grey, Big Ben* and the marches *Kensington* and *Blue Devils*. A few of his works, besides *The Devil's Galop*, were adopted as signature tunes: *Voice of London* (for the QHLO), *Majestic Fanfare* (Australian TV), *The Old Clockmaker* ('Jennings at School') and the march *Girls in Grey* (BBC TV newsreel).

WILLIAMS, Gerrard (1888-1947). A prolific arranger for almost every medium, especially for orchestra and the BBC Military Band, he was also quite lavish with his original compositions. These were sometimes 'serious', including two string quartets, the second (1923) praised by Cobbett; his large output for voices was often popular in aim, sometimes being suitable for children's voices (*Playbox*) and nearly always concise in format. His orchestral music included the ballet *The Wings of Horns* (1928) and the suite *Ring up the Curtain*; he also dabbled in the theatre with the operetta *The Story of the Willow Pattern Plate* and the ballad opera *Kate the Cabin Boy*, produced at the Kingsway in 1924 in the wake of the success of *The Beggar's Opera* from 1920.

WILSON, Alexander Galbraith (Sandy) (1924-). Educated Harrow and Oxford University. Contributed songs to various West End shows before achieving success with the 1920s spoof musical *The Boy Friend* (1953-4: frequently revived and later filmed). Later productions such as *The Buccaneer* (1955), *Valmouth* (1958), *Pieces of Eight* (1959), *Aladdin* (1979) and *Divorce Me Darling* were rather less successful. His music for the TV series *The World of Wooster* did well.

WILSON, Henry Lane (1871-1915). Singer and songwriter, born in Gloucestershire and trained at the RAM. His song output divides roughly into two parts: arrangements of old (usually 18th-century) English songs foretelling perhaps the popularity of *The Beggar's Opera* revival in the 1920s, and 'originals', though the dividing line is blurred because the old style influenced his own writing (the cycle *Dorothy's Wedding* though original, was based on old dance forms). Another cycle, *Flora's Holiday*, comprised arrangements entirely. Other popular songs were the duet *Tenor and Baritone, To the Dance, Soldiers and Sailors, The Lovers* and *Carmena*. Wilson also wrote a few pieces for chorus, and an orchestral *Meditation*.

WINTERBOTTOM, Frank (1861-1930). From a family of military musicians. Directed Royal Marines Plymouth Band 1890-1910, later instructor at Kneller Hall. Composed ballets *Jorinda* and *Phantasma*, the *Seven Ages* suite (after Shakespeare) and many fine military band arrangements, still used.

WOLSTENHOLME, William (1865-1931). Like Alfred Hollins (*qv*) a blind concert organist. Some of his organ output (he also wrote orchestral and chamber music and songs) reflects his need to entertain, as well as instruct, audiences: two Concert Overtures, *Barcarolle* in C, *The Question and the Answer* and the *Allegretto*, later transcribed by Tertis for viola. Friendly with Elgar.

WOOD, Gareth H. (1950-). Educated RAM. Double-bass player with RPO for many years. Compositions include *Suffolk Punch*, *Fantasy on a Welsh Song* and the overture *Cardiff Bay* for orchestra and *Culloden Moor* for brass band.

WOOD, Sir Henry Joseph (1869-1944). Noted conductor and founder of the Proms, for many years a major outlet for light, as well as other, music. His compositions, many of them songs, are mostly early, but he deserves mention for his inventive arrangements, notably the *Fantasia on British Sea Songs* (1905).

WOOD, Thomas (1892-1950). Born Chorley, Lancs. Studied Exeter College, Oxford, and RCM. D Mus Oxon, 1920. Taught at Tonbridge School and Exeter College. Settled in Essex. Composed much choral music, especially on nautical themes (*Master Mariners*, *Merchantmen* and *The Rainbow*; *A Tale of Dunkirk*); on the lighter side he composed the marches *St George's Day* (orchestra, with bugles) and *Six Bells* (brass band), the concert overture *Suffolk Punch* and, for two pianos, *Waltzing Matilda: A Frolic Founded on an Australian Tune*.

WOODFIELD, Ray (1931-). Director of Music, Royal Marines, then (1974-91) a peripatetic tutor with Doncaster Local Education Authority. A very prolific and inventive arranger. A clarinettist, has composed miniatures for that instrument; he regards his best original works as the two euphonium solos *Varied Mood* (an anagram of its dedicatee David Moore) and *Caprice*, the marches *Walkabout*, written for his student band in Doncaster, and *Amsterdam*, a concerto in E flat for trumpet and the virtuoso piece *Trumpet Eclair*. Not afraid to write good tunes.

WOODFORDE-FINDEN, Amy (1860-1919). Born Amy Ward, Valparaiso (Chile). Married an officer in the Indian Army and lived in India, perhaps the inspiration for the very popular, ballad-like *Indian Love Lyrics* of 1902, which were followed by other exotic-sounding song-cycles, *A Lover in Damascus*, *Little Japanese Songs*, *A Dream of Egypt*, *Stars of the Desert*, *The*

Pagoda of Flowers (with chorus) and *On Jhelum River*, plus other less oriental (and less popular) ballads.

WOODGATE, Hubert Leslie, OBE (1902-61). Educated RCM. Chorus Master to BBC; musical director of the LNER and several provincial choral societies; festival adjudicator. Prolific arranger of popular tunes for chorus, composer of an oratorio and many shorter choral compositions (including several for the LNER), solo songs, chamber music and orchestral items: the 'impression' *Caerdydd*, *Romance* (full orchestra) and *English Dance Suite* (strings).

WOOLFENDEN, Guy Anthony (1937-). Educated Whitgift School and Christ's College, Cambridge. A conductor and Head of Music RSC; has composed 150 play-scores in an approachable style for that company and others for theatres abroad, plus ballet scores for *Anna Karenina, The Three Musketeers, La Traviata* and *The Queen of Spades* and music for films, radio and TV. Many of his Shakespearean scores have been arranged for the concert hall, especially for wind band, eg, *Illyrian Dances, Deo Gracias* and *Gallimaufry*; or brass quintet, eg, *Full Fathom Five*. Has also composed *SPQR*, a suite inspired by roads, ancient and modern, for concert band, plus three musicals, a children's opera, concertos and chamber music.

WRIGHT, Denis, OBE (1895-1967). Studied at RCM and taught music in schools. Associated with brass bands from 1925, producing several major works for them (eg, *Music for Brass, Tintagel, Tam o'Shanter's Ride, Overture for an Epic Occasion*) and classical arrangements often used as contest test-pieces. He adjudicated hundreds of contests himself. General Music Editor for Chappell 1930-6; with BBC 1936-66 and composed *Cornish Holiday* and *Casino Carnival*, both for orchestra and brass band, for the Light Music Festivals of 1957 and 1958. Conductor; founded National Youth Brass Band of Great Britain 1952. Produced over 1000 scores for brass (including arrangements), 800 of them published, some under pseudonyms W Stewart, Frank Denham, etc., plus songs and, for orchestra, *Dance Suite; Two Arthurian Sketches* and *Suite in 18th Century Style*.

WRIGHT, Frank, MBE (1901-70). No relation to Denis. Australian-born, well-known in brass band circles as adjudicator, conductor and arranger. Music Director to the GLC 1955. Fewer brass works (about 100) than Denis and fewer original pieces, among the latter being *Preludio Marziale, Sirius*, the suite *Old Westminster* and the march *Whitehall*.

WRIGHT, Kenneth Anthony, OBE (1899-1975). No relation to foregoing two composers. Joined BBC in 1922, for whom he held various positions including Deputy/Acting Director of Music (1944-8) and Head of TV Music (1951-9). After retiring from BBC went into films. Composed widely, especially for orchestra: a fantasy *Bohemia, Tobacco Suite*, for the BBC's 1st Light Music Festival in 1949, and many single-movement genre pieces like *Dainty Lady, Dancing With the Daffodils* and *Perky Pizzicato*. His list of works also includes *Six Fantasy Pictures from a Pantomime* and other pieces for piano, many songs and works for brass and military band, *Pride of Race* and *Peddar's Way* being adoped as test-pieces for major brass contests.

YORKE, Peter (1902-66). Educated Trinity College, London. Pursued a career in dance music in the 1920s and formed the Peter Yorke Concert Orchestra in 1937. Broadcast regularly. Composed songs, music for brass band *(The Shipbuilders* suite, written for a BBC Light Music Festival, *Gallions Reach* and the overture *The Explorers)* and for orchestra, of which output we may instance the suite *In My Garden* and the novelty movements *Caravan Romance, Miss in Mink, Midnight in Mexico, Fireflies, Parade of the Matadors, Flyaway Fiddles and Faded Lilac*, a 'waltz intermezzo'. Wrote the theme music for TV's *Emergency Ward 10*.

SELECT DISCOGRAPHY

This discography refers to CDs which were available at the time of the book's first publication in 1997. Since then there have been many more releases and the reader is referred particularly to the catalogues of ASV, Hyperion, and Naxos.

BILLY MAYERL

ACADEMY ASV CD WHL 2071	The Nimble-Fingered Gentleman: Phillip Dyson (piano).
CHANDOS CHAN 8560, 8848, 9141	Eric Parkin Plays the Piano Impressions of Billy Mayerl, Vols 1 to 3.
PRIORY PRCD 399	Piano Music of Billy Mayerl: Peter Jacobs.
PRIORY PRCD 466-8	Billy Mayerl Piano Transcriptions: Eric Parkin.
STOMP OFF CD 1313	The Nimble-Fingered Gentleman: Tony Caramia (piano).
EMI CDM 5 65596 2	British Piano Music of the Twenties and Thirties (Billy Mayerl, plus Gerrard Williams, Walton, Lambert, Bliss, etc). Richard Rodney Bennett (piano), English Sinfonia/ Neville Dilkes
PRIORY PRCD 544	Puppets: A tribute to Billy Mayerl. Eric Parkin (piano)

MARCO POLO RECORDINGS

8.223732	Richard Addinsell: BBC Concert Orchestra / Kenneth Alwyn.
8.223515	Ronald Binge: Slovak RSO/Ernest Tomlinson.
8.223445	Eric Coates: Czecho-Slovak RSO / Adrian Leaper.
8.223521	Eric Coates: Slovak RSO / Andrew Penny.

8.223516	Samuel Coleridge-Taylor: RTE Concert Orchestra / Leaper.
8.223425	Frederic Curzon: Czecho-Slovak RSO / Leaper
8.223517	Trevor Duncan: Slovak RSO / Penny
8.223401	Robert Farnon: Czecho – Slovak RSO / Leaper.
8.223419	Edward German: Czecho – Slovak RSO / Leaper.
8.223518	Ron Goodwin: New Zealand SO/Goodwin.
8.223886	Anthony Hedges: (RTE Sinfonietta/ Hedges).
8.223694	Archibald Joyce: RTE Concert Orchestra/Penny.
8.223442	Albert Ketèlbey: Slovak Phil. Male Chorus, Czecho-Slovak RSO / Leaper.
8.223514	Billy Mayerl: Slovak RSO / Gary Carpenter.
8.223444	Roger Quilter: Czecho-Slovak RSO / Leaper.
8.223413	Ernest Tomlinson, Vol 1: Czecho-Slovak RSO/Tomlinson. Ernest
8.223513	Tomlinson, Vol. 2: Slovak RSO/Tomlinson
8.223591	Ernest Tomlinson Vol 3: New Zealand SO/Tomlinson
8.223443	Sidney Torch: BBC Concert Orchestra / Barry Wordsworth.
8.223837	Robert Docker (RTE Concert Orchestra/Knight)
8.223402	Haydn Wood: Czecho-Slovak RSO / Leaper
8.223605	Haydn Wood: Slovak RSO / Tomlinson
8.223522	Miniatures: RTE Concert Orchestra/ Tomlinson (Anthony Collins, Mark Lubbock, Armstrong Gibbs, Benjamin Frankel, Vivian Ellis, Arthur Benjamin, Robert Docker, Edward Elgar, Harry Dexter, Ken Warner, Gordon Jacob, Thomas Arne, Gilbert Vinter, Geoffrey Toye.

8.223806	Eric Coates: Songs. Richard Edgar-Wilson (tenor), Eugene Asti (piano).
8.223271	Frederic Cowen: CSSR State Philharmonic/Leaper.
8.223370	Edward German piano music: Alan Cuckston.
8.223695	Edward German orchestral music: RTE Concert Orchestra / Penny.
8.223726	Edward German orchestral music: NSO of Ireland/Penny
8.223458	Armstrong Gibbs songs: Nick Hancock-Child (bar), Rosemary Hancock-Child (piano).
8.223699-700	Ketèlbey: Piano Music, Vols 1 and 2. Rosemary Tuck.

OTHER MODERN ISSUES

ACADEMY ASV CD WHL 2069	Robin Hood County: East of England Orchestra / Malcolm Nabarro (Komgold, Coates, Nabarro, Curzon, Goodwin)
ASV CD WHL 2075	Four Centuries: Music of Eric Coates Vol. 2. East of England Orchestra/ Malcolm Nabarro
ASV CD WHL 2107	Eric Coates: BBC Concert Orchestra / John Wilson. Includes world premiere of the recently discovered *Coquette* and premiere recordings of *The Unknown Singer, Idyll, Rhodesia* and the *Two Light Syncopated Pieces*.
BENTLEY PRODUCTIONS BCP 101 (Cassette only)	'Shipmates o'mine': Ralph Meanley (baritone), David Mackie (piano) (ballads by Montague Phillips, Stanford, Ireland, Sanderson, Kennedy Russell, W H Squire, Loder, Gordon Temple, Ernest Longstaffe and G.F. Cobb).
CAMBRIA (US) CD-1084	Leigh Kaplan plays Madeleine Dring
CHANDOS CHAN 8797	Ron Goodwin: My Kind of Music. Bournemouth Symphony Orchestra/ Goodwin
CHANDOS CHAN 8856	Salon to Swing. Palm Court Theatre Orchestra /A Goodwin (Joyce,Haydn Wood, Ancliffe, Ketèlbey, etc).
CHAN 9142	Marilyn Hill-Smith sings Ivor Novello

CHAN 9243	William Alwyn: Film Music. LSO / Richard Hickox
CHAN 9110	Edwardian Echoes. Marilyn Hill-Smith (sop), Southern Festival Orchestra/Robin White (German, Monckton, Bucalossi, Montague Phillips, Fletcher, Caryll, Finck, Ancliffe, Baynes)
CHANDOS FBCD 2000	Test Card Classics. Various orchestras. Music written to accompany the TV test card by Gordon Langford, Ernest Tomlinson, Brian Couzens, Frank Chacksfield, Jack Strachey, etc.
EMI 0777 7 99638 2 9	'Music For A Country Cottage'. Various orchestras and conductors (Coates, C. Williams, Collins, Tomlinson, Melachrino, Jacob, Binge, Gardner, Farnon, A. Langford, Hanmer, Coleridge-Taylor, Bayco, A. Gibbs).
HARLEQUIN HAR 1125 CD	English Landscapes. Rigid Containers Group Band/John Berryman (Maurice Johnstone, Ernest Tomlinson, Gordon Langford, etc.)
HMV 7 67800 2	Light Music Classics (Charles Williams, Melachrino, Binge, Hanmer, Frederick Bayco, Armstrong Gibbs, Farnon, etc.)
HYPERION CDA 66818	'Bird Songs at Eventide'. Robert White (ten.), Stephen Hough (piano) (ballads by Coates, Quilter, Haydn Wood, Woodforde-Finden, Lehmann, Brahe, del Riego, etc.)
CDA 66868	British Light Music Classics. New London Orchestra/Ronald Corp (Coates, Toye, Collins, Farnon, Baynes, Curzon, Binge, Charles Williams, Armstrong Gibbs, White, Ketèlbey, Joyce, Ellis, Ancliffe)

HYPERION CDA 66968	British Light Music Classics, Vol. 2. New London Orchestra / Ronald Corp. (Coates, Curzon, Docker, Farnon, Frankel, Wood, Ketèlbey, Tomlinson, Duncan, Vinter, Benjamin, Bucalossi, Finck, Richardson, White, Binge, Ellis, Fletcher, Hartley, Elgar).
MERIDIAN CDE 84308	Music for the Theatre (by Alfred Reynolds). Singers, London Salon Ensemble.
CDE 84322	Liza Lehmann Songs Henry Wickham
NAXOS 8.553495	20th Century English Ballets (Carl Davis, Philip Feeney, Dominic Muldowney). Northern Ballet Theatre Orchestra / John Pryce-Jones.
8.553515	'Elizabethan Serenade' – the best of British light music. Selected from various Marco Polo releases.
8.553526	Malcolm Arnold: English, Scottish, Cornish, Irish and Welsh Dances. Queensland Symphony Orchestra / Penny.
PRIORY PRCD 489	The Complete Organ Works of Percy Whitlock, Vol. 1. Graham Barker. (Includes the Phoebe March, Holiday Suite and Balloon Ballet).
SWINSTY FEW 128	'Lilacs in the Rain'. Reginald King piano music. Alan Cuckston.
UNICORN-KANCHANA UKCD 2057	Laurie Johnson, London Brass, Coldstream Guards Band, LPO/ Johnson.

HISTORIC RECORDINGS REISSUED

CONIFER CDHD 211/212	The Music of Eric Coates (Coates' own recordings with various orchestras 1912-35).
EMI CDEMS 1554	Vintage Themes. Various orchestras and conductors. (Farnon, Ronald Hanmer, Coates, Charles Williams, Peter Yorke, Laurie Johnson, Louis Levy, Clive Richardson, etc.)
GROSVENOR CD GRS 1265	Billy Mayerl Favourites (Mayerl's piano recordings 1925-39).
HMV CDP 7 99256 2	Sidney Torch and his Orchestra (Torch, Farnon, Haydn Wood, Duncan, Clive Richardson, Ellis, Coates, Angela Morley, John Addison, Hanmer, etc.)
PEARL GEMM CD 9965	Coleridge-Taylor. Various orchestras and conductors.
CD 9973	Eric Coates. Various orchestras, conductors and soloists.

SELECT BIBLIOGRAPHY

JBMS = Journal of British Music Society

Colin Bayliss (ed), *The Music of Anthony Hedges* (Humberside Leisure Services, 1990).

James Brown, 'Edward German' in JBMS Vol 7 (1985), pp. 11-16.

Eric Coates, *Suite in Four Movements:* An Autobiography (Heinemann, 1953, reprinted in revised edition Thames 1986).

Peter M. Cooke, Eric Ball: *The Man and the Music* (Egon, revised edition 1992).

Ro Hancock-Child, *A Ballad-Maker: the life and songs of C. Armstrong Gibbs* (Thames, 1993).

Ro Hancock-Child, *Madeleine Dring* (MicroPress, 2000).

Michael Harth (ed), *Lightning Fingers: Billy Mayerl, The Man and His Music* (Paradise Press, 1995).

Trevor Hold, *The Walled-In Garden: The Songs of Roger Quilter* (Thames, 1995).

Robert and Nicola Hyman, *The Pump Room Orchestra, Bath* (Hobnob Press, 2011).

Arthur Jacobs, *Henry J. Wood, Maker of the Proms* (Methuen, 1994).

Beryl Kington, *Rowley Rediscovered* (Thames, 1995).

Valerie Langfield, *Roger Quilter* (Boydell, 2002).

Stephen Lloyd, *Sir Dan Godfrey: Champion of British Composers* (Thames, 1995).

Roy Newsome, *Doctor Denis: The Life and Times of Dr Denis Wright* (Egon, 1995).

Barbara Parker, 'John Gerrard Williams' in JBMS Vol 9 (1987), pp. 19-31.

Brian Reynolds, *Music While You Work* (Book Guild, 2006)

Malcolm Riley (ed.) *The Percy Whitlock Companion* (Percy Whitlock Trust, 2007).

E. Ann Rust, 'Cecil Armstrong Gibbs (A Personal Memoir)' in JBMS Vol 11 (1989), pp. 45-66.

John Sant, Albert W. Ketèlbey, *From the Sanctuary of His Heart* (Manifold, 2000)

Philip L. Scowcroft, 'Wilfrid Sanderson: Songwriter, Organist and Conductor' in JBMS Vol 3 (1981), pp. 50-59.

Philip L. Scowcroft, 'Alfred Reynolds: Man of the Theatre' in JBMS Vol 10 (1988), pp. 37-46.

Geoffrey Self, *In Town Tonight: A Centenary Study of Eric Coates* (Thames, 1986).

Geoffrey Self, *Hiawatha Man: The Life and Work of Coleridge-Taylor* (Scolar Press, 1995).

Geoffrey Self, *Light Music in Britain Since 1870* (Ashgate, 2001).
Kenneth Shenton, 'From A to B: Kenneth Alford and Hubert Bath' in JBMS Vol 17 (1995), pp. 49-60.
John Trendell, *Colonel Bogey to the Fore: A Biography of Kenneth J. Alford* (Blue Band Magazine, 1991).
Stuart Upton, *Eric Coates: A Biographical Discography* (Vintage Light Music Society, 1980).
Eric Wetherell, *Gordon Jacob – A Centenary Biography* (Thames, 1995).
Edmund Whitehouse, *London Lights: A History of West End Musicals* (This England, 2005).
John Williams (ed.) *TV Composer Guide* (Variations, 1996; new edition due 1997).
Daphne Woodward (ed), *Essex Composers* (Essex Libraries, 1985) (includes Armstrong Gibbs at pp. 27-32).
Andrew Youdell, 'Storm Clouds: A Survey of the Film Music of Arthur Benjamin', in JBMS Vol 18 (1996) pp. 19-27.

LIGHT MUSIC SOCIETIES

All these societies issue informative newsletters/journals and sometimes other publications.
Billy Mayerl Society, 'Shellwood', St Leonard's Road, Thames Ditton, Surrey, KT7 ORN.
British Music Society, 40 Roding Court, Mill Road, Ilford, Essex, IG1 2FH.
International Military Music Society, Amberstone, Pyrford Road, Pyrford, Surrey, GU22 8UP.
Percy Grainger Society, 6 Fairfax Crescent, Aylesbury, Bucks, HP20 2ES.
Percy Whitlock Trust, 32 Butcher Close, Staplehurst, Tonbridge, Kent, TNl2 OTJ.
Robert Farnon Society, 'Stone Gables', Upton Lane, Seavington St Michael, Ilminster, Somerset, TA19 OPZ.
William Alwyn Society, 51 Bailey Street, Old Basford, Nottingham, NG6 OHD.
Eric Coates Society, geoffsheldon@yahoo.co.uk

***

Light Music Society, Lancaster Farm, Chipping Lane, Longridge, Preston, Lancs, PR3 2NB. Administers the extensive Library of Light Orchestral

Music, founded 1984, which includes printed music and manuscript special arrangements for light orchestra, also much instrumental and vocal music. The library, which houses 16000 orchestral scores, has been of value to many orchestras and small groups and for the Marco Polo British Light Music CDs and other recordings.

* * *

Other libraries of light music also exist, among which may be mentioned that held by Nick Barnard (5 High Park Road, Farnham, Hampshire, GU9 7JJ, nickbd@hotmail.com), primarily for the use of his Tin Pan Alley Orchestra, which specialises in light music of all kinds.